MANY RIVERS TO CROSS

Black Migrations in Brazil and the Caribbean

Edited by

Elaine P. Rocha

*The University of the West Indies,
Cave Hill Campus, Barbados*

Critical Perspectives on Social Science

VERNON PRESS

Copyright © 2024 by the Authors.

All rights reserved. No part of this publication may be reproduced, stored in a retrieval system, or transmitted in any form or by any means, electronic, mechanical, photocopying, recording, or otherwise, without the prior permission of Vernon Art and Science Inc.
www.vernonpress.com

In the Americas:	*In the rest of the world:*
Vernon Press	Vernon Press
1000 N West Street, Suite 1200,	C/Sancti Espiritu 17,
Wilmington, Delaware 19801	Malaga, 29006
United States	Spain

Critical Perspectives on Social Science

Library of Congress Control Number: 2023946573

ISBN: 978-1-64889-934-8

Also available: 978-1-64889-767-2 [Hardback]; 978-1-64889-830-3 [PDF, E-Book]

Product and company names mentioned in this work are the trademarks of their respective owners. While every care has been taken in preparing this work, neither the authors nor Vernon Art and Science Inc. may be held responsible for any loss or damage caused or alleged to be caused directly or indirectly by the information contained in it.

Every effort has been made to trace all copyright holders, but if any have been inadvertently overlooked the publisher will be pleased to include any necessary credits in any subsequent reprint or edition.

Cover design by Vernon Press.

TABLE OF CONTENTS

Foreword — vii
Darién J. Davis
Middlebury College

List of Figure and Tables — xvii

Introduction: Paths on the Margins of History — xix
Elaine P. Rocha
The University of the West Indies, Cave Hill Campus, Barbados

PART I
SLAVERY AND FORCED MIGRATIONS — 1

CHAPTER ONE
The Atlantic Slave Trade and the Portuguese-Brazilian Slavocrat Social Formation — 3
João-Manuel Neves
Centro de Estudos Comparatistas, Universidade de Lisboa, Portugal

CHAPTER TWO
Fugitive Slaves in an Unstable Border Region: Patterns of Nineteenth-Century Slave Flight from Brazil to Uruguay and Argentina — 23
Karl Monsma
Universidade Federal do Rio Grande do Sul, Brazil
Patrícia Bosenbecker
Universidade Federal da Grande Dourados, Brazil

CHAPTER THREE
Slavery and Cassava in the Atlantic World: Commercial and Cultural Relationship between Rio de Janeiro and Angola in the Nineteenth Century — 49
Nielson Rosa Bezerra
Universidade do Estado do Rio de Janeiro, Brazil

PART II
BLACK AGENCY IN THE POST ABOLITION 71

CHAPTER FOUR
The Great Migration in Brazil: Blacks Families and Households. Rio de Janeiro, (1888-1940) 73
Carlos Eduardo Coutinho da Costa
Universidade Federal Rural do Rio de Janeiro, Brazil

CHAPTER FIVE
Life after Slavery: Migration, Work and Culture in Brazil 1900-1929 91
Lúcia Helena Oliveira Silva
Universidade Estadual Paulista, Brasil

CHAPTER SIX
Historical Aspects of Forced and Free Black Migrations in the ABC Islands 105
Marco A. Schaumloeffel
University of British Columbia, Canada

PART III
UNWANTED PEOPLE WITH DANGEROUS IDEAS 119

CHAPTER SEVEN
The Antillean Immigration in Cuba: Labor and the Politics of Race 121
Kátia Couto
Universidade Federal do Amazonas, Brazil

CHAPTER EIGHT
No Ugly People in The Paradise: Undesirable Immigrants in the Brazilian Racial Democracy 133
Elaine P. Rocha
The University of the West Indies, Cave Hill Campus, Barbados

CHAPTER NINE
Diasporic Echoes in the Global South: The Italo-Ethiopian War and Brazil 155
Petrônio Domingues
Universidade Federal de Sergipe, Brazil

Contributors 171

Index 175

Foreword

Darién J. Davis
Middlebury College

It is a peculiar sensation, this double consciousness... one ever feels his two-ness, an American, a Negro; two souls, two thoughts, two unreconciled strivings; two warring ideals in one dark body, whose dogged strength alone keeps it from being torn asunder.

W. E. B. Dubois, *The Soul of Black Folks*

There is a direct connection between the pioneering work of W.E. B. Dubois and this important volume entitled *Many Rivers to Cross: Black Migrations in Brazil and the Caribbean*. Dubois developed a theory of dual consciousness, or "two-ness," to describe the African American experience. He focused on North American territorial boundaries, but he also thought about the role of Black migration. In his 1917 article in *Crisis*, the official magazine of the National Association for the Advancement of Colored People (NAACP), Dubois anticipated the impact of the movement of Black Americans from the south to the north. This phenomenon would later be called 'The Great Migration.' Dubois would also become increasingly interested in the global African diaspora and Pan-Africanism. This volume engages and expands upon many of Dubois' ideas, including dual and multiple consciousness, transnationalism, and other 'great migrations.' By focusing on Brazil and the Caribbean, two geographical regions that have received more African migrants than anywhere else in the Atlantic world, this work offers students multiple possibilities to expand their knowledge on Black migrations in the global south.

My excitement about this volume connects to my incessant quest to find and promote good sources about African descendants. Like Dubois and many scholars studying the Black experience, my research was initially nationally bound. I began my scholarly career by studying nation-building and race in Cuba, the largest Caribbean nation. Learning Portuguese and moving to Brazil in the late 1980s exposed me to a rich new historiography and way of understanding the Black experience from a comparative perspective. Meeting Abdias do Nascimento and many other Afro-Brazilians interested in making diasporic connections helped shape my scholarly trajectory and that of many of my peers. Our attendance at multi-lingual conferences and connections to networks preparing for the United Nations World Conference against Racism, Racial Discrimination, Xenophobia and Related Intolerance in 2001 also advanced our understanding of the commonalities and differences of the transnational Black experience.

In one of my conversations with Nascimento, he spoke warmly of his friendships and admiration for many African American and Caribbean writers and activists, including Marcus Garvey, who wanted to form a branch of his Universal Negro Improvement Association (UNIA) in Brazil, and Léon Damas, one of the founders of the Negritude movement. Nascimento also talked about his connection to Africa and his participation in the Second World Black and African Festival of Arts and Culture in Dakar, Senegal, in 1977. He was interested in Brazil's migratory connections to the major regions associated with the trans-Atlantic slave trade well before the field of Black migration studies had emerged as a bonified field of inquiry. His self-imposed exile in the United States in the 1960s also allowed him to educate Americans on Afro-Brazilian struggles and expand the global reach of Black Studies.

Nevertheless, even in the early twenty-first century, most historians interested in diffusing knowledge about African descendants in Latin America and the Caribbean utilized the nation-state as the framework of analysis. Works on Afro-Mexicans, Afro-Columbians, and Afro-Cubans began to multiply. My 2000 work, *Afro-Brazilians Hoje*, followed this model. These works did not explicitly study the experience of Black Latin Americans through the lens of migration.

Indeed, before the wide availability of the internet as a research tool, historians had limited access to archives and historiographical information from different cultures. Travel constraints and limited language training also made transnational historical studies more challenging to produce. Moreover, history graduate programs often dissuaded students from pursuing comparative or transnational history dissertations. Nevertheless, edited volumes by historians from different national perspectives often allowed students to make broad cross-national comparisons and inter-regional connections. As early as the 1940s and 1950s, scholars such as Frank Tannenbaum attempted to compare Latin American slave societies with the United States. Stanley Elkins followed with a study that argued that slavery in the U. S. was a result of rampant capitalism. At the same time, in Latin America, the presence of the Church and laws of manumission engendered a different societal dynamic (Tannenbaum).[1] These broad comparisons did not explicitly examine slavery as forced migration. However, they helped pave the way for the fields of migration and diaspora studies that would later alter the Academy.

---

[1] See also Carl Degler, Neither Black nor White: Slavery and Race Relations in Brazil and the U.S (New York: Macmillan, 1971).

As students began to receive training in several languages and had access to multiple archival materials, historians such as Robert Brent Toplin in the 1970s and Rebecca Scott published comparative analyses of slavery, abolition, and race in English. Their work also appeared in edited volumes alongside other scholars (Toplin; Scott). These studies provided further knowledge for the early development of Black migration studies *avant la lettre*.

Students also benefitted from scholars who wrote on the global Black experience. Stuart Hall's essays on Black representation, policing, and transnational Black popular culture (Hall) and Paul Gilroy's *Black Atlantic: Modernity and Double-Consciousness* (1993) provided ways of thinking about diaspora, migration, and circulation of black cultures. However, the edited volume and special journal editions with diverse articles dedicated to the Black experience in Latin America and the Caribbean still represent the best forums for providing in-depth scholarship on the transnational connections among African descendants or Afro-Latin Americans. *No Longer Invisible: Afro-Latin Americans Today* (1996) was a significant milestone. That edited volume combined scholarly and journalistic views on the formation of diverse Afro-Latin American communities.

The edited publication *Beyond Slavery: The Multifaceted Legacy of Africans in Latin America and the Caribbean* explored different national themes from a continental perspective (Davis 2006). Black mobility from colonial to contemporary times emerged as a theme in this volume, but only one essay focused specifically on Black transnational migration. Bobby Vaughn and Ben Vinson III provide an insightful analysis of Afro-Mexican migrants in the United States. George Reid Andrew's 2004 *Afro-Latin America* was a pioneering work in a different sense, as it created a grand narrative for students to imagine a general field of Afro-Latin American studies. Still, Andrew's work does not focus on migration.

The development of the internet, digital access to archives, increased interconnectivity across national borders, and the strengthening of African-descendant networks allowed for more transnational research in the twenty-first century. At the same time, the development of diaspora theory, which explores the triad among homeland, host land, and diasporic groups, and migration studies, which examines push/pull factors and migration networks, helped historians to study migration and mobility throughout history.

Migration studies emerged as an interdisciplinary field of inquiry that analyzes forced and voluntary movement across regional, national, linguistic, and cultural boundaries. Migration studies also includes the movement of commodities, ideas, and cultural products. Works on Black migration by historians follow these trajectories, enhancing our knowledge and analysis of the mobility of racialized Black subjects or African descendants. *Many Rivers to*

Cross: Black Migrations in Brazil and the Caribbean represents a vital contribution to this scholarship.

According to voyages.org, between 1514 and 1866, Brazil received more than three million enslaved Africans, while the Caribbean received almost four and a half million. Those numbers represent a significant percentage of the diaspora compared to the seven thousand deported Africans who arrived in Europe and the over three hundred thousand forced to go to the United States. Despite the geographical proximity and shared histories of colonization, slavery, indentured servitude, and migration, few scholars have studied the commonalities between the Caribbean and Brazil or the exchanges between the two regions. This volume helps fill that lacuna and opens new dialogues about the transnational Black experience. *Many Rivers to Cross: Black Migrations in Brazil and the Caribbean* encourages readers to contemplate the implicit and explicit connections and commonalities through the lens of Black migration.

In her essay, "Defining Diaspora, Defining a Discourse," Kim Butler reminds us that the diasporic experience is predicated on the scattering of peoples over more than one generation and throughout various geographical experiences (Butler, 191-215). However, the literature on Black migrations in English has focused mainly on migration streams to the global north. Research on migrants in the United States is particularly robust. In her essay on Black American tourism to Bahia, Brazil, Patricia Pinho advises scholars to avoid overemphasizing the Black experience in the United States as the most critical experience. She suggests that students examine the multiple African diasporic experiences and their ways of seeing and experiencing the world (Pinho). In this project, Rocha has assembled a group of scholars who help us do just that.

In her introduction, Rocha explains that she chose 'Black migration' to speak about Brazil and the Caribbean because of the specific meaning of Blackness in the Brazilian and Caribbean contexts. Interrogating 'Black migration' in Brazil and the Caribbean as opposed to 'African descendants' or migrants of 'African descent' introduces a specific set of epistemological and discursive queries related to hybridity, visibility, and cultural African-ness, which has shaped both regions. "Black subjects," as scholars such as Mintz and Price tell us, are *de facto* Afro-Creoles, peoples forcibly separated from their specific ethnic African cultures who creatively drew on materials and practices from other cultures and reconstituted a new culture in the Americas (Mintz and Price). Stuart Hall also informs us that Black popular culture and, by extension, Blackness constitutes "a contradictory space," a site of strategic contestation that cannot be generalized but must be mapped out in specific historical and geographical spaces (Hall 1993, 51-52).

The essays in this volume do not explicitly engage the philosophical debates surrounding identity or color within the Black community. Instead, they explore Black migrations through paradigms of agency, labor, production, and power within colonial, imperial, and national frameworks. The authors also center the experience of black subjects as migrants and as part of a diaspora with lasting connections to Africa, even as they carve out new lives and networks outside of Africa across generations. The chapters explore diverse types of migrations and employ different nomenclatures as they refer to forced enslaved and freed labor to internal migrations within national borders.

Forced migration was the driving force that undergirded the trans-Atlantic slave trade. The end of the slave trade slowed the flow of involuntary migration, but the illegal flow of captives continued clandestinely to the Caribbean and Brazil. For its duration, forced African migration provided local white elites with cheap labor for diverse economic, social, and cultural activities. The enslaved toiled in homes, on plantations, and on public works and infrastructure. Africans and their descendants' engagement in self-emancipation also entailed migrating to maroons, quilombos, or cimarrones away from European-dominated centers of power.

With the abolition of slavery, African descendants often continued to perform the same tasks for meager salaries or in exchange for accommodation or basic needs. Others left their homes and places of worship in search of new opportunities. Cities and towns across the Americas often responded to the flow of Afro-Descendants across the region with anti-Black regulations, including vagrancy laws, curfews, and registration laws. Others criminalized Blackness, prohibited Black assembly, and eventually institutionalized Black mass incarceration.

Despite these obstacles, people of African descent remained inspired to preserve their cultural inheritance, seek lives of dignity, and pursue economic sustainability within and across national borders and bodies of water. Formal state emancipation occurred in the Caribbean and Brazil, beginning in 1791 in Haiti and ending in 1888 in Brazil. The first waves of migration after abolition saw the formerly enslaved take advantage of their new access to mobility. More specific studies need to be conducted on Black migrants and the saliency of race as migrants moved from areas of drought, poverty, and violence to areas of better opportunity and freedom.

Black Migrations and the Caribbean

The Caribbean is a multi-geographical region shaped by migratory flows from Africa, Europe, Asia, and the Middle East. It includes the islands between North and South America and the littoral countries of South and Central American mainland. However, Caribbean migrant communities can be found in diverse places in the Americas, from Canada to Chile. Writers of the Greater Caribbean have exposed the legacies and contradictions of these migrations.[2]

The unequal exchanges among diverse peoples, nonetheless, initiated a series of cultural and religious fusions, syncretism, and social intermingling, which led to mixed or Creole American cultures. In the French Caribbean, the rhetoric of *creolité* promotes this view of the Caribbean and parallels the notion that Brazil is a culturally syncretic *mestiço* country. As Rocha indicates, the cultural reality and celebration of cultural mixing often clash with the official state and elite anti-Blackness in Brazil. This may also be true of certain Caribbean nations. (Davis 2022, 127-148).

Migrations from southern Europe, the Middle East, and Asia also played distinct roles in constructing the national houses, to paraphrase the metaphor utilized by José Luis Gonzalez in his essay *The Four-Storeyed House*. However, the politics of migration has often led to exclusion and xenophobic national policies. At the same time, the economic costs of caring for local underprivileged populations or migrants often pose significant challenges for post-colonial countries such as Brazil and nations in the Caribbean.

Brazil

Since the birth of the Brazilian nation at the beginning of the nineteenth century, Brazilian leaders have traditionally focused on augmenting the country's status on the world stage through bilateral relations with the world's most potent hegemons in Europe and North America. Historically, building relationships with the Caribbean was hardly a priority. As in the Caribbean, waves of migration have played critical roles in shaping Brazilian nationhood. Yet, migration has not become a significant part of the national discourse on identity. Essays in this volume may help change that. Several authors clearly illustrate that the forced and voluntary movement of Black migrants played vital roles in shaping individual and community relationships to empire and nation.

Whether discussing the flight of enslaved cowboys across or within Brazil or the movement of Black subjects within the Caribbean and Brazil, this volume establishes dialogues with well-known processes and historiographies in the United States. Carlos Eduardo Coutinho da Costa's use of "The Great Migration" to refer to Brazil, for example, allows us to reconceptualize meanings of phenomena often associated with the United States. The historical contextualization of

---

[2] See the works of Garcia Marquez in Colombia, Maryse Condé in Martinique to Martin Dobru in Surinam, Julia Alvarez from the Dominican Republic, and Edwidge Danticat from Haiti.

Black Haitian migration to Cuba and Brazil by Couto and Rocha also helps us expose the dynamics of colorism and nativism, issues that can be applied to Black migrations elsewhere.

Rocha also wisely includes essays focusing on the connection between transnational or transregional Black mobility and the movement of commodities and bodies (cassava and penal culture are two examples). She also includes a chapter that explores the importance of Ethiopia as a symbol of Africa among the African diasporic community. The migration and exchange of ideas among African descendants across the Atlantic give us new insights into transnational exchanges, circulation, and "Currency of Blackness." (Davis and Williams 2006, 143-170).

While the Caribbean has not figured prominently in Brazil's political or economic development, countries such as Haiti, Jamaica, and Cuba have often captured the Brazilian popular imagination. These islands' historical revolutionary roles have captivated Brazilians for generations. Bordering mainland nations close to Brazil, such as Guyana, French Guiana, and Surinam, have influenced border dynamics. Hopefully, this work will inspire future works on these and other borders with Brazil.

Conclusion

The legacies of colonialism and slavery have shaped contemporary dynamics in Brazil and the Caribbean. Plantation economies and extractive processes benefitted European colonizers at the expense of local communities. Endemic class and racial-based color prejudice dominated the Caribbean and Brazilian landscapes for centuries. Brazil eventually emerged as a linguistically unified geocultural and political entity, while the distinct Caribbean nations generated multiple political and linguistic realities. Migrations, forced and voluntary, have played a critical role in all these processes. European migrations to the Americas often led to the destruction or transformation of the people and landscapes of the First Peoples. The subsequent migrations of Africans and their descendants left their imprint on various sectors of the Caribbean and Brazilian societies.

A note on terminology

It is also worth noting that the scholars in this volume currently work and reside outside of the United States and Europe. In other words, they are scholars working on the periphery. The fact that they write about migration for an English-reading audience from that perspective also represents a call for transnational dialogue. Readers will come across racial and cultural terms that come out of the Caribbean and Brazilian historical contexts. Terms such as "moreno," "Euro-mestizo," "mulato," or "métis," for example, cannot be adequately translated into English without specific contexts. At the outset, Rocha explains why she chose to title the volume "Black migrations" rather than use the term "African descendants" in the title. Other scholars in this volume utilize many racial terms to refer to black people in different contexts. As we have seen from Stuart Hall, "Black" continues to be a contested term, and that argument is part of lack migration history writ large. There is no global authority that sets the boundaries and definitions across languages and cultures.

Readers may also note the different contemporary uses of words such as *slave* and *enslaved*. Among scholars writing in the United States and the United Kingdom, there is a growing preference for 'enslaved' where possible. This choice is not mere political correctness. Rather, this attention to language represents an earnest attempt by scholars to be more precise and to acknowledge that *enslaved person* refers to an individual deported and forced to work against *their* will.[3] Enslaved Africans came from all strata of society and practiced multiple professions before their enslavement. Many scholars often aim to employ *slave* to refer to the status *or* description of the economic system. Yet this convention and sensibility is hardly universal. Moreover, translating racialized and gendered terms presents an additional challenge. For example, consider translating the Spanish term *esclavo fugitivo* (literally "escaped or fugitive slave"), a term that necessarily legitimizes the slave condition as an original status. Is 'self-emancipated African descendants' better or does it distort the historical record? Like many historians working in the field, scholars in this volume navigate these linguistic challenges as they provide insightful analysis. They embrace multidimensional issues that will engender discussion and debate.

Migration studies forums are also grappling with language. For example, migrant activists in the English-speaking world encourage students to use the term "migrant" rather than "immigrant," the latter of which implies the movement of a subject into a specific national space or host land. Migrants often move to, from, and through multiple geographical spaces and cross many boundaries. Is it best to refer to Haitians moving from Brazil to Argentina and Chile as immigrants in each case or migrants over many borders or both?

---

[3] 'Their, they, them' as substitutes for his/hers, he/she, and him/her also represents another language shift that does not necessarily enjoy universal appeal in the United States or elsewhere. These non-gendered terms are particularly challenging and often problematic in gendered languages such as Portuguese, Spanish, and French.

Immigration policy, after all, is the purview of nations. Scholars in the text use 'migrant' and 'immigrant.'

Whatever the terminology, Hannah Arendt has shown us that the nation-state's construction of rights and laws does not apply to many migrants, including the stateless (Arendt 1951, 276-280). Additional studies of enslaved Africans as migrants compared to other migrants and poor whites will reveal regional idiosyncrasies. National policies in the post-abolition era will provide other insights. Beyond the possibilities for linguistic debates, this volume invites readers to engage the history of Black migrations from multiple viewpoints. Rocha helps provide valuable historical sources and frameworks that expand on previous historical studies. *Many Rivers to Cross: Black Migrations in Brazil and the Caribbean* also complements the contemporary migration analysis across many disciplines. This work is a valued addition to migration studies and a must-read for students interested in the history of Black migrations.

Darién J. Davis,
29 October 2023

Bibliography

Arendt, Hannah. "Statelessness and the Refugee Problem." *The Origins of Totalitarianism* (New York: Harcourt Brace, 1979.

Butler, Kim. "Defining Diaspora, Defining a Discourse." *Diaspora* 10: 2 (2001), 191-215.

Davis, Darién J. "Migraciones, mezclas y poder en el Caribe: Apuntes transnacionales para entender el multiculturalismo poscolonial," *Procesos Históricos. Revista de Historia*, 41, enero-junio, 2022, 127-148 Universidad de Los Andes, Mérida (Venezuela) https://dialnet.unirioja.es/servlet/revista?codigo=5924.

Davis, Darién J.; and Williams, Judith. "Pan-Africanism, Negritude, and the Currency of Blackness," *Beyond Slavery: The Multilayered Legacy of Africans in Latin America and the Caribbean* Jaguar Books on Latin America, 2006.

Degler, Carl. *Neither Black nor White: Slavery and Race Relations in Brazil and the U.S.* New York: Macmillan, 1971.

Elkins, Stanley. *Slavery, a Problem in American Institutional and Intellectual Life.* New York: Macmillan, 1971.

Hall, Stuart. *Selected Writings on Race and Difference.* Durham: Duke University Press, 2021.

Hall, Stuart. "What Is This "Black" in Black Popular Culture?" *Social Justice*, Spring-Summer 1993, Vol. 20, No. ½, 51-52.

Mintz, Sidney W.; and Price, Ricard, *The Birth of African American Culture: An Anthropological Perspective.* New York: Beacon Press, 1992.

Santana Pinho, Patricia. *Mapping Diaspora: African American Roots Tourism in Brazil.* Chapel Hill: University of North Carolina Press, 2018.

Scott, Rebecca. "Exploring the Meaning of Freedom: Post Emancipation Societies in Comparative Perspective," *The Abolition of Slavery and the Aftermath of Emancipation in Brazil.* Durham: Duke University Press, 1988.

Tannenbaum, Frank. *Slave and Citizen: The Negro in the Americas.* New York: Vintage Books, 1946.

Toplin, Brent. *Slavery and Race Relations in Latin America.* Westwood, Connecticut: Westwood Press, 1974.

List of Figure and Tables

Figure

Figure 2.1. Map of Rio Grande do Sul and Uruguay in 1856, by Herrmann Rudolf Wendroth.   26

Tables

Table 2.1. Percentage of male and female slaves listed as escaped in probate records of estates including escaped slaves - southern Rio Grande do Sul, 1822-1888.   29

Table 2.2. Percentage of slaves listed as escaped, by origin and sex, in probate records of estates including escaped slaves in southern Rio Grande do Sul, 1822-1888.   30

Table 2.3. Percentage of male slaves listed as escaped in probate records of estates including escaped slaves, by occupational category, southern Rio Grande do Sul 1822-1888.   30

Table 2.4. Percentage of male slaves listed as escaped in probate records of estates including escaped slaves, by occupational category and origin, southern Rio Grande do Sul 1822-1888 (among slaves with birthplace identified).   31

Table 2.5. Escaped slaves listed in probate records of Four Municipalities in southern Rio Grande do Sul, by five-year intervals.   34

Table 2.6. Age distributions of male and female runaway slaves on 1851 list.   38

Table 2.7. Age distributions of runaway male slaves on 1851 list, by birthplace.   39

Table 2.8. Occupational distribution of male runaway slaves on the 1851 list.   40

Table 2.9. Occupational distribution of male runaway slaves on the 1851 list by birthplace.   40

Table 3.1. Agricultural production in *Reconcavo* (1769-1779).   58

Table 5.1. Birthplace (states) of migrant prisoners in 1894.   95

Table 5.2. Data on migrants arrested between June and September of 1894.   97

Introduction:
Paths on the Margins of History

Elaine P. Rocha

The University of the West Indies, Cave Hill Campus, Barbados

This book is a collection of essays that focus on Black migrations in Brazil and the Caribbean. The Americas, since the first contact with Europeans, is as much a continent of immigrants as a continent of continuous migrations. As part of the colonial project, Latin America was colonized by immigrants coming from Europe and by those brought by force from Africa. Colonization also included the movement of indigenous people from one region to another, taken by force as the colonizer demanded more labor and enslaved the natives or as part of their resistance to colonial oppression and enslavement.

The transit of people between continents and countries is the backbone of modern cultures. It has influenced every aspect of culture, transformed politics, established borders, and generated societies marked at the same time by miscegenation and racial prejudice. Also, under colonial rule, British colonies received immigrant workers from China and India during the nineteenth and early twentieth centuries. Researchers estimate that more than 45 million immigrants have entered the United States of America from its independence to 2021 (Ward and Batalova 2023), while Canada has received more than 17 million immigrant workers between 1867 and 2016[1]. Among countries of Latin America, in Brazil, millions of immigrants arrived from the Americas, Europe, the Middle East, Africa, and Asia. Since the 1820s, other Latin American countries also received a great number of immigrants, with a predominance of Europeans. (Gonzalez Navarro 1994; Modolo 2016; Wermuth 2020).

After independence, Spanish and Portuguese-speaking nations of the Americas embraced immigrants coming from Europe, with public investment made towards that end. The immediate aim was to increase the white population, and also important was to attract European workers, considered superior based on those increasingly popular theories of racial hierarchy that dominated the period. (Skidmore 1974; Schwarcz 1995; Rocha 2006). The policies supporting European immigration promoted the assumption that more European workers and a predominantly white population would accelerate the modernization

---

[1] According to Statistics Canada. www.150.stacan.gc.ca accessed June 15, 2023.

process. After their arrival, a system of preferences benefited the white immigrants to the detriment of other groups. All newly independent countries of Latin America rejected black immigrants.

The historiography, also a product of the nation-building process, selected the history of white immigrants as the major focus of its migration studies, with indigenous nations and black people for a long time denied a place in the historiography, unless as supporting actors in the histories of conquest, colonization, and economic development. For decades, historical evidence of the experiences of black people – as much as of indigenous people – along with their own narratives and experiences were rejected by historians, except where they rebelled to the point of jeopardizing the national project. Likewise, for a long time, studies of migrations have been separated from studies of slavery, neglecting the impact of the traffic of humans all around the world, especially the intensive African modern slave trade, which lasted more than five centuries. Patrick Manning called the trade of enslaved Africans "a system of forced labor migration" (Manning 1990, 255), an idea which he further reinforced:

> The movement of Africans to the Americas from the seventeenth to the nineteenth centuries may be accounted as mankind's second largest transoceanic migration. This migration, along with the concurrent African migration to the Middle East and North Africa, was distinct from other major modern migrations in its involuntary nature, and in the high rates of mortality and social dislocation caused by the methods of capture and transportation. (Manning 1993, 279).

Manning's approach to the history of the African Diaspora as a history of African migrations includes the transoceanic movement of people and the continued involuntary movement of slaves through the continents. In the case of the Americas, as he emphasizes, enslaved people brought to one port of entry could be further transferred to other ports and then moved to various regions by land or rivers through centuries of involuntary migrations. To this view, I want to add that during the time of slavery, there were also voluntary migrations, as enslaved people managed to escape captivity, seeking refuge in other places. During the nineteenth century, people ran away from places like Texas and estates of the Mississippi Valley, seeking refuge in Mexico, where slavery was abolished after independence. (Kelley 2004). Similarly, in Brazil, people running away from enslavement have crossed the territorial border of provinces and colonies, looking for a place where they could be free. Flavio Gomes traces the routes of runaways from northern Brazil into the Guianas, crossing various provinces from the seventeenth to the nineteenth centuries, establishing settlements and an extended network with family ties across the borders (Gomes 2005) and as Monsma and Bosenbecker present here, enslaved persons fled from Brazilian southern states, seeking freedom in Uruguay.

Therefore, to include the topic of the slave trade in the historiography of migrations is to recognize the agency of individuals who were dehumanized under the classification of slaves. As we acknowledge the impact of the movement of individuals through geographic areas in the making of societies and culture, being those free or enslaved workers, we aim to contribute to the decolonization of the historical methodology.

Why Black migrations?

For a while, the title of this book was under consideration. In the end, the option for "Black migrations" instead of "African Diaspora" presented itself as more appropriate for a book that focuses mostly on Brazil. Black identity for Brazilians is beyond African identity and, though it includes African identity and representations of Africanness, it is focused on colorism and a concept of Blackness that has been built for centuries, that is marked by misrepresentations while at the same time determining the struggle for equality.

Black migrations are more than the transit of people between countries and regions and from rural areas to urban centres. It includes the construction of networks that made survival possible, that created neighbourhoods and cultural expression, impacted dietary habits, the exchange of crops and agricultural techniques, and the uplifting of families from slavery and misery to ownership, education and political representation. These migrations – like other types of migrations – have influenced local, regional and national societies, in culture and politics. See, for example, the religious practices centered in the cult of *orixas* in Brazil, Colombia, Haiti and Cuba, which have influenced the culture beyond the area of religion. The same things could be said with music and language, but nothing is more visible than the biological influence of the Black migrations through the mixed people of African descent, called *Morenos*, and the *Afro-Latinos* and Caribbeans of all physical features, that have marked the economy, society and politics in the Americas.

However, for decades, studies of Black migrations in the Americas were placed at the margins of national historiographies, where migration studies focused on European immigrants and their contributions to the economy and society. Hobsbawm (1975), for example, in the seminal work *The Age of Capital 1848-1875*, produced a chapter about migrations without mentioning African migrations and Black migrations in general. Historiographies of Costa Rica, Panama, Colombia, and Brazil only recently have incorporated studies about Black migrations, internal and foreign.

In Brazil, for example, one of the most important themes in Brazilian historiography is the immigration wave that, between the 1870s and 1940s, brought thousands of foreigners to the country, and how those groups of immigrants were incorporated into society, the landscape and popular memory. A positive image of the European immigrant was established in early years, heavily influenced by racist ideologies and contested scientific studies. Those views lead to a mythification of that immigrant as a progressive element, a more efficient and reliable worker, with whom ideas of modernity and civilization were often associated.

It was only in recent decades that historical studies about non-European immigrants in Latin America started to gain visibility. Among those studies, special attention has been given to Black immigrants, especially after the latest crisis in Haiti in 2010, when hundreds of thousands of Haitians departed the island of Hispaniola with various and multiple destinations, which included Colombia, Brazil, Mexico, the United States and Canada. Negative reactions to Haitian immigrants gained visibility in newspapers and social media, revealing racist attitudes towards the Black immigrants in those countries.

American-born Haitian descendant Natasha Lucas compared the type of reception given to Cubans, who for more than half a century have been privileged through the "wet foot, dry foot" policy and received permanent visas within a year of living in the United States. Similarly, since the war in Ukraine, immigrants from that country have been well-received in the United States and have had their visas processed fast and drama-free. Haitians, on the contrary, have faced abuse, violence and discrimination as try to enter the United States, moving away from poverty, disaster and the insecurity that has plagued their homeland since 2010.

> Back in September (2021), nearly 15,000 mostly Haitian immigrants were camped under a bridge at the Del Rio, Texas border. Nearly 30,000 migrants have passed through since last Sept. 9, according to Homeland Security Secretary Alejandro Mayorkas. Photos of border patrol agents on horses forcefully preventing immigrants from crossing the border—visuals I can only associate with slavery and the roles of slave patrols—have gone viral. President Joe Biden called the border patrol agents' actions "horrible," but his administration has done little to bring them to heel.
>
> (…)
>
> Cuban immigrants fled repression to establish communities in South Florida and elsewhere in the U.S. Ukrainians are fleeing an active war zone. Haitian migrants are fleeing a country that lacks infrastructure, medicine, a stable economy or political system and adequate housing. The major difference is that most of the Haitian immigrants are Black while most of the Ukrainians and Cubans before them are not. (Lucas 2022).

Introduction

The diverse status of immigrants as seen in the United States, is also prevalent in other countries. Factors of discrimination include nationality and religion, race and color. Even in a country that applies the "one drop rule" when defining blackness, it is important to note that Cuban immigrants, although many have African ancestors, have a better status than Haitians.

In many ways, Black workers have contributed to the construction of societies in the Americas as well as to the economic development of the region. Even greater is their influence on the politics and policies that have marked the Americas for more than a century, from the racist policies of segregation and negative discrimination that inspired legislation and unwritten rules to the challenge and ascension to political power and the spreading of dangerous ideas of equality and liberty. For example, in the past 30 years, African Americans and African immigrants in the United States with direct ties to African nations have pressured the government to better foreign relations with African nations. (Blyden and Jones 2020). In Brazil, a growing presence of Afro-Brazilians in the universities allied to the increasing presence of African international students in undergraduate and graduate programs – thanks to policies like affirmative action and scholarship opportunities for students from Africa and the Caribbean – have contributed to new academic research and debates, which resulted in changing the views of Brazilians about Africa and the African Diaspora.

For more than five centuries, dangerous ideas of freedom and citizenship spread fear of change and social revolution among colonial and independent states in the Americas. In an attempt to control this, countries promoted discrimination and criminalization of people of color with support from elites and middle classes struggling to hold on to their privileges. The Haitian Revolution spread fear through the entire region, especially from those whose economy relied on slavery. In the newly independent United States, as well as in the British, Spanish, French and Dutch colonies of the Caribbean and the soon-to-be independent countries of continental Latin America, the idea of Blacks taking arms and ending the colonial system based on plantation and slavery affected private estate owner as much as politicians and military leaders (Reis 1995; Blackburn 2006). It also influenced enslaved people in Brazil, who carried necklaces with the image of Dessalines in the streets of Rio de Janeiro (Mott 1982). For Reis, "these are signs of elasticity, adaptability, and the extended information networks that characterized, in war and in peace, slave cultures of the New World" (Reis 1995, 48). A few decades later, the abolition of slavery in the British colonies influenced abolitionists and enslaved persons in Brazil, Cuba, Colombia and Venezuela. In 1850, a newspaper in Colombia reprinted an article first published in Jamaica, entitled "Of the African Race and its descendants," which praises leaders of African descendants from Mexico,

Venezuela and Cuba, as well as the leader of the Haitian revolution, as part of the Colombian abolitionist campaign. (Lohse 2001). During the first half of the XIX century, it was common to find Africans from various nations, enslaved and free, as well as Black sailors from foreign lands in the ports of Brazil. The interaction between those men and women contributed to the dissemination of ideas of rebellion and disobedience that led many to prison. When examining documentation from the prison system of Rio de Janeiro, Soares found that Black Brazilian and foreigners' socialization extended beyond the port to villages of the interior and runaway communities (Soares 1998; Soares and Gomes 2006).

The interaction of Africans and people of African descent born in various places outside Africa indicates the circulation of knowledge that influenced the mainstream, like in the case of rebellions or demands for rights, and in local and individual spheres, as part of the knowhow that made possible adaptation and survival in slave societies.

Over the years, the identity moved away from Africa, assuming a diverse meaning among Caribbeans and Brazilians. In the case of the Caribbean, blackness became part of the national identity and by the twentieth century, the image of Caribbean people is associated with Black people. Among Caribbeans and Afro-Latinos, the idea of blackness combines physical features and the historical experience of slavery, colonization and racial discrimination, in addition to the culture that was preserved or forged in the diaspora.

Black Migrations and Black History

The twentieth century emergence of Black History in the United States as a valid line of research is related to the rise of a decolonized African historiography, particularly after the end of WWII. In that same period, and influenced by what was happening in the United States and some African countries, philosophers, sociologists, anthropologists and historians from the former colonies in Africa and the Caribbean also started to re-examine their past, proposing new approaches and new problems to historians. Black History, therefore, is itself a product of migrations of peoples and ideas.

As Goebel (2013) reminds us, it is important to overcome the notion that migrations are a movement of people from point A to point B, as it is very common for persons to undergo multiple migrations during their lifetime.

> Contrary to common assumptions about migration as a linear movement from a point of origin to a destination, migratory circuits involved much return migration (typically around fifty percent of the total flow), back-and-forth movements (especially by seasonal workers), as well as on-migration within the overall receiving region. (Goebel 2013, 15).

Introduction xxv

Obviously, Goebel is referring to voluntary migrations because although forced migrants can also be moved from multiple destinations in their lifetime (Manning 1993), it is mostly unlikely that an enslaved person could manage to return to their original place. Also, in Goebel, the concept of migratory networks connecting the sending and receiving regions is very important to understand the phenomenon. However, that to understand the dynamics of migratory movements and the historical events that they involve, one must go beyond the traditional framework of history, utilizing methods and data from sociology, anthropology, geography, political science, and legal studies (Goodman 2015). To those, I would add semiotics, demographic and cultural studies.

A very important part of Black History is the study of the African Diaspora, including migrations within Africa, from Africa to other continents, between countries and continents, and within the same country, as is the case of the Great Migrations in the United States and the Caribbean Migrations. The major trend of Black migrations between the 1870s and the 1960s in the United States also happened in Brazil and within the Caribbean archipelago and from the islands to the American and European continents. In all cases, individuals and families moved away from their origin to pursue a better life, gaining access to jobs, property, education, and rights. In that context, racist politics were a common obstacle to the adjustment of the immigrants in their places of destination as much as a major factor in the emigration. Racism itself and the representations of Africa, Africans and African descendants played important roles in the making of racist rules and practices, as much as in the construction of alliances to resist them. Racism and representations of *the other* have been central to studies of various mainstreams of migration, like the Chinese to the United States, Indians and Pakistanis to the United Kingdom and Japanese to Brazil; but it is especially important for studies of Black migrations because of the way that Black history and today's representations of Black people are still influenced by experiences of slavery, segregation, and colonization that have impacted on the economic development, political rights and social inclusion of Africans and their descendants. As Mae Ngai reminds us, including discussions of race and racism is crucial to the history of immigration. (Ngai 2012).

New communities, sometimes imagined, as proposed by Anderson (1991), were formed in the new locations can be based on racist definitions like the Black ghettos of the United States. They could also be based on nationalities, like the Nigerian community of New York City, which includes Nigerians from various ethnic groups and is located in a region of the big city; the Haitian community of Montreal; the communities of West Indians – which include people from various islands – formed in Costa Rica, New York, Brazil, and Panama, for example. Other forms of solidarity in the diaspora, based on race, culture, and nationality, were formed. That is the case of Black migrants that moved from Sao Paulo, Bahia and Minas Gerais into Rio de Janeiro, where they greatly influenced the building of samba schools. These networks include employment, housing, marriage opportunities and cooperation, as those formed by Italian immigrants in New York, Germans in Santa Catarina, Lebanese in Sao Paulo, or Cubans in Miami.

No doubt, Black migrations have a great impact in the places of origin, for demographic reasons as much as for the importance of remittances sent by emigrants, which contributed to enhancing opportunities for housing and education for family members who stayed behind, resulting in social, economic, and political transformation. They also impacted the places of destination, starting with the pressure created in the housing market – the birth or transformation of entire neighborhoods – as was the case of the capital of Rondonia state, in northern Brazil. In general, demographic change had a great influence on society, economy, culture and politics.

Historians have recognized the importance of these migrations in global, national, transnational, regional, and local histories and the particularities in the dynamics of Black migrations. It is, however, a relatively new field of studies in Latin America, as it is Black History in general. In part because of Latin America's struggle to recognize the protagonism of its Black population in history, as much as in acknowledging the prevalence of racist ideologies in their culture and politics. The exception is the Caribbean, where the predominance of Black people – and their rise to power after independence – made the decolonization of history a major demand in the nation building after the 1960s, reaffirming the influence of regional and transcontinental migrations.

The colonial enterprise in the Caribbean, as well as disputes among empires, is responsible for early modern migrations of Africans and their descendants within the archipelago and from the islands to continent, as was the case of West Indian migrations to British Guiana from 1870s. In general, West Indian workers were a cheaper labor force, hired by plantations and construction projects from the late 1800s to the 1930s, creating seasonal and definitive migrations. (Chomsky 1996; Harpelle 2001; Lasso 2007; 2021; McLeod 1998; Newton 2004; Thomas-Hope 2009; Putnam 2002; 2013). However, the theme of black migration in Latin America is fairly new among historians, especially when examining South America.

Sometimes voluntarily, sometimes coerced, people have moved from one place to another, carrying with them history and important cultural traditions such as language, music, and religion. Moreover, ideas have traveled as well - political projects to defeat imperialism and dangerous ideas of liberty and equality would spread through the African Diaspora. Since the early days of colonization, Africans and their descendants living in the Americas maintained their places of origin, and also Africa in general, as the reference for their cultural practices. Especially from the early twentieth century, Black intellectuals have acknowledged their connections to a broad African diaspora.

As pointed out by Patterson and Kelley (2000, 13), "their political and cultural vision crisscrossed the Atlantic, from the U.S. to Africa, from the Caribbean to Europe". In the aftermath of World War II, struggles against racial discrimination in the Americas, wars for decolonization of Africa, and the movement for independence in the Caribbean, together with the increasing impact of Africans and Blacks in the politics, arts, sports, sciences and philosophy, resulted in a strong network, and beyond that, a sense of common background, challenges and goals.

> Scholars' efforts to understand the black world beyond the boundaries of nation-states have profoundly affected the way we write the history of the modern world. The making of a "black Atlantic" culture and identity, in general, and Pan-Africanism, in particular, was as much the product of "the West" as it was of internal developments in Africa. Racial capitalism, imperialism, and colonialism – the processes that created the current African diaspora – shaped African culture (s) while transforming Western culture itself. In saying this, we are not speaking of the "black Atlantic" as merely "countercultural," but as an integral part of the formation of the modem world as we know it. (Patterson and Kelley 2000, 13).

The network of ideas and studies on the Black experience, together with strategies to defeat racism, relies on decolonial perspectives on history, sociology, arts, literature, anthropology, and other fields of academic knowledge. Paul Gilroy, in his seminal work *The Black Atlantic* (1993), discusses the reciprocity and multiplicity of voices crossing the Atlantic as part of the struggle to decolonize the Western perception of Africa and the African Diaspora, as well as to support struggles against racism. According to him, the journal *Presence Africaine*, created in 1947, had an important contribution "in the developing awareness of the African diaspora as a transnational and intercultural multiplicity" (Gilroy 1993, 195).

Following Gilroy's proposal, this book intends to bring to a broad audience some of the work that has been done in the field of Black migrations, focusing on those who had South America as their destination and locus. It includes coerced and voluntary migrations, migrations within the same State and the same colonial empire, and migrations between places of diverse culture and politics. It discusses social and political inclusion and the building of communities and networks, as well as the traveling of ideas and representations of Africa and freedom. It will also present evidence of the extended traffic of African people to Brazil and the criminalization of Blacks and Africans in Rio de Janeiro to discuss the movement between the islands of the Caribbean, which, although it contributed to the building of a regional identity as the Caribbean, did not succeed in creating a Federation. It incorporates a diverse framework of analysis, like transnationalism, diaspora, colonialism and postcolonialism (Ngai 2012), and it extends over more than four centuries of history.

The collection of chapters is focused on history, but it benefits from the contribution of linguistics and sociology as well. Authors contributed to a variety of methods and sources, examining demographics, laws, policies, personal and public archives, and newspapers, among other types of data. The time framework is also extended, from early slavery to the 21st century, with the aim of offering a kaleidoscopic view of Black migrations in their multiple aspects and diverse experiences. The book combines continuity and discontinuity, which are often synchronous in human history (Jaago 2014). Take, for example, the experience of African inmates in the late nineteenth century in Rio de Janeiro as a continuity from the extended slavery period in Brazil's history or the rejection of the Black immigrants in Cuba and in Brazil as a continuous process in which Black people were classified as dangerous people. The discontinuity of the Afro-Caribbean migrations to Brazil and Cuba, because it was concentrated in a few decades of the twentieth century, has its continuity in the memories and the reclaimed identity of the descendants of those immigrants. Similarly dangerous ideas of dignity, rights, and racial solidarity found in the discourse of Barbadian immigrants in Brazil, Jamaican immigrants in Cuba, and in the discourse about Ethiopia that influenced Afro-Brazilian intellectuals were direct responses to attitudes of racism, economic and political oppression, and to representations of Africa as a colonized continent, land of poverty and misery.

The organization of this book

Although historical processes are also connected to other processes, and many times events and experiences overlap while they mutually influence each other's processes, we made an effort to group the articles of this book according to three major themes: slavery, post-abolition, and unwanted people with dangerous ideas. The themes also reflect moments of the Black migrations in Brazil and the Caribbean, from coerced migrations under enslavement to the post-abolition restrictive laws which resulted in massive criminalization of Black people and to the construction of migration networks that moved people, always seeking a better life.

The first part of the book, *Slavery and Forced Migrations*, is opened with the article by João-Manuel Neves' which is key to understanding the origins of racial inequality with its terrible consequences for the world and its ties to slavery and the development of the mercantilist economy based on sugar cane monoculture. In this work, he explains that "the association of sugar production with slavery during the Middle Ages in the Mediterranean was to take the form of a huge tragedy for the sub-Saharan African populations, since the second half of the fifteenth century, at the hands of the Portuguese." Therefore, to understand the origins of the problem in the Americas, it is important to examine its origins in Portugal. Neves also explores the presence of African slaves in Europe, particularly in the Iberian Peninsula, but also in places like Genoa, Flanders and Antwerp, amplifying our understanding of the African Diaspora. His analysis includes views from Europe, Africa and the Americas in understanding the trading of African slaves and the construction of social norms based on racialized views about the labor force that sustained the colonial enterprise.

The transit of persons escaping slavery in Brazil across the borders of Argentina and Uruguay is the topic of the chapter written by Karl Monsma and Patrícia Bosenbecker. Their article breaks with the traditional views of slavery in the plantation economy or in the mines of Brazil, introducing the figure of the enslaved cowboy and his equivalent in southern Brazil, the *gaúcho*. Monsma and Bosenbecker also examine the commerce in slaves between Argentina and Brazil during the first half of the nineteenth century and the preference for boys and young men who could be easily trained to work on the *ranchos*. Once trained, those enslaved men would become able horsemen, competent with knives, machetes, bolas and lassoes, "which made fugitives dangerous men." Some of them would be recruited to fight in wars, with the promise of freedom at the end. Not only cowboys crossed the borders escaping slavery; some other Afro-Brazilians went on foot to Uruguay while others escaped by boat. The transit of enslaved persons from Brazil into Argentina and Uruguay increased after both countries abolished slavery, which lasted until 1888 in Brazil. Like Neves, the authors examine the issue of slavery and resistance to slavery from a transnational perspective.

In "Slavery and Cassava in the Atlantic World: Commercial and Cultural Relationship between Rio de Janeiro and Angola, nineteenth century," historian Nielson Rosa Bezerra examines the extended commerce between Brazil and Angola, the importance of cassava in the Atlantic slave trade and how this trading affected economic and social life on the outskirts of Rio de Janeiro. Bezerra's study challenges the theory of the Triangular Trade, showing that a solid and dynamic exchange developed between Rio de Janeiro and Angola, lasting some three centuries, and which did not involve Portugal. Beyond the numbers of the transatlantic trade, Bezerra presents information on some of the lives of free and enslaved persons affected by such commerce.

The book's second part comprises articles tackling themes related to the period known as *Post-Abolition*. The authors used qualitative and quantitative sources to examine the experiences of Black people in the late years of slavery and in the decades following the abolition. The dynamics of black families during the Great Migrations in Brazil in the valley located between the cities of Rio de Janeiro and São Paulo are examined by Carlos Eduardo Costa, who has dedicated his studies to understanding black migrations in post-emancipation Rio de Janeiro. According to him, in that period, the population of Rio de Janeiro city and the surrounding areas increased greatly because of the influx of black immigrants from regions of plantation agriculture seeking a better life. Those immigrant workers left a life of oppression, marked by disfranchisement, economic exploitation and violence, to build a new life in Rio de Janeiro, where they influenced the birth of street carnival and, more importantly, of samba schools. Moreover, they found work in the port and took other menial jobs in Rio or engaged as peasants in the orange groves on the capital's outskirts, seeking better housing and access to education for their children.

Lucia Helena Silva also discusses Black migration in post-abolition Brazil. In her work, she dialogues with Costa in examining Black migrants in Rio de Janeiro. However, Silva's research focuses on the records of the Rio de Janeiro *Casa de Detenção*, Rio's largest jailhouse, to trace the trajectory of those migrants, most of them first-generation free men, who were arrested and registered between 1888 and 1920. She points out that the incidence of imprisonment went up on festive days such as carnival, Christmas, and holidays, mainly because of fights and drunkenness. Women were also affected, imprisoned for drunkenness, prostitution and public fighting. The majority of detainees were under 30 years of age, implying that most immigrants were young men and women in their most productive years, looking for a better life away from the plantations.

Marco Aurelio Schaumloeffel examines the ABC islands – Aruba, Bonaire and Curaçao – located in the southern region of the Caribbean archipelago. These islands, although they "functioned as an entrepôt for enslaved Africans, and the slave traders operated there as "middlemen" in the lucrative business of human trafficking", were not drawn into the plantation economy. Schaumloeffel starts with a discussion about the importation of African people from various regions during the period in which the Dutch were heavily involved in slave trading, moving onto the arrival of Portuguese-Brazilian Sephardic Jews and their enslaved workers, which had a great impact in the islands. After the abolition of slavery, black people started to move from the islands to the continent, but the migrations increased during the twentieth century when workers moved from the ABC islands to parts of the British and Spanish Caribbean. He shows that movement in the region did not take place in only one direction, as people from other islands moved to Curaçao and Aruba, attracted by economic

Introduction   xxxi

opportunities after oil was found in the region. This intra-Caribbean migration had a huge impact on the cultural identity of the region.

The third part of this book, *Unwanted People with Dangerous Ideas*, is reunited with three articles that examine the impact of Black immigrants and their foreign ideas in the politics of Brazil and Cuba. Katia examines Caribbean migrations, particularly the presence of Haitians and Jamaicans in Cuba in the early twentieth century, focusing on how those immigrant workers affected the struggles of the Cuban working class. Their presence was seen by Afro-Cuban workers as competition for jobs and by the Cuban elite as a social hazard, increasing the black population and bringing in foreign traditions, putting national values at risk. Employers, however, saw in the immigrant workers the opportunity to lower salaries and increase their profits. Couto shows that, despite being foreign immigrants, many of those called *Antillanos* actively participated in the struggle of the working class.

In "No Ugly People in the Paradise: Undesirable Immigrants in the Brazilian Racial Democracy," I examine the Brazilian historical rejection of black immigrants, starting from the nineteenth century and continuing through the twentieth century until 2010, when a wave of Haitian immigrants caused great debate among Brazilians, divided into those who rejected what they considered undesirable immigration and those who argued for a more humanitarian reception of immigrants escaping from hardship exacerbated by the earthquake. The first important wave of black immigrants – post slavery – arrived in Brazil between 1900 and 1915, during the implementation of projects of modernization in the Rain Forest region. Those Caribbean immigrants entered Brazil despite the prohibition, some illegally, some as immigrant workers under temporary contracts. Their presence, although not significant in numbers, has left its mark on the history of places like Manaus, Belem and Porto Velho. This work is part of an ongoing project about the West Indian migrations to Brazil in that period.

Finally, Petronio Domingues brings us his contribution. He is a highly respected professor who has been developing research on African Diaspora populations in Brazil and the Americas, post-emancipation, social movements, identities, biographies, multiculturalism and racial diversity in Brazil. His text discusses the Italian invasion of Ethiopia in October 1935, which sparked a mass wave of debates around the world, particularly in the Atlantic world of the African diaspora. He analyzes the repercussions of the Italo-Ethiopian War among Afro-Brazilians, based on the documentation produced by agencies of political repression and particularly articles published in Brazil's black press. This study focuses on the debates among Afro-Brazilians regarding the war in Africa, assessing the stances and actions taken in light of the dialog conducted in the transnational network of the Black Atlantic. Domingues's work examines the transit of ideas and facts and how representations of Africa influenced antiracist discourses in Brazil.

In general, the objective of this book is to contribute to studies of Black migrations in a transnational perspective, with views from diverse perspectives on how populations have transited between regions, countries and continents, carrying their ideas, costumes, beliefs, and strategies for survival. In their trajectories, they built communities, created religions, musical traditions, languages and much more. The lives of those migrants influenced politics, contributed to revolutions and wars, and influenced the economy and societies. For centuries, the official history of Latin America has pushed the histories of black immigrants to the margins, keeping them in the shadows and denying their importance in the construction of the modern world. The works brought together in this book aim to contribute to breaking this pattern, bringing the experiences of Black migrants from the margins to the centre.

References

Anderson, Bendict. *Imagined communities on the origins and spread of Nationalism.* London: Verso, 1991

Blackburn, Robin. "Haiti, Slavery, and the Age of the Democratic Revolution". *The William and Mary Quarterly* 63, no. 4 (2006): 643-674.

Blyden, Nemata; Jones, Jeannette. "Between Africa and America. Recalibrating Black American's relationship to the Diaspora". *Perspectives on History* 58, no.6 (2020): 21-23.

Chomsky, Aviva. *West Indian Workers and the United Fruit Company in Costa Rica, 1870-1940.* Baton Rouge: Louisiana State University Press, 1996.

Gilroy, Paul. *The Black Atlantic. Modernity and double consciousness.* Massachusetts: Harvard University Press, 1993.

Goebel, Michael. *Overlapping geographies of belonging: migrations, regions, and nations in the Western South Atlantic.* Washington, DC: American Historial Association, 2013.

Gomes, Flávio Santos. A hidra e os pântanos. Mocambos, quilombos e comunidades de fugitivos no Brasil (séculos XVII-XIX). São Paulo: UNESP/Polis, 2005.

Gonzalez Navarro, Moises. *Los extranjeros en Mexico y los mexicanos en el extranjero.* Mexico: El Colegio de Mexico, 1994.

Goodman, Adam. "Nation of migrants, historians of migrations". *Journal of American Ethnic History* 34, no.4 (2015): 7-16.

Harpelle, Ronald. *The West Indians of Costa Rica: Race, Class and the Integration of an Ethnic Minority.* Kingston: McGill-Queens University Press, 2001.

Hobsbawn, Eric. *The age of Capital, 1848-1875.* New York: Charles Scribner's Sons, 1975.

Jaago, Tiiu. "Discontinuity and Continuity in Representations of twentieth Century Estonian History". *Culture Unbound* 6 (2014): 1071-1094.

Kelley, Sean. "'Mexico in his head': Slavery and the Texas-Mexico border, 1810-1860". *Journal of Social History* 37, no.3(2004): 709-723.

Lasso, Marixa. "Race and ethnicity in the formation of the Panamanian identity: Panamanian discrimination against Chinese and West Indians in the thirties". *Revista Panameña de Política*, no. 4 (2007): 61-92.

Lohse, Russell. "Reconciling freedom with the rights of property: slave emancipation in Colombia, 1821-1852, with special reference to La Plata". *The Journal of Negro History* 86, no.3 (2001): 203-227.

Lucas, Natasha. "Why are Haitian Immigrants not treated like Ukrainians? The U.S. needs to extend the same generosity to the Haitian immigrants". *The Root*. Last modified July 23, 2022. Digital. https://www.theroot.com/why-are-haitian-immigrants-not-treated-like-ukrainians-1849199271

Manning, Patrick. "Migrations of Africans to the Americas: the impact on Africans, Africa and the world". *The History Teacher* 26, no.3 (1993): 278-296.

Manning, Patrick. "The slave trade: the formal demography of a global system". *Social Science History* 14, no.2 (1990): 256-279.

Modolo, Vanina. "Análisis histórico-demográfico de la inmigración en la Argentina del Centenario al Bicentenarioigracion y Desarrollo: el caso de Argentina", *Papeles de Poblacion* 22, no.89 (2016): 201-222.

McLeod, Marc. "Undesirable aliens: race, ethnicity, and nationalism in the comparison of Haitian and British West Indian immigrant workers in Cuba, 1912-1939", *Journal of Social History* 31, no.3 (1998): 517-543.

Newton, Velma. *The Silvermen: West Indian Labour Migration to Panama 1850-1914*. Kingston: Ian Randle Publishers, 2004.

Ngai, Mae. *Immigration and ethnic history*. Washington, DC: American Historical Association, 2012.

Patterson, Tiffany; Kelley, Robin. "Unfinished Migrations: Reflections on the African Diaspora and the Making of the Modern World". *African Studies Review* 43, no. 1 (2000): 11-45.

Putnam, Lara. *The company They Kept. Migrants and the Politics of Gender in Caribbean Costa Rica, 1870-1960*. Chapel Hill: The University of North Carolina Press, 2002.

Putnam, Lara. Radical Moves. *Caribbean migrants and the politics of race in the Jazz Age*. Chapel Hill: the University of North Carolina Press, 2013.

Reis, João José. Slave rebellion in Brazil. The Muslim uprising of 1835 in Bahia. Baltimore: John Hopkins, 2005.

Schwarcz, Lilia. *O espetáculo das raças. Cientistas, instituições e questão racial no Brasil 1870-1930*. São Paulo: Companhia das Letras, 1995.

Skidmore, Thomas. *Black into white. Race and nationality in Brazilian thought*. New York: Oxford, 1974.

Soares, Carlos E. L.; Gomes, Flavio. "Revoltas, marinehiros e sistema prisional no Arsenal de Marinha: notas sobre o trabalho compulsórioe cultura política num Rio de Janeiro Atlântico (1820-1840)". *História Social* 12 (2006): 11-33.

Soares, Carlos E. L.. *Zungú: rumor de muitas vozes*. Rio de Janeiro: Arquivo Público do Estado do Rio de Janeiro: 1998.

Thomas-Hope, Elizabeth (ed.) *Freedom and Constraint in Caribbean Migration*. Kingston: Ian Randle Publishers, 2009.

Ward, Nicole; Batalova Jeanne. "Frequently asked statistics on immigrants and immigration in the United States". Spotlight. Migration Policy Institute. Last modified Mach 14, 2023. https://www.migrationpolicy.org/article/frequently-requested-statistics-immigrants-and-immigration-united-states

Wermuth, Maiquel Angelo. "As políticas migratórias brasileiras do século XIX ao século XXI: uma leitura biopolítica do movimento pendular entre democracia e autoritarismo". *Direito e Praxis*, 11, no. 4 (2020): 2330-2358.

PART I

SLAVERY AND FORCED MIGRATIONS

CHAPTER ONE

The Atlantic Slave Trade and the Portuguese-Brazilian Slavocrat Social Formation

João-Manuel Neves

Centro de Estudos Comparatistas, Universidade de Lisboa, Portugal

Abstract

This essay is part of a contextual introduction to the analysis of denial in recent Portuguese historical novels related to the plantation system. The authoritarian perception of Africans by current Portuguese culturalist discourse is rooted in Portugal's own predatory activity and systematic destruction of Africa, carried out from the fifteenth century onwards. Relationships of domination derive from the slave plantation system and the African oceanic slave trade, which initially focused on the subtropical and intertropical East Atlantic islands. The expansion of the plantation system into Brazil from the end of the sixteenth century, followed by the advent of mining exploration in Minas Gerais, principally during the first half of the eighteenth century, created a unique slavocrat social formation. This complex entity would completely interlink Portugal, Brazil and various territories in Africa and India, having its heyday in the seventeenth and eighteenth centuries.

Keywords: Portuguese Empire, Slave Trade, Colonial Slavery, Brazilian Studies, Portuguese Africanist Discourse

***

At the core of my current research project on contemporary Portuguese literature relating to the Empire is an analysis of the hypertextual representations of stereotypical racist fictions within these aesthetic narratives. This fantasist imaginary establishes an original and insurmountable racial inequality, introducing hierarchical differences that suppose a positive or negative identification between morphology and culture. An array of rhetorical forms of justification of injustice is rooted in this naturalizing of inequality, mainly articulated by present-day Africanist discourse. Within a genre of imperial revivalism that emerged in the last years of twentieth-century Portugal, several works of historical fiction represent the massive deportation of Africans to Brazil and the slavery as the result of a biological/cultural racial inequality, bondage viewed cynically as an opportunity created by the masters to lift Africans from savagery. This topic has been present in Portuguese literature since the seventeenth century, mainly in the writings of António Vieira (1954). The image of the African and of the Métis, whether in modern colonial literature or the contemporary Portuguese literature related to the old imperial space, has resulted from a steady increase in depictions of the colonized in Africanist discourse. This imaginary has been consistently elaborated, simultaneously in Portugal and in all regions of her pre-modern empire, over the 450 years that preceded the Berlin Conference.

Medieval Slavery, the Sugar Economy and the Slave Trade

After the fall of the Roman Empire, slavery would persist in vast regions on the shores of the Mediterranean. The caliphate of Cordoba used slave labour on a large scale, based both on the enslavement of prisoners of war as well as on the regular trade originating in Eastern Europe. The Slavic populations are in fact, at the origin of the term "slave", used by the West European and the Muslim brokers of the trade (Verlinden 1970; Heers 1996; Blackburn 2010). The crusades and the conquest of the Levant would increase the use of forced labour in the Mediterranean in the Middle Ages. Then, and indeed before, two quite different types of slavery existed - domestic and sexual slaves and those used for heavy work such as mining or agriculture. The latter included the production of sugar on large estates requiring very heavy labour. Sugarcane, endemic to a vast area from New Guinea to Punjab, was first cultivated in India, expanding to the East, to Southern China by the eighth century, and to the West to Mesopotamia by the seventh and eighth centuries, where huge plantations were cultivated using slaves originating from Eastern Africa (Dockès 2012; Godinho 1982, IV; Popovic 1999). After the tenth century, sugarcane plantations began to be introduced in the Muslim parts of the Mediterranean, first in Egypt, Syria, and Palestine, then to the Eastern islands of the Mediterranean, and later, in the twelfth century, to Morocco (Godinho 1982, IV).

After the Crusades, the Venetians cultivated sugarcane in Tir from the twelfth century; Teutonic Knights and the Templars did the same in Tripoli, in the Levant. In Cyprus and Crete, sugarcane was cultivated on large estates, always using slave labour. Sicily would also become an important area for sugar production in the fourteenth century (Verlinden 1970; Mintz 1986; Heers 1996). On the Iberian Peninsula, sugar was produced in Motril, on the coast of

Granada, from the twelfth century on, and later, particularly in the region around Valencia (Phillips Jr. 2004). In the Algarve, sugarcane plantations existed at least from the twelfth century, as mentioned by German travelers, and also around Coimbra from the fifteenth century (Godinho 1982, IV). Slavery, at the end of the Middle Ages, had expanded to all the Western islands of the Mediterranean, particularly to Majorca and to the south of Italy. Charles Verlinden estimated the number of slaves in Majorca in 1328 at around 21,000, about 36% of the population (Heers 1996; Verlinden 1955).

Until the arrival of the Ottomans in the Eastern Mediterranean in the second half of the fourteenth century, one of the main routes for the trade in slaves to the West passed through the Black Sea, based on Venetian, and especially Genovese, trading posts, particularly Tana and Caffa in the Crimean Peninsula, from where flowed an important traffic originating in Eastern Europe and the Caucasus. The other main lines of the slave trade were the trans-Saharan routes running to Egypt, Cyrenaica or Morocco. In the first half of the fifteenth century, the Turkish presence made the slave trade from East to West quite impracticable, while the conquest of the main strongholds on the Moroccan Atlantic coast by the Portuguese caused a major disruption in traffic coming out of Western Sahara (Heers 1996; Godinho 1982, IV).

The association of sugar production with slavery during the Middle Ages in the Mediterranean took the form of a huge tragedy for sub-Saharan African populations after the second half of the fifteenth century at the hands of the Portuguese *fidalgos-mercadores* (merchant noblemen; see Godinho 1975, 103). The introduction of sugarcane into Madeira coincided with the arrival in the markets of southern Portugal of the first contingents of African slaves in the 1440s. The importance of slavery in Iberian social formations was significant throughout the Middle Ages (Verlinden 1955), particularly as a result of the large number of prisoners of war taken in the wars between the Christian kingdoms and Muslim powers. Valencia and Seville, meanwhile, and above all Barcelona, kept up a regular slave trade from Eastern Europe and the Eastern Mediterranean (Heers 1996). During the first phase of the cultivation of sugarcane in Madeira, the workforce came mainly from the Canaries, where the native population, the Guanches, had been totally reduced to slavery in the fourteenth century. Huge contingents of Guanches had already supplied the sugar plantations of the Iberian Peninsula (Heers 1996; Godinho 1981, I). A significant number of the slaves on the islands or shipped to the peninsula were captured on the Atlantic coasts of North Africa.

Four factors in the fifteenth century were to determine the beginning of a quite rapid development in human trading from the sub-Saharan African coasts. The relative importance of each factor can only be understood within its reciprocal contextual interdependence. First, following Blackburn, it should be noted the importance of the European trade in commodities arising specifically from slave production and the ever-greater need for labour in these sectors. Godinho is certainly right in emphasizing the lack of manpower caused by the Black Plague in the fourteenth century, which is itself related to a third factor, the impossibility of obtaining slaves in the Eastern European markets due to the Ottoman arrival in the Mediterranean (Blackburn, Robin. 2010; Godinho 1982, IV). The need for labour will be the origin of various laws destined to force people into agricultural work while allowing peasants to negotiate a reduction in feudal privileges. Nicolau Clenardo, a Flemish humanist who lived for five years in Portugal from 1533, where he was the preceptor of the royal prince, explicitly associates the impressive numbers of African slaves present in southern Portugal with acute labour shortages (Clenardo 1926). None of these factors alone can explain the recourse to the trade in Africans. To this set of complimentary circumstances is added a fourth factor, technical progress in navigation (Mauro 1989, I; Godinho 1981, I). This historical context would permit continued oceanic exploration by the Portuguese and the development of a sugar economy, first on the island of Madeira, then later in Cape Verde and especially in Sao Tome, through the use of an even greater number of enslaved Africans.

Sugar exports from Madeira began between 1450 and 1455, from Sao Tome in the 1490s, reaching a significant volume, and from Cape Verde by the beginning of the sixteenth century, though only in tiny quantities. Madeira produced around 20,000 *arrobas* (230 metric tonnes) in 1470, rising to a peak of some 200,000 *arrobas* (2,300 t) by 1515. Walvin mentions 230,000 *arrobas* (2,645 t) during the years 1500-1510. Sao Tome would produce 150,000 *arrobas* (1,725 t) by the mid-sixteenth century, with a peak of 200,000 by 1580 before declining (Godinho 1982, IV; Walvin 2018). The Spanish would also start sugar production in the Canary Islands in the 1490s, then later in the Caribbean and on the American continent, in Mexico and Peru, from the sixteenth century, using the initial experiences of Majorca, the south of Italy, the Iberian Peninsula and Madeira (Vieira 2004; Godinho 1982, IV; Pétré-Grenouilleau 2006). The number of enslaved Africans in the Spanish sugar industry was quite substantial, and though the majority of enslaved in the Caribbean and in the Americas were still Amerindian, the Spanish colonies were the main market for the slave trade in those years. Between 1526 and 1550, some 21,736 Africans were shipped to the Spanish Americas, a number which was to double during the years 1551 to 1575.

The Portuguese started the oceanic trade in human beings from the African coasts at the beginning of the fifteenth century and continued to control this traffic exclusively until the end of the sixteenth century. Their monopoly of the slave trade would be established in 1494 by the Treaty of Tordesillas, signed by Portugal and Spain under the auspices of the Pope. The two kingdoms thus divided up the world, with Portugal keeping the rights over Africa. The evolution of the sugar economy confirms the analysis of Verlinden who pointed out that slavery would feed itself. Actually, as we have seen, the process of the constant expansion of this form of labour was connected to the important growth of the pre-modern economies of Western European societies, where the importance of sugar consumption, as well as of other tropical commodities, grew incessantly. Meanwhile, the sudden demographic decline of Europe in the fourteenth century, as well as the non-viability of the slave markets from Eastern Europe, would contribute to the development of the trade in enslaved Africans on European soil. Right from the start, Lisbon became the crossroads for selling Africans in considerable numbers from the 1440s (Saunders 1994). A large number of these enslaved were destined for the Spanish market, whose main centres continued to be Seville, Valencia and Barcelona, and for the Italian market, centred chiefly in Genoa. Flanders also took a considerable part of the Portuguese trade. According to Pétré-Grenouilleau (2006), after Lisbon, Antwerp in the sixteenth century was the European city with the most African residents·

In Portugal, Africans made up 84% of the slave population in the sixteenth century and almost 93% in the seventeenth century, according to data gathered by Jorge Fonseca in his study on slavery in the south of the country. The other slaves were mainly of "Moorish" origin (9.3% and 4.6%) and Asian, mainly Indians (6.5% and 1.7%) (Fonseca 2002). Saunders suggests a total number of 35,000 slaves in Portugal in the mid-sixteenth century, representing around 10% of the population of Lisbon, Evora and the Algarve, some 5% of the population of the southern countryside, and 1% to 2% in the north. The proportion of slaves among the total Portuguese population would be 2.5% to 3%, comparable to the 4% of Sicily which at this time was regularly supplied by the trans-Saharan routes (Saunders 1994). The estimate of Jorge Fonseca leans towards an average of 8% in Lisbon, 7% in Evora and between 3% and 5% of the total population of Alentejo (2002). In Seville, in 1565, there were about 6,000 slaves, nearly 7% of the 85,000 inhabitants, with the Africans acquired in Lisbon making up the majority of the enslaved population of the city (Thomas 1997).

The importance of the slave labour force in Lisbon, the largest European city at this time with a total population of 100,000 inhabitants, was far from negligible. Saunders sees the social condition of the slaves in Portuguese seignorial society as being the lowest position on the hierarchical scale of servitude. The social situation of the slave or the *liberto* (freedman) would be that of a lower *criado* (domestic or manual servant, often born and raised in the master's house). Meanwhile, various rights of the master over his property demarcated the social condition of the slave in relation to the *criado*. Even if the master in Portugal was not allowed to sell baptised slaves (Godinho 1982, IV), they remained goods which could be passed on, given that they had been the object of an initial transaction, bought and sold. The master could give them away or pass them on through inheritance. The slave generally was obligated to live in guarded residences, was forbidden to go to taverns or places that sold drink and was subject to summary judgement in the case of robbery. The punishments meted out to slaves might comprise branding with hot irons or mutilation. In principle, the master was supposed to punish the slave with "humanity," but in practise, no one would dare interfere in cases of extreme violence. The slave did not benefit from ecclesiastical shelter, and the owner could pursue him into the premises of the Catholic church. The arrangements designed to prevent violence or sexual harassment, provided in the *Ordenações* (Ordinances), the legislative codes of the Old Regime, were applicable to all categories of women, including "white" slaves (probably "Moors") but did not apply to African or Métis slaves. These women were at the disposal of all men and could be raped at any time. Among numerous other constraints, it is important to note that the testimony of a slave was not recognised in law but that any free man could use his condition against a non-free man or against an African or a Métis *liberto* (Godinho 1982, IV; Saunders 1994; Aguiar 1930).

Saunders does not seem to take into account the clear distinction between two forms of slavery, domestic and heavy labour. The majority of slaves in the fields and a large part of those who lived in the cities certainly found themselves in the second category. In any case, the possession of slaves was a clear sign of wealth or social success with the more slaves and the more varied their origins, the greater the respect for the fortune of the owner (Saunders 1994). Hugh Thomas gives two examples of bequests of slaves in the mid-sixteenth century. Baltasar Jorge d'Évora, in Lisbon, in 1546, expressed his wish to leave an inheritance of two captives who came from Gujarat in India, as well as two Chinese, one of them a tailor and the other from Caffa, a former Genoese slave trading outpost in Crimea. Maria de Vilhena, in 1562, expressed the wish to free ten slaves, one Chinese, three Amerindians, two "Moors," a white man from Eastern Europe, an African, a dark-skinned person and a Métis, a *mulato* (Thomas 1997). Also, around this time, there developed another type of activity in Lisbon and Seville, the reproduction of slaves for sale. Clenardo mentions this practise in his description of Portugal in the sixteenth century, and Oliveira Martins, in his *History of Portugal*, published in 1879, reminds us that this activity was still very common in the mid-eighteenth century (Clenardo 1926; Martins, 1972).

The Slavocrat Social Formation of the Seventeenth and Eighteenth Centuries

The production of sugar was to become the paradigm of the plantation economy. This activity required considerable investment in land conquered and run as a seignorial dominion. It meant an economy mainly structured around two levels of reproduction of capital: the trafficking of African slaves, which made up two-thirds of the labour force on seventeenth-century plantations (Godinho 1982, IV), and trade in commodities produced with slave labour. During the second half of the fifteenth century, the trade in gold in Western Africa and the trafficking of slaves to Madeira and above all to European markets, as well as the sugar trade, had allowed a certain accumulation of capital by the crown, a large part of the aristocracy and the Portuguese traders. These latter comprised a sizeable contingent of *cristãos-novos* (New Christians) or *conversos*, i.e., converted Jews. Their place within the social formation is quite specific and would become crucial in the expansion of the plantation economy, although the whole process exceeded any explicit intent of the community. Through their capital and their capacity to organise across transnational networks, the New Christians appeared indispensable to the functioning of this embryonic Portuguese mercantile activity, which was very dependent on commercial circuits that first went through Genoa and then later through Flanders (Wilke 2007). Meanwhile the stigma of *judeu marrano* (forcibly converted Jew) allowed the seignorial aristocracy and the merchants to prevent the New Christians from consolidating their social position, with the Inquisition the main weapon used by the aristocracy to keep them under constant political threat. This social group was therefore never able to unite the emerging trader bourgeoisie, whose power would always be neutralized (Wilke 2007; Godinho 1975).

From the end of the fifteenth century until the last quarter of the sixteenth century, the trade in Eastern spices constituted the main economic resource of Portugal. The slave trade, the West African trade in gold and the production of sugar, particularly in Sao Tome, where the other major components of the Portuguese economy at the time. Nevertheless, even though the trade in spices destined for Europe remained in Portuguese hands, the organisation of production was largely beyond their control. Moreover, this trade was based on relentless military might whose incessant violence ravaged the entire Indian Ocean during this time (see e.g. Subrahmanyam 2005; 2012). One aspect ignored by many authors researching the slave trade, including almost all consulted here, has to do with the role played by African captives in Portuguese military power in the East throughout the sixteenth century. Charles Boxer emphasises the importance of Africans as cannon fodder as a central part of the elementary Portuguese military tactic. This consisted, whether in local skirmishes or on the battlefield, of forcing large contingents of alcohol-fed African slaves against an enemy that in most cases, was overwhelmed and suffocated by their large numbers. The adversaries were then slaughtered by Portuguese soldiers whose indiscipline, disorganisation and lack of other military tactics were compensated for by the effectiveness of the large numbers of Africans sent in the first waves to break the enemy lines (Boxer 1973).

Besides the slave trade destined for the East, the Portuguese, in the sixteenth and seventeenth centuries, organised huge traffic of slaves across the Indian Ocean and the Far East. Godinho points out that, in the sixteenth century, some 4,000 to 5,000 Indians were reduced to slavery each year, most ending up in the galleys but with a significant number used for ransom. As with Goa and the other strongholds in India, the Portuguese trading outposts of the Malay Archipelago, Malacca and the Moluccas, and of the Far East, Macau or the settlements in Japan, were slavocrat microcosms. The *fidalgos-mercadores*, and the Portuguese soldiers all had slaves in abundance and lived with captive concubines. A very important traffic was to supply Manila, from Malacca, with slaves destined mainly for Spanish America (Godinho 1982, IV). A report sent in 1550 by a Jesuit to Ignacio de Loyola tells of a man in Malacca who had 24 concubines of "various races" at his disposal. For the Portuguese in the East, it was common, according to this report, to have four, eight or ten slave women and "to sleep with them all" (Boxer 1973).

Although the spice trade continued to grow in absolute value, at least until 1640 (Mauro 1989, v. II), despite the loss of some markets in the East at the end of the sixteenth century, its economic importance became much less relevant at the beginning of the seventeenth century given the increasing influence of the sugar trade. Brazil, where sugar cane was introduced in 1540 through the network of the New Christians (Wilke 2007), would rapidly replace the island of Sao Tome, which had become virtually ungovernable as a result of attacks by Corsairs and especially slave revolts that became endemic after 1580 (Mauro 1989, I; Godinho 1982, IV; Henriques 2000). The yearly production of sugar in Brazil would be 180,000 *arrobas* (2,070 t) in 1570, 900,000 (103,500 t) in 1627, and 2,000,000 (230,000 t) in 1670, making the Portuguese colony the almost exclusive exporter of this commodity into Europe up to the last quarter of the seventeenth century, given that the Spanish production was largely for the internal market. A considerable part of this sugar was initially traded in Antwerp, but also particularly in Amsterdam, the major European centre for the distribution of the commodity (Mauro 1989; Godinho 1982, IV; Marcadé 1991).

In the first phase, the labour force on the Brazilian plantations was mainly Amerindian, as it had been on the plantations of Spanish America. To a large extent, the overall processes of Spanish and Portuguese colonisations of the Americas would lead to the genocide of the original populations (Green 2012). As Charles Boxer notes, "there is no doubt that the Portuguese often exterminated whole tribes in a singularly barbarous way." (Boxer 1962). The revolts of the Amerindian slaves, the high mortality due to the diseases transmitted by Europeans and Africans, and the pressure from Jesuits for the manumission of the remaining local captives, or at least their supervision, would lead to the importation of ever more significant contingents of African slaves (Schwartz 1985; Boxer 1962). By the mid-1580s, their numbers would be equivalent to one-third of the slaves on the Pernambuco plantations, around 2,000 out of an estimated total of 6,000 slaves. Bahia, which was to become the second sugar region of Brazil in the seventeenth century, presented the same proportions among the slave population by the 1590s (Schwartz 1985; Godinho 1982, IV). Contrary to what happened in the spice trade, the capitalists, noblemen, or merchants, had direct control over the production of sugar. The organisation of the plantation and the slave mode of production were inseparable from the trade in the commodity.

The United Provinces, whose economic expansion at the start of the seventeenth century was backed by major naval and military might, were denied access to Portuguese markets after the Iberian Union in 1580 and had, in the meantime, occupied several of the Portuguese outposts in the East. From 1621 on, with the creation of the Dutch West India Company, the Low Countries began to express a huge interest in Brazilian territory. The collaboration between Protestant and Jewish or New Christian networks in Lisbon, Madrid and Amsterdam began to take shape from the beginning of the seventeenth century in Africa, where they dealt in slaves destined for Brazilian plantations (Green 2012). The seizure by the Dutch Company of Bahia in 1624, then Recife and later the entire Northeast, the main sugar regions of Brazil, depended on the participation of these networks. A Jewish emigration, directly related to the expansion of the sugar economy, started towards Dutch Brazil, taking on a Messianic character. Successive revolts by Catholic planters from 1638 on led to the formation of a Portuguese-Brazilian armada in 1645 that would succeed in forcing the Dutch West India Company to completely evacuate the territory in 1654 (Marcadé 1991). Under the Dutch administration, the Jews and the New Christians had experienced an "ephemeral Jewish-Brazilian golden age" (Wilke 2007). Around 1645, according to a probably exaggerated calculation, this community would reach some 1450 people, a number equivalent to the Dutch living in the colony, and would participate actively in developing the production and trade in sugar for the Amsterdam market and in the slave trade and the trade in European products. When the Dutch Company was forced to leave Brazil, the Jews and New Christians went with them to New Amsterdam (Manhattan) and later to Curaçao in the Caribbean (Wilke 2007; Mauro 1989, II). Their technical knowledge of the sugar economy was highly sought after and their interest in the slave trade very important (Wilke 2007; Thomas 1997; Green 2012).

The departure of the Dutch from Pernambuco marks the beginning of the Caribbean production of sugar, which was based mainly on French and English investment. The exponential increase in production after 1660, a phenomenon some called the "sugar revolution" (A. Ly *apud* Célimène and Legris 2012, 214), is related to the growing consumption in Europe of colonial products, especially coffee, tea or chocolate, always associated with sugar (Thomas 1997). The plantation system and the slave trade saw a rapid expansion after the last quarter of the seventeenth century. In a very short while, the "contracted labourers" of European origin who had worked the lands in Barbados or the southeast of North America were replaced by African slaves producing sugar or tobacco. France was to follow closely with the setting up of an ever-greater number of plantations in Saint Domingue or in the Lesser Antilles (Williams 1994; Klein 2010; Thomas 1997). This transfer of the Portuguese Brazilian model of the slave production of sugar to the Caribbean would be the origin of the impressive figures of the slave trade in the eighteenth century and the subsequent development of other colonial products both in the islands and on the North American continent. Despite the rapid growth in Dutch, English and French plantations in the Caribbean and the economic depression of the years 1670 and 1690, the production of sugar would continue relatively stable in Brazil (Mauro 1989, I; Marcadé 1991). Throughout the seventeenth century, the slave production of sugar and (less importantly) tobacco in Brazil would constitute the economic motor for the Portuguese Brazilian imperial social formation, which integrated Portugal, the American colony, the slave trade and the eastern trade. During this century, nearly 1,004,752 slaves were shipped to the Americas from the Western coasts of Africa and, after 1643, from the Mozambican coast (Capela 2002). Brazil was to receive 130,850 slaves during the century, mainly from West and Central West Africa. The population of European origin in the colony was around 30,000 in 1600 and did not exceed 100,000 by the end of the century (Martinière 1991). The total number of slaves in 1630 could be estimated at 35,000, according to Schwartz, who gives a figure of 350 mills in activity at that time in all Brazilian *capitanias* (provinces), which demanded an average of 100 slaves for each plantation (Schwartz 1985). According to Klein and Luna, by 1620, the slave workforce in the Brazilian plantations was already almost entirely of African origin, but the instability in supplying slave markets during the Dutch period would lead to another cycle of massive Amerindian enslavement (Klein and Luna 2010). The figure of 28,385 Africans shipped to the colony in the years 1641 to 1650 is an indicator of the significant economic growth during this period, with a corresponding increase in the enslaved among the Amerindian population.

The population of Portugal stagnated somewhere between 1,100,000 inhabitants in 1580 and 1,200,000 in 1639, according to Mauro (1989, II), due in large part to epidemics but above all because of emigration to Brazil. Godinho, for his part, estimated the population of Portugal at 2,000,000 in 1640 and asserted that the migratory flow from Portugal to Brazil would amount to between 5,000 and 6,000 departures per year. Madeira and the Azores at this time had around 150,000 inhabitants, mainly of Portuguese origin, and the number of Portuguese in the Eastern strongholds and outposts never exceeded 12,000 (Godinho 1975). By that time, a few Portuguese also cohabited with significant and often rival free creole populations in the slaving entrepôts of Cape Verde and Sao Tome archipelagos, in the Upper Guinea or the Slave Coast trade outposts and in those located along the Central West African coasts, mainly Luanda and later Benguela (Green 2012; Miller 1988). Among the slaves in Brazil, the number of children was very low, with two-thirds of the captives being very young men. The renewal of the slave population with Africans was ongoing, given the high rate of mortality and the low birth rate.

Godinho, using data from a poll carried out in Spain at the end of the sixteenth century on men able to carry weapons, draws paradoxical conclusions which are believed to be applicable to Portugal in the Old Regime. In fact, the economic situation created by the flow of precious metals was similar to that in Portugal, firstly with the spices, then even more with the sugar trade and above all in the eighteenth century with gold from Brazil. In these pre-industrial societies, where agriculture should have occupied a central economic position, it turned out that only a third of the male population of active age was found to be involved in agricultural work. The clergy, aristocrats, and merchants made up 36.8% of the population giving, if we add domestic workers and older men, a total of 40.5% of people not involved in productive activities. The tertiary sector had a disproportionate weight for the epoch with a massive rise in sumptuous expenses prefiguring the future secular Iberian stagnation (Godinho 1975; Anderson 1974). In these conditions, Iberian societies found themselves completely incapable of developing manufacturing activities, engendering a chronic dependence on European products.

The demographic picture of the Portuguese Brazilian space, defined by these estimates for the middle of the seventeenth century, allows us to ask central questions about the typology of social formation, which suggests a strong interdependence between Portugal, Africa and Brazil. The relationship between a predominately colonial male population, probably accounting for around 60,000 slaves monitored by an equivalent number of predominantly young male Portuguese (Martinière 1991), compared to a population of between 1,200,000 and 2,000,000 inhabitants in Portugal, comprising many women, children and old people, confirms on the demographic level Frédéric Mauro's economic analysis of the Portuguese-Brazilian space between 1570 and 1670. As was pointed out, this author regarded the Brazilian economy as the motor of the Atlantic empire in the seventeenth century (Mauro 1989, II). In fact, slave production and trade in colonial commodities involved probably the equivalent of one-half of those directly participating in productive activities in the metropolis. Moreover, agricultural production in Portugal was mainly oriented to basic sustenance. The parasitic character of the

Portuguese economy relative to the trade in Asiatic spices, so evident throughout the whole sixteenth century, would worsen even more in the seventeenth century with the production and trade of Brazilian sugar. Portugal became a largely unproductive space within Europe, more geared towards predatory or basic agricultural activities. At the same time, it provided a huge yearly contingent of 5,000 to 6,000 able-bodied men destined for military or police duties and largely implicated in the terror on the plantations.

The seignorial Portuguese regime of the seventeenth century, parasitic and unproductive, was thus integrated into the broader Atlantic space of a social formation dominated by a slave mode of production of colonial commodities. The predatory character of the colonial relationship reached, in the case of the Portuguese Brazilian space, a dimension which went beyond any historical parallel. For more than two centuries, the terror on slave plantations would feed the non-productivity of two-fifths of the population of the European home-country, while a large part of the other three-fifths barely survived of subsistence, goodwill or banditry (Godinho 1975). On the whole, the Portuguese-Brazilian space of the seventeenth century was made up of a seignorial-slavocrat social formation. In Portugal itself, at the end of the seventeenth century, the African slaves comprised between 7 to 9% of the population of two of the most important boroughs of Lisbon (Lahon 1999). The economic stagnation proved even more structural since the New Christian merchants were under constant threat from the lordly class through the Inquisition. In fact, as we have seen, within the ruling class, dominated by an aristocracy of *fidalgos-mercadores*, the elite of the old Jewish population was the only strata capable of becoming the hub for a possible bourgeoisie and of advancing the economy. A French report of 1684 characterises the ruling Portuguese stratum:

> Even though the Portuguese are all spiritual, their self-importance always ends up surprising us. They have no education and they have learnt nothing from the other countries and only speak of the greatness of their houses and the good deeds of their predecessors. They believe there is no nobility more illustrious than theirs, nor a nation where there are so many great men. Those who wish to study the sciences learn them very easily, though they are few amongst these lords. The natural inclination they have for depravity, which they give into from a very young age, takes away the will to train and to travel. They are very shrewd, all phony, extremely lazy and very suspicious (Torcy 1960).

The discovery of gold in the present-day Brazilian state of Minas Gerais at the beginning of the eighteenth century was to bring an extraordinary and unexpected bonanza to the lordly Portuguese class. At the same time, it caused a dramatic increase in the violence of the mode of production and the forms of terror used over the slaves. Boxer refers to the statement of Martinho de

Mendonça, who carried out exhaustive inquiries in Minas Gerais in 1734, concluding that owners normally expected twelve years of work from their slaves (Boxer 1962); a figure similar to the estimates of Klein and Luna (2010). In the case of more dangerous tasks, down in the mines, for example, life expectancy shortened considerably (Boxer 1962). Pétré-Grenouilleau (2006) seems to neglect this reality in his appreciation of Brazilian slavery. This author has a tendency to minimise the importance of the Portugues- Brazilian space within the economic whole that makes up the Atlantic commercial capitalism of the eighteenth century. His view that there would be a fall in sugar production in Brazil in the eighteenth century, given the competition of Caribbean sugar on the European market, is wrong. According to Klein and Luna, in 1760, Brazilian sugar accounted for 17% of the total production, making the Portuguese colony the third largest producer (Klein and Luna 2010). There was an enormous increase in the consumption of sugar and other colonial products in Europe, with production in Brazil remaining stable (Stols 2004). The chief analytical error of Pétré-Grenouilleau was his consideration of slave labour only in the framework of the sugar economy. Despite the evidence of the figures for the slave trade cited in his work, some 6,000,000 Africans abducted during the eighteenth century, of whom 2,000,000 sent by the Portuguese to Brazil, this author completely overlooks the importance of the labour force used in the mines which would have made up the majority of slaves during the first half of the eighteenth century (Boxer 1973). This equivocation by Pétré-Grenouilleau prevents him from understanding the real reason for the natural growth in slavery due to the increase in the birth rate in Minas Gerais at the end of the eighteenth century, by which time the mines had run dry for over half a century. Actually, it was partly the result of the diminution of the grueling violence of the working conditions in a region where the plantation system had not seen wide development and the number of available slaves after the closure of the mines remained significant (Pétré Grenouilleau 2006).

Brazilian gold would play a crucial role in the accumulation of capital, carried out chiefly by England at the start of the Industrial Revolution at the end of the eighteenth century. In 1703, at the time of the signing of the Treaty of Methuen, England was already the main supplier to the Portuguese Brazilian space of agricultural and, especially, manufactured products. Giving trade privileges to English products in exchange for preferential treatment for Portuguese wines in the English market, the Treaty would very quickly deepen the Portuguese trade deficit with England. The gold served to plug the deficit, causing a drastic deterioration of the predatory and unproductive nature of the Portuguese economy. Between 1558 and 1694, England had minted nearly 15,000,000 pounds sterling in gold, and the Portuguese Brazilian trade would allow the same amount to be minted between 1694 and 1727, in the 33 years of extensive exploitation of the Brazilian mines. This constant flow and minting of gold would allow England to secure monetary stability during the eighteenth century and to launch her industrial growth by the end of the century (Vilar 1978). Between March 1740 and June 1741, the Falmouth packet boat, the main line of entry to England of gold from Lisbon, imported the equivalent of 444,317 pounds sterling in gold. Nearly half of Portuguese imports from England were paid for in gold at the beginning of the eighteenth century. Besides this, Portugal did not have enough shipping capacity, so a considerable part of her trade had to be done using British ships, reinforcing the bonds of dependence. There was also a large negative balance in relation to other European suppliers to the Portuguese Brazilian Empire, particularly France and the Low Countries, with the latter having practically a monopoly on the diamond trade of Brazil. During the eighteenth century, Brazil would have furnished more than 800 tons of pure gold, which was to have a determinant role in the economic growth of Europe, accelerating the expansion of its markets (Marcadé 1991).

Brazilian gold would thus allow embryonic capitalism to accomplish all the accumulation of wealth necessary to carry out the Industrial Revolution, ushering in the Modern Age. This prodigious injection of precious metal into the economies of north-western Europe had its origin in the hellhole of slavery in Minas Gerais. The exploitation of gold mobilised a large part of the 1,463,652 Africans shipped to Brazil during the eighteenth century as well as the 800,000 Portuguese needed to monitor them for the benefit of a parasitic lordly class averse to any form of productive activity. The archaism and ridicule of the court and the Portuguese ruling classes were proverbial amongst their counterparts in Europe, as Oliveira Martins was to describe in his *History of Portugal* published a century later (Martins, 1972; Chantal 2005).

The promise of gold throughout the entire eighteenth century would enable the consolidation of the slavocrat social formation that developed in the second half of the seventeenth century, leaving Portugal at the start of the nineteenth century with a weak and completely unindustrialized economy. In addition, Brazil, which became independent in 1822, would remain submerged in the inhumanity of a system of slavery perpetuated by the Bragança dynasty. The demographic picture of the Portuguese Brazilian space in the eighteenth century reveals the importance of slavery in the imperial society. Between 1700 and 1775, an annual average of 13,500 Africans was shipped to Brazil, while some 10,000 Portuguese, mainly young men, left Portugal each year. The population of Portugal grew from 2,000,000 in 1700 to 2,500,000 in 1758 and 3,000,000 at the end of the century. Without counting free Amerindians, Brazil, by 1750, had around 1,500,000 inhabitants, of whom one-third to half were slaves (Martinière 1991). At the beginning of the nineteenth century, Brazil had 3,000,000 inhabitants, of whom a third were slaves. During all of the eighteenth century, between 1,000 and 2,000 slaves were shipped each year from Africa to Portugal destined for heavy labor or domestic duties (Godinho 1975). By 1750, the weight of the slave mode of commodity production in the Portuguese Brazilian economic space was overwhelming. Actually, in one century, Brazil's slave population had increased from 60,000 to 750,000, mainly young males. The principal difference, in the mid-eighteenth century, had to do with the significant number of free inhabitants, around 750,000 to a million. Klein and Luna estimate the total Brazilian slave population in 1800 at one million, while free Africans and Métis amounted to half a million. Only 10 percent of slaves resided in urban areas, the vast majority being confined to the plantation and other agricultural and mining activities. The free population was more balanced in gender and age, including many non-Europeans and featuring an important young European component (Klein and Luna 2010). For its part, Portugal had a population of two and a half million inhabitants, consisting of a large number of women, children, and older men.

The slave mode of production in the Americas started to disintegrate after 1775. The revolution in Haiti became, from 1791, the tipping point of the permanent resistance of Africans to slavery all around the Atlantic from the inception of the trans-Atlantic slave trade in the fifteenth century. The impact in the Americas of the disintegration of the French colonial system would be huge on the spirits of the masters as much as of the slaves. The Haitian revolution would influence the abolitionist processes that occurred throughout the nineteenth century (James 2001). In Brazil, resistance to slavery had been endemic and generalised ever since the arrival of the first Europeans in the sixteenth century. However, a variety of circumstances would allow its survival until 1888. The successive disruptions in the production of colonial commodities, caused by the crises and the disintegration of slavery in other parts of the Atlantic, would have the effect of increasing Brazilian exports. The slave mode of production was thus reinforced under the Bragança regime, established in Brazil after 1808 when the Portuguese court fled Europe from the Napoleonic armies.

The average annual number of Africans shipped to Brazil was to increase until it reached 23,635 between 1791 and 1800, then reaching 33,321 between 1801 and 1810, and 47,418 between 1811 and 1820, while in the 1820s, there would be 54,898 slaves shipped per year to the new Empire of the Portuguese royal house. Between 1820 and 1920, there was an annual average emigration to Brazil of 10,000 Portuguese, 14,000 Italians, 5,000 Spaniards and 5,600 of other nationalities. In the 1850s, the vast majority of the 4,000 Portuguese who entered Brazil each year were destined to replace African slaves in the coffee plantations (Pereira 1981). They would be about 12,000 a year in the decade after 1870 and 14,000 a year in the decade after 1880 (Godinho 1975; Mauro 1980). The definitive abolition of slavery in 1888 and the fall of the Braganças in 1889 coincided with growing interest in Africa from the Portuguese ruling classes and with the beginning of land conquests which were to constitute the future colonies of Angola and Mozambique. As we have seen, Portuguese specificity consisted in the continuation of the plantation system and the slave mode of production uninterruptedly from ancient times to the nineteenth century on the very European soil of Portugal and on a colossal scale in Brazil, following on from the fifteenth-century experiences of the East Atlantic islands. The Portuguese Brazilian space, consisting of the complete interdependence of Portugal, Brazil and parts of Africa and India, was really an economy dominated, throughout the seventeenth and eighteenth centuries, by a slave mode of production of colonial commodities. This economy was, however, entirely structured by the market circuits of commercial capitalism of northwestern Europe in the Old Regime. Aníbal Quijano (2008) has properly characterised the social formation that developed in Central and South America as colonial capitalism. In fact, the slave mode of production and the colonial seignorial political framework are completely integrated within an economic capitalist system, but it is important to stress that the prevailing social mores, at least in the Portuguese Brazilian space, were indeed of a slavocrat type. The African Empire of Portugal in the twentieth century reproduced, to a large extent, the main characteristics of the Portuguese Brazilian social formation of the preceding centuries. The modern discursive appropriation of Africa relies largely on the imaginary developed throughout the centuries-old slavocrat experience. The plantation system with forms that arose from slave labour relations would be implemented by Portugal in Africa up to the last quarter of the twentieth century. Plantation and colonial racialized slavery can be found today at the core of the representations articulated in everyday life within Portuguese contemporary colonial discourse on Africa.

References

Aguiar, Asdrúbal António de. *Crimes e delitos sexuais em Portugal na época das Ordenações (sexualidade normal)*. [Separata]. Lisboa: Instituto de Medicina Legal, 1930.

Anderson, Perry. *Lineages of the Absolutist State*. London: NLB, 1974.

Blackburn, Robin. *The Making of New World Slavery: From the Baroque to the Modern, 1492-1800*. London and New York: Verso, 2010.

Boxer, Charles. *The Golden Age of Brazil, 1695-1750: Growing Pains of a Colonial Society*. Berkekey, Los Angeles and London: University of California Press, 1962.

_____. *The Portuguese Seaborne Empire, 1415-1825*. Harmondsworth: Penguin, 1973.

Capela, José. *O tráfico de escravos nos portos de Moçambique*. Porto: Afrontamento, 2002.

Célimène, Fred and André Legris. "L'économie coloniale des Antilles françaises au temps de l'esclavage". In *L'économie de l'esclavage colonial: Enquête et bilan du XVIIe au XIXe siècle*, edited by Fred Célimène and André Legris, 209-245. Paris: CNRS, 2012.

Chantal, Suzanne. *A vida quotidiana em Portugal ao tempo do terramoto*. Lisboa: Livros do Brasil, 2005.

Clenardo, Nicolau. "Cartas". In *Clenardo*, edited by Gonçalves Cerejeira. Coimbra: Coimbra Editora, 1926.

Dockès, Pierre. "Le paradigme sucrier (XIeXIXe siècle)". In *L'économie de l'esclavage colonial: Enquête et bilan du XVIIe au XIXe siècle*, edited by Fred Célimène and André Legris. Paris: CNRS, 2012.

Fonseca, Jorge. *Escravos no Sul de Portugal: Séculos XVIXVII*. Lisboa: Vulgata, 2002.

Godinho, Vitorino Magalhães. *Estrutura da antiga sociedade portuguesa*. 2nd rev. ext. ed. Lisboa: Arcádia, 1975.

_____. *Os descobrimentos e a economia mundial*. 2nd rev. ext. ed. 4 vol. Lisboa: Presença, 1982.

Green, Toby. *The Rise of the Trans-Atlantic Slave Trade in Western Africa, 1300-1589*. New York: Cambridge UP, 2012.

Heers, Jacques. *Esclaves et domestiques au Moyen âge dans le monde méditerranéen*. Paris: Hachette, 1996.

Henriques, Isabel Castro. *Sao Tomé e Príncipe: A invenção de uma sociedade*. Lisboa: Vega, 2000.

James, Cyril L.R. *The Black Jacobins: Toussaint L'Ouverture and the San Domingo Revolution*. London: Penguin, 2001.

Klein, Herbert S. *The Atlantic Slave Trade*. 2nd ed. New York: Cambridge UP, 2010.

Klein, Herbert S. and Francisco Vidal Luna. *Slavery in Brazil*. New York: Cambridge UP, 2010.

Lahon, Didier. *O negro no coração do Império: Uma memória a resgatar: Séc. XV-XIX*. Lisboa: Secretariado Coordenador dos Programas de Educação Multicultural, 1999.

Marcadé, Jacques. "O quadro institucional e imperial". In *O império luso-brasileiro: 1620-1750: vol. VII: Nova história da expansao portuguesa*, edited by Frédéric Mauro. Lisboa: Estampa, 1991.

Marques, João Pedro. "Uma cosmética demorada: as Cortes perante o problema da escravidão (1836-1875)". *Análise Social* 81 (2001): 209-247.

Martinière, Guy. "A implantação das estruturas de Portugal na América (1620-1750)". In *O império luso-brasileiro: 1620-1750: vol. VII: Nova história da expansao portuguesa*, edited by Frédéric Mauro, 91-261. Lisboa: Estampa, 1991.

Martins, Oliveira. *História de Portugal*. 16th ed. Lisboa: Guimarães, 1972.

Mauro, Frédéric. *La vie quotidienne au Brésil au temps de Pedro Segundo, 1831-1889.* Paris: Hachette, 1980.

———. *Portugal, o Brasil e o Atlântico: 1570-1670.* 2 vol. Lisboa: Estampa, 1989.

Menezes, Sr. Mary Noel. 1988. "The Madeiran Portuguese and the Establishment of the Catholic Church in British Guiana, 1835-98". *Immigrants & Minorities: Historical Studies in Ethnicity, Migration and Diaspora* 7, no.1 (1988): 57-78.

Miller, Joseph. *Way of Death: Merchant Capitalism and the Angolan Slave Trade, 1730-1830.* Madison: University of Wisconsin Press, 1988.

Mintz, Sidney W. *Sweetness and Power: The Place of Sugar in Modern History.* Harmondsworth: Penguin, 1986.

Pereira, Miriam Halpern. *A política portuguesa de emigração: 1850 a 1930.* Lisboa: A Regra do Jogo, 1981.

Pétré-Grenouilleau, Olivier. *Les traites négrières: Essai d'histoire globale.* Paris: Gallimard, 2006.

Phillips Jr, William D. "Sugar in Iberia". In *Tropical Babylons: Sugar and the Making of the Atlantic World, 1450-1680*, edited by Stuart B. Schwartz, 27-41. Chapel Hill (NC) and London: University of North Carolina Press, 2004.

Popovic, Alexandre. *The Revolt of African Slaves in Iraq in the 3rd/9th Century.* Princeton: Markus Wiener, 1999.

Quijano, Aníbal. "Coloniality of power, Eurocentrism and Latin America". In *Coloniality at Large: Latin America and the Postcolonial Debate*, edited by Mabel Moraña, Enrique Dussel and Carlos A. Jáuregui, 181-224. Durham (NC) and London: Duke UP, 2008.

Saunders, A. C. C. M. *História social dos escravos e libertos negros em Portugal (1441-1555).* Lisboa: Imprensa Nacional, 1994.

Schwartz, Stuart B. *Sugar Plantations in the Formation of Brazilian Society: Bahia, 1550-1835.* Cambridge: Cambridge UP, 1985.

Stols, Eddy. "The Expansion of the Sugar Market in Western Europe". In *Tropical Babylons: Sugar and the Making of the Atlantic World, 1450-1680*, edited by Stuart B. Schwartz, 238-288. Chapel Hill (NC) and London: University of North Carolina Press, 2004.

Subrahmanyam, Sanjay. *The Portuguese Empire in Asia: 1500-1700: A Political and Economic History.* 2nd ed. Chichester: Wiley Blackwell, 2012.

———. *From the Tagus to the Ganges.* Dehli: Oxford UP, 2005.

Takaki, Ronald. *Pau Hana: Plantation Life and Labor in Hawaii.* Honolulu: University of Hawaii Press, 1983.

Thomas, Hugh. *The Slave Trade: The History of the Atlantic Slave Trade, 1440-1870.* London: Papermac (Macmillan), 1997.

Torcy, Colbert de. "Estat du royaume du Portugal en 1684". *Boletim da Biblioteca da Universidade de Coimbra* 30 (1960).

Verlinden, Charles. *L'esclavage dans l'Europe médiévale: Vol I: Péninsule Ibérique, France.* Brugge: Tempel, 1955.

———. *The Beginnings of Modern Colonization.* Ithaca (NY) and London: Cornell UP, 1970.

Vieira, Alberto. "Sugar Islands: The Sugar Economy of Madeira and the Canaries, 1450-1650". In *Tropical Babylons: Sugar and the Making of the*

Atlantic World, 1450-1680, edited by Stuart B. Schwartz, 42-84. Chapel Hill (NC) and London: University of North Carolina Press, 2004.

Vieira, Padre António."Sermão Décimo Quarto (Da série 'Maria, Rosa Mística')". *Obras escolhidas: Volume XI: Sermões (II)*, 146. Lisboa: Sá da Costa, 1954.

Vilar, Pierre. *Or et monnaie dans l'histoire: 1450-1920*. Paris: Flammarion, 1978.

Walvin, James. *Sugar: The World Corrupted: From Slavery to Obesity*. New York and London: Pegasus, 2018.

Wilke, Carsten L. *Histoire des juifs portugais*. Paris: Chandeigne, 2007.

Williams, Eric. *Capitalism & slavery*. Chapel Hill (NC) and London: University of North Carolina Press, 1994.

CHAPTER TWO
Fugitive Slaves in an Unstable Border Region: Patterns of Nineteenth-Century Slave Flight from Brazil to Uruguay and Argentina

Karl Monsma
Universidade Federal do Rio Grande do Sul, Brazil

Patrícia Bosenbecker
Universidade Federal da Grande Dourados, Brazil

Abstract

This paper discusses patterns of slave flight in the southern borderlands of Brazil, based primarily on lists of runaway slaves in post-mortem inventories of masters in the border region. It addresses variations in the kind of slave who fled (birthplace, occupation, gender, age), as well as variation over time in response to wars and the abolition of slavery in neighboring countries. It also considers how fugitive slaves supported themselves, as well as the change over time in the nature and degree of state support for masters attempting to capture alleged runaways and the difficulties and hazards faced by both fugitive slaves and slavecatchers. Rising prices after Brazil effectively ended the importation of enslaved Africans in 1850 produced renewed efforts by slaveowners to locate fugitives, as well as greater Brazilian diplomatic pressure on Uruguay and Argentina for the return of fugitives.

Keywords: Slavery, Black Cowboys, runaways, Brazil, Uruguay

***

Introduction

Patterns of nineteenth-century slave flight in the southernmost Brazilian province of Rio Grande do Sul are particularly interesting given its borders with Uruguay and Argentina, which both abolished slavery before Brazil. A significant number of slaves worked as cowboys and could flee on horseback, while the frequent civil and international wars in the region produced both unique opportunities for flight and specific dangers for fugitives. For a long time, historians have denied the existence of enslaved cowboys in nineteenth-century Rio Grande do Sul: in part because this history is inconsistent with the image the *gauchos* (from Rio Grande do Sul) held of themselves, in contrast to the rest of Brazil, as freedom-loving, republican and white; in part because historians and historical social scientists, especially those influenced by Marxism, long thought that it was impossible to use slaves as cowboys given the facility for escape and the fact that the tools of the job, such as knives, lassoes, and bolas (*boleadeiras*), easily became weapons. In the past two decades, however, increasing evidence, especially statistical evidence, has clearly demonstrated the widespread presence, if not prevalence, of enslaved cowboys on the ranches of nineteenth-century Rio Grande do Sul (Bell 1998; Farinatti 2003, 2010; Monsma 2012; Osório 2007).

In one of the most influential books on rural *gaúcho* history, Paulo Zarth claims that ranchers were forced to use slaves because public land in the forested parts of the province available for informal occupation by free people – approximately half of the territory – created a shortage of free workers (Zarth 2002). According to Zarth, it was only after the land law of 1850, which made informal occupancy more difficult, in combination with European colonization schemes that expropriated much of the land already occupied by *caboclos* (rural people of indigenous or mixed descent), that an increasing number of free workers became available for the ranches.

In a comparative article, however, Monsma shows that in the first decades of the nineteenth century, ranchers in both Buenos Aires Province, Argentina and southern Brazil actually preferred slaves as permanent workers, in combination with fluctuating numbers of free workers, hired on a temporary basis for seasonal tasks (Monsma 2012). Ranch slavery declined in the Platine republics solely as a function of abolition laws and the wars of independence, for which many slaves were drafted as soldiers and freed if they survived. Ranchers who could afford slaves preferred them as permanent workers because, over the long run, they cost considerably less than the wages of free workers and, in many cases, were considered more reliable, largely because they were much more dependent on their masters than were free cowboys, who often quit to tend their own herds and fields, or simply to look for better conditions under another employer. With the declining availability of slaves, ranchers in Buenos Aires turned increasingly to migrant workers from Paraguay and the northern provinces of Argentina. In combination with the radical simplification of ranches and the availability of enormous expanses of high-quality land newly conquered from indigenous peoples, the migrant workers helped Buenos Aires ranchers prosper in the early to mid-nineteenth century, prior to the introduction of fencing.

The ranchers of Rio Grande do Sul could have used migrant workers from the same origins, which are closer to Rio Grande do Sul than to Buenos Aires, but they continued using enslaved cowboys because they were more profitable and because slavery continued in Brazil. If anything, the preference for enslaved cowboys was even more marked in Rio Grande do Sul than in the Platine republics because the survival of the slave trade until 1850 made slaves cheaper there. At the beginning of the 1830s, a slave in Rio Grande do Sul cost about the same as 4.6 years of salary for a free ranch worker (Maestri 2008). The ranching economy and the fact that cowboy skills of riding, roping, castration and the like were best learned by young men, produced a particularly high demand for enslaved boys and youths, both Brazilian- and African-born, in Rio Grande do Sul (Caratti 2013).

Enslaved cowboys necessarily rode horses and could easily escape. They were also armed with knives, machetes, bolas and lassoes, which made fugitives dangerous men. In addition, the proximity of international borders with Argentina and Uruguay provided obvious destinations for highly mobile fugitives on horseback. Uruguay was by far the most common destination because it was closer to most of the ranches, much of the border was easily crossed by land or by fording small rivers – unlike the Brazil-Argentina border, defined by the large Uruguay River – and the various civil and international wars in Uruguay meant that cowboys, especially, could easily gain freedom by joining one of the rival armies. Interaction across the Rio Grande do Sul-Uruguay border was so intense in the early and mid-nineteenth century that it is perhaps emblematic that a map drawn in 1856 does not even show the borderline (Figure 2.1).

Figure 2.1. Map of Rio Grande do Sul and Uruguay in 1856, by Herrmann Rudolf Wendroth.

Source: Herrmann Wendroth, "Mapa da Província de São Pedro, c. 1852. Aquarela". *Tetraktys. Wikimedia Commons*, 2008.
(http://commons.wikimedia.org/wiki/Category:Herrmann_Rudolf_Wendroth).

Both Argentina and Uruguay began the abolition process in the 1810s with "free womb" laws and prohibitions on the international slave trade (Borucki, Chagas, and Stalla 2004; Isola 1975). These laws were sometimes interpreted to mean that any slave brought to the country by his or her master should be considered free, but Brazilian ranchers established in northern Uruguay brought their slaves into the country and were able to keep them in captivity until the 1840s. The Uruguayan-born children of slaves were officially free, but Brazilian ranchers invented subterfuges to keep them in bondage, often bringing them to Rio Grande do Sul for baptism and then using the baptism certificate as "proof" that the child was born in Brazil (Monsma and Fernandes 2013). Although fugitive slaves were not officially considered free, most employers did not ask questions, and armies were always eager for new recruits. Once a fugitive found employment or joined an army – or was forced into an army – he, or sometimes she was generally treated as free. Final Uruguayan abolition was decreed for Montevideo and its environs in 1842 by the Colorado government in power there and in 1846 by the rival Blancos, who controlled the rest of the country. After 1846, until Brazil forced Uruguay to sign a treaty providing for the return of fugitive slaves in 1851, all escaped slaves who reached Uruguay were officially free (Palermo 2013). After the fugitive slave treaty went into effect, many Brazilian masters and government officials believed that it applied retroactively to all fugitives who had previously entered Uruguay, whereas the predominant Uruguayan interpretation was that it applied only to fugitives who entered the country after the treaty. Even after this treaty, escaped Brazilian slaves who entered military service or found employment on a ranch could often count on the protection of their new Uruguayan employers, who could hide them when Brazilian slave catchers approached.

Slaves of all origins and occupations escaped. Horses were common in the livestock-raising province of Rio Grande do Sul, and not only cowboys could ride. Some captives also entered Uruguay on foot. Another highly mobile category was enslaved sailors, common on the boats that sailed the Brazilian great lakes Lagoa dos Patos and Lagoa Mirim, connecting the three largest cities of the province, Rio Grande, Pelotas, and Porto Alegre, as well as river destinations such as Sao Leopoldo, Rio Pardo, and Jaguarão, along tributaries of these lakes. In some cases, enslaved sailors stole boats and sailed to Uruguay, which could be reached by way of the Sao Gonçalo Canal and the Lago Mirim without risking the open ocean. Other sailors fled when their boats were in Uruguayan ports or at points close to Uruguay. The greatest concentration of enslaved workers in the province was in and around Pelotas, the center of the jerked beef industry. Many of the jerked beef plant, or *charqueada*, workers were Africans who had never learned to ride horses, but the border at Jaguarão was only about 130 kilometers from Pelotas, so a determined fugitive could walk to the border in a few days.

In this chapter, we examine which kinds of slaves (occupation, gender, origin) were most likely to flee, as well as variation over time in response to wars, the ending of the international slave trade after 1851, and international treaties for the return of escaped slaves. We use evidence drawn from three datasets: lists of slaves in posthumous inventories of masters in the border region, which generally noted if a slave was a runaway at the time of the inventory; a list of supposedly escaped slaves that a Brazilian slavecatcher produced in court to defend himself against charges of enslaving free people in Uruguay after the Farroupilha civil war in Rio Grande do Sul between 1835 and 1845; and a list, compiled by the provincial government, of "slaves" that people who claimed to be their masters had reported as escaped to Uruguay during this war. We also draw on evidence from the personal correspondence of an important ranching family and from criminal trial records resulting from violence between escaped slaves and those attempting to capture them.

Influence of gender, birthplace, and occupation on propensity to flight

We coded data from the probate records (posthumous inventories) of four municipalities in southern Rio Grande do Sul: Pelotas, Piratini, Bagé and Jaguarão. The probate records provide a valuable general picture of patterns of escape because they cover the entire period from 1810 up to the end of slavery in 1888, although, for most of the analyses reported below, we only include data from 1822 (Brazilian independence) onward because the number of pre-independence inventories is limited. These records generally list escaped slaves along with all other slaves, apparently because heirs wanted to be able to reclaim them if they were located at some later time. As a record of the contemporary pattern of escapes, this source is limited by the fact that, in many cases, fugitives had escaped years before the death of their master, and the inventories were only compiled after the master's death. Some slaves are undoubtedly counted twice as well because it was common, at least in rich families, to protect the rights of heirs by compiling two inventories, one after the death of a first spouse and another after the death of the other.

We also cannot be sure that all of these "escaped" slaves had really fled from Rio Grande do Sul. In the wake of the Portuguese occupation of the Banda Oriental/Província Cisplantina (later Uruguay) in 1816, many Brazilian ranchers had acquired properties in the northern expanses of this territory and taken slaves there to work on their ranches (Borucki, Chagas, and Stalla 2004; Palermo 2013). Because many of the wealthier ranching families had properties on both sides of the border, some of the people listed as "escaped" could actually have been freed by the 1846 Uruguayan abolition law. For Brazilians who refused to accept Uruguayan abolition, listing such ex-slaves as escaped would have been a strategy to recover their human "property".

These records include the inventories of 2,626 masters, with 19,803 slaves, of whom 191 were listed as escaped and still missing at the time of the inventory. The number who had escaped at some time in their lives is undoubtedly much larger because many were recaptured or voluntarily returned after a temporary absence. Thus, these data over-represent long-term fugitives, presumably the same group that headed for an international border rather than stay close to the ranch, farm, *charqueada*, workshop, or house from which they had fled. We produced two datasets with this information, one in which the unit of analysis is the deceased master, with variables such as the total number of slaves and the number who had escaped, and another more detailed dataset with information on the individual slaves of deceased masters with at least one escaped slave, which includes 2,086 enslaved individuals, and permits comparison of the characteristics of escaped slaves with those of nonfugitives who worked for the same masters.

Using this second dataset, Table 2.1 shows, unsurprisingly, that men were substantially more likely to escape than women, who were less likely to ride horses, more likely to be employed in domestic work, more likely to be raising children, and more vulnerable to sexual or other forms of violence when on their own. But some women did escape as well, sometimes, as will be seen below, accompanying men or taking along their children. Considering the great distances of the Campanha ranching region as well as the distances between towns, the separation of families or lovers constituted a clear motive for escape. A letter from Francisco Vieira Braga, a rancher in Boqueirão, to his brother Vicente on the Sao João ranch states, "My negro Israel fled some days ago, and I suppose he has gone to Sao João, the place of his love, and he probably is sheltered by the others."[1]

Table 2.1. Percentage of male and female slaves listed as escaped in probate records of estates including escaped slaves - southern Rio Grande do Sul, 1822-1888.

	% escaped	Total
Men	11.3	1346
Women	3.3	518
Total	9.1	1864

$\chi^2 = 29.1$, 1 d.f., $p < ,001$

Source: Arquivo Público do Estado do Rio Grande do Sul (APERS) 2010.

These data include information on place of birth for about only half of the slaves listed. Table 2.2 suggests that, among men, those born in Brazil were more likely to escape than those from Africa, whereas the relationship is reversed among female slaves, although the relationship between birthplace and percentage escaped is not statistically significant for men or for women. If the observed relations are not simply the result of random events, the greater propensity to escape of Brazilian-born men could result from the fact that they were more likely to work with horses, as cowboys or horse breakers, or at least know how to ride them, and the lesser propensity to escape of Brazilian born women could be a result of a greater tendency for employment in domestic, and thus more closely controlled, labor.

---

[1] Francisco Vieira Braga to Vicente Vieira Braga, Arroio Grande, 28 March 1859. Biblioteca Rio-Grandense (BRG), Arquivo Vieira Braga (AVB), Lata 27, Correspondencia de 1856 a 1860.

Table 2.2. Percentage of slaves listed as escaped, by origin and sex, in probate records of estates including escaped slaves in southern Rio Grande do Sul, 1822-1888.

Birthplace	Men	Total	Women	Total
Africa	9.8%	357	4.5%	67
Brazil	12.6%	333	2.3%	177

N=934

χ^2(men)=1.4, 1 d.f., non-significant; ^{2}(women)=0.9, 1 d.f., non-significant
Source: APERS 2010.

The next table presents the percentages of escaped male slaves by occupational category. Cowboys were more likely to flee than slaves of any other occupation – although we do not have adequate data to estimate the chances of flight for enslaved sailors, another highly mobile occupation that probably also had high rates of escape. The correspondence of ranchers reveals that slave flight was a constant preoccupation, and ranchers treated enslaved cowboys better than other captives to inhibit flight (Monsma 2013). Even so, many did run away, almost invariably heading for one of the international borders, especially the southern border with Uruguay, which at most points is either a land border or one with small, easily fordable rivers, in contrast to the Argentine border, which was both more distant from most ranches and defined by the large Uruguay River.

Charqueada workers were particularly unlikely to escape. Many, if not most, were Africans who did not ride horses and were unfamiliar with the geography of the interior of the state. The enslaved workers of these protoindustrial operations also suffered closer supervision than many other workers, such as artisans or cowboys. Perhaps surprisingly, male agricultural workers were also relatively likely to escape, although this percentage is based on a small number of individuals. These workers necessarily worked in the countryside, where horses were readily available that some undoubtedly could ride, facilitating escape.

Table 2.3. Percentage of male slaves listed as escaped in probate records of estates including escaped slaves, by occupational category, southern Rio Grande do Sul 1822-1888.

Occupation	% escaped	Total
Cowboy	15.2	151
Agricultural worker	13.2	38
Jerked beef worker	3.1	195
Other	4.7	359
All occupations	6.9	743

χ^2=25.8, 3 d.f. p<,001
Source: APERS 2010.

Table 2.4 presents the same information as Table 2.3, but separately by birthplace (with agricultural workers here included in the category "others" due to their small numbers). As expected, enslaved African *charqueada* workers were particularly unlikely to escape, but cowboys born in Africa were over twice as likely to escape as their Brazilian-born counterparts. Apparently, if they had a real opportunity for a successful escape, Africans were even more likely than Brazilians to attempt to regain freedom. This is consistent with the idea that those who grew up in slavery were somewhat more resigned to it or learned to gain small advantages within the system and thus had something to lose if they tried unsuccessfully to escape. However, it is important to note that the great majority of the African cowboys would have been purchased as boys or adolescents, affording them the opportunity to master cowboy skills. Unless they escaped soon after purchase, when they were still very young, these Africans would have been able to learn how the system worked just as well as the Brazilian-born cowboys. Although based on small numbers, these results seem to suggest that Africans captured, even when quite young, remembered their former lives and were more determined than those born in slavery to regain freedom if they had a chance to do so.

Table 2.4. Percentage of male slaves listed as escaped in probate records of estates including escaped slaves, by occupational category and origin, southern Rio Grande do Sul 1822-1888 (among slaves with birthplace identified).

Occupation	Brazilians	Total	Africans	Total
Cowboys	13.6%	44	28.1%	32
Charqueada workers	5.4%	37	1.2%	86
Others	7.6%	79	4.5%	111

N=359

χ^2(Brazilians)=2.0, 2 d.f., nonsignificant; ^{2}(Africans)=29.2, 2 d.f., p<,001
Source: APERS 2010.

Certainly, slaves ran away primarily because they wanted freedom, which is to say that the principal cause of slave flight was slavery. But specific situations or events often precipitated escape. As in many other contexts, flight was often a response to punishments felt by captives to be unjust or excessive. João Congo, an agricultural laborer on the ranch of Luisa Gomes de Oliveira in Arroio das Cabeças, municipality of Rio Grande, told the judge that he "had fled [in 1852] because of the unjust punishment that they gave him."[2] Some fugitives stayed in Rio Grande do Sul, often near the ranches from which they had escaped, depending on a network of contacts among slaves and free blacks to survive. João Congo had fled with the cowboy Antonio Cassange, but they remained relatively close by, in the forests of Machado Island.[3] Others went to

---

[2] APERS, Caixa 418, Processo 25, Rio Grande, 1852.
[3] Ibid.

the cities. The cowboy and laborer João fled at the end of 1874 or beginning of 1875 from his master's farm, apparently near Pelotas, but stayed in the city of Pelotas, where he was later recognized.[4]

For many other fugitives, especially those who rode horses, the international border was the logical destination. On arrival in Uruguay, they could receive the protection of a large rancher or one of the rival armies, although they did not always willingly sign up for military service (Aladrén 2009). Just the fact that they were in a foreign country made it more difficult for masters to capture them and bring them back to Brazil. Between 1846 and 1851, they were officially considered free under Uruguayan law.

But flight to Uruguay or Argentina was not as easy as it may seem. Many fugitives were recaptured before reaching the border. Those who did not ride horses could easily be pursued by riders, except during the special conditions created by the Farroupilha civil war, in which royalist masters were often restricted to the cities. Even those who fled on horseback often were recaptured before reaching the border. Ranchers knew they were heading for the border, knew the logical escape routes, and sent other, generally free, workers after them. At the beginning of 1835, Adão and Jose Caxaxa fled the Muzica ranch near the Uruguayan border, but the ranch administrator took "measures," and the two were recaptured a couple of days later. Adão was on the brink of death, apparently from wounds suffered during capture, but his master João Francisco Vieira Braga celebrated: "with the news that the escaped slaves were seized I was happy despite the expense they caused; however, it was good to catch them to give a good example to the others."[5]

Even fugitives who reached Uruguay were not completely safe. During the Portuguese and then Brazilian occupation of the Banda Oriental, or Cisplatine Province (later Uruguay), from 1816 to 1823, slave catchers from Rio Grande do Sul could freely enter this territory. In 1821, slave catcher Juan Bautista Latargas hunted fugitives along the coast of the Negro river and around Colônia. Among those he captured was José, a slave of João Francisco Vieira Braga, who had fled three months before "to avoid serving the administrator" and had joined residents in the forest near Colonia, who cut firewood for sale in Buenos Aires.[6]

---

[4] APERS, Caixa 006.0329, Pelotas, Tribunal do Júri, Processo 1033, 1875.

[5] João Francisco Vieira Braga to João Fernandes da Silva, Rio Grande, 23 and 29 Jan. 1835. BRG-AVB, Lata 27. "Copiador de todas as cartas qᵉ tenho escrito a João Fernandes da Sᵃ Capataz da Estᵃ da Muzica"

[6] Juan Bautista Latargas to João Francisco Vieira Braga, Montevideo, 25 May 1821, BRG - AVB, Lata 25, Correspondência de 1821.

During the long periods of war in Uruguayan territory, escaped slaves risked forced recruitment by the various armies or even joined them voluntarily, which implied obvious physical risks and subjection to military discipline but also provided protection against recapture. In 1851, Brazil and Uruguay signed the Extradition Treaty, which provided for the return of fugitive slaves. Brazilians previously established in Uruguay who had lost their human property to Uruguayan abolition, or the heirs of these ex-slaveowners, also commissioned slavecatchers to kidnap these freedmen and women in Uruguay and bring them to Rio Grande do Sul, where they could be re-enslaved (Monsma and Fernandes 2013). In some cases, these slavecatchers or bandit gangs randomly kidnapped Black Uruguayans with the hope of selling them into slavery in Rio Grande do Sul (Caratti 2013; Grinberg 2016; Lima 2009).

Recaptured fugitives could face horrible punishments. In 1821, José da Costa Santos, a rancher in Sao Lourenço do Sul and father-in-law of Francisco Vieira Braga wrote that he had been delayed by "the flight of two slaves, and only after five days were they caught, with great expense, and when they arrived I had them punished in a manner that they are sure to remember for a long time."[7] In the case mentioned above, in which the slave Israel had fled from the ranch of Francisco Vieira Braga to visit a woman on another Vieira Braga family ranch, Francisco offered an ounce of gold to whoever caught and returned Israel, "because I am eager to whip him."[8] Those who repeatedly escaped from ranches could be sold to the *charqueadas* of Pelotas, where working conditions were much worse. Still others were sold to the coffee planters of southeastern Brazil, suffering separation from family and friends, in addition to hard, regimented labor on the coffee plantations (Machado 1987).

Patterns of slave flight over time

The data presented above address the characteristics of the enslaved people most likely to flee and not return or be recaptured by the time those claiming to own them died. Events also influenced the likelihood of flight because they influenced the chances of success in gaining permanent freedom. Using the data on all enslaved people listed in the probate records of the same four southern municipalities, Table 2.5 shows the number of slaves who escaped in five-year intervals from 1821 to 1885. It is important to remember that there was a lag between when someone escaped and the completion of their former

---

[7] José de Costa Santos to João Francisco Vieira Braga, "Fazenda", 12 November 1821. BRG,-AVB, Lata 25, Correspondência de 1821.

[8] Francisco Vieira Braga to Vicente Vieira Braga, Arroio Grande, 28 March 1859. BRG-AVB, Lata 27, Correspondência de 1856 a 1860.

master's *posthumous* inventory, both because masters could die many years after the escape and because the inventories could be delayed for years. Even so, some suggestive patterns emerge in this table.

Table 2.5. Escaped slaves listed in probate records of Four Municipalities in southern Rio Grande do Sul, by five-year intervals.

Interval	Escaped slaves	Number escaped per 1,000 listed	Total slaves listed
1821-25	4	4.59	871
1826-30	9	6.68	1,348
1831-35	4	3.89	1,027
1836-40	0	0	182
1841-45	14	24.22	578
1846-50	25	10.79	2,318
1851-55	33	13.96	2,364
1856-60	17	8.47	2,008
1861-65	23	11.78	1,953
1866-70	12	5.21	2,304
1871-75	15	6.56	2,285
1876-80	21	13.57	1,548
1881-85	8	8.75	914

Source: APERS 2010.

The table shows a clear increase in both the listed absolute and the relative numbers of escaped slaves during and after the *Farroupilha* War of 1835 to 1845. This was the only Brazilian war of this period fought largely on *riograndense* soil, and it thus dramatically increased opportunities for escape and reduced the risk of recapture. The separatist and republican *farrapos* also controlled much of the countryside of Rio Grande do Sul for long periods and promised that slaves who escaped from their royalist enemies to join them would be given post-war freedom. Royalist masters were often afraid to leave the major cities and some, such as João Francisco Vieira Braga, had even left the province.

After the initial years of the war, during which very few inventories were completed, probably due to disruption of the justice system and *Farroupilha* control of much of the province's interior, the final years of the war and the first ten years thereafter saw sharp increases in both the absolute number of escapees listed and the number per 1000 slaves. Many if not most of the escapees listed in probate records from the ten years after 1845 undoubtedly had escaped during the war. Given that these data are from only four municipalities, the total number of escaped slaves from the entire province must have been much larger.

Table 2.5 also provides a hint that escapes increased around the beginning of the Triple Alliance War in 1864, when rich men could avoid military service by donating slaves to the army (Toral 1995). Although slaves sent to the war were officially freed, this probably did not stop some of them from escaping to avoid the hazards of forced military service, just as men drafted from the free population often did. Finally, the table suggests that slave escapes increased again in Rio Grande do Sul in the second half of the 1870s, when it was becoming increasingly evident that the official end of slavery was just a matter of time. Other provinces, especially Sao Paulo, saw increasing slave flight and rebellion during the 1870s and the 1880s (Azevedo 1987; Machado 1994; Monsma 2016). The decrease in escapes in these four municipalities in the early 1880s could be related to the decrease in the total number of people still enslaved, as increasing numbers were able to purchase their freedom under the terms of the 1871 Rio Branco law, and many *riograndense* slaveholders attempted to use conditional manumission as a strategy to impede flight and keep their unpaid workers for a few more years. In no other period in this series was there a peak in slave flight so large as that of 1841 to 1855, almost certainly due to the *Farroupilha* War and its aftermath. The rest of this chapter focuses on the special conditions of the *Farroupilha* period and what slave flight at that time reveals about relations with masters and slaves' ability to understand and take advantage of international conflicts.

Slave escape to Uruguay and Argentina during the *Farroupilha* period

With greater opportunity for gaining permanent freedom, slaves did not need specific events or provocations, such as excessive punishment, to stimulate them to flight. Enough slaves believed the *Farroupilha* promise of liberty to make a significant contribution to the war effort. Skilled horsemen were particularly valued, and the separatists set up two corps of Black Lancers on Horseback (*Lanceiros Negros a Cavalo*), with a total of about 400 men (Carvalho 2013; Leitman 1979). Other slaves served as foot soldiers. The correspondence of the ranching Vieira Braga family in this period regularly refers to escaped slaves who had presumably joined the *Farrapos*. In 1838, Joaquim Vieira Braga wrote to his mother that there were no more enslaved cowboys left on the two ranches she and her children owned, the enormous São João and Santa Isabel ranches, along the Camaquã River. "Recently the following have fled: Antonio Coçamba, the boy Daniel, and João Jagoarão, these, according to what I have been informed, went to the Republican Army, and there they signed up."[9] After their defeat by the Imperial army, the Farrapos did not defend the liberty of the

---

[9] Joaquim Vieira Braga to Maria Angelica Barbosa, Fazenda de São João, 20 Oct. 1838, BRG-AVB, Lata 26, Correspondência de 1836 a 1840.

escaped slaves who had fought with them. Many were betrayed by Republican commander David Canabarro and killed by Imperial forces at the now infamous *Porongos* massacre. Many others were sent to Rio de Janeiro for forced labor on public works (Carvalho 2013). Vieira Braga's family documents show that others were simply returned to their former masters.

Many enslaved people had already fled to Uruguay or Argentina during the war, either escaping from their masters or deserting the *Farroupilha* army. At the end of the war, in 1845, many of the Black *Farroupilha* soldiers, realizing that their freedom was not guaranteed, fled to Uruguay, often going directly to Uruguayan military commanders to sign up for service there, which was the best way to guarantee protection from recapture by former masters or slavecatchers employed by them (Palermo 2013). Uruguay at the time was in the middle of the 1839-1851 Guerra Grande civil war between the *Colorados*, led by Fructuoso Rivera and the *Blancos*, led by Manuel Oribe, and both sides needed more recruits.

Many Brazilian slaveholders established in Uruguay tried to claim exemption from Uruguayan abolition, decreed in 1842 for Montevideo and its surroundings controlled by the *Colorados*, and in 1846 for the rest of the country controlled by the *Blancos*. However, such protests through official channels met with little success, and many Brazilians attempted to take their former slaves back to Brazil for re-enslavement or hired slavecatchers to enter Uruguayan territory and capture them (Borucki, Chagas and Stalla 2004; Grinberg 2017; Monsma and Fernandes 2013).

There was some initial confusion among Uruguayan authorities about whether Brazilian fugitive slaves should be returned after the 1846 abolition, but Oribe clarified that all slaves present in or entering Uruguayan territory, including fugitives from Brazil, should be freed. Both sides had abolished slavery to draft freedmen for the war, with the promise of future compensation for their former masters. Most fugitives who arrived prior to the 1851 treaty for the return of fugitive slaves apparently gained freedom, especially if they joined the Blanco army. Brazil forced this treaty on the *Colorado* government of Uruguay after the Guerra Grande in exchange for Brazilian help in defeating the *Blancos*. The Uruguayan government understood that it only applied to escaped slaves who entered the country after ratification of the treaty, whereas many Brazilians thought it should apply retroactively and continued to send slavecatchers after those who had fled earlier (Borucki, Chagas, and Stalla 2004; Palermo 2013).

In the atmosphere of frontier lawlessness during and immediately after the Guerra Grande, slavecatchers and bandit gangs also captured freeborn Uruguayans and those who had been freed by Uruguayan abolition for enslavement or re-enslavement in Brazil. Random kidnapping of Afro-Uruguayans was apparently common in association with the *califórnias*, or cattle rustling and pillage expeditions into northern Uruguay carried out by *riograndense* frontier elites after the *Farroupilha* War, when cattle for the Pelotas *charqueadas* were scarce and Blanco authorities, who controlled the Uruguayan countryside, had banned cattle drives to Brazil because the Pelotas jerked beef industry was supplying meat to the *Colorados* in Montevideo, then under siege by the *Blancos* (Borucki, Chagas, and Stella 2004; Palermo 2013).[10]

Two other data sources provide important information on those who fled to Uruguay during the *Farroupilha* war and its aftermath. The first is a list of supposedly runaway slaves that the slavecatcher Manoel Marques Noronha presented during his 1854 trial in Pelotas for kidnapping a ten-year-old free Black Uruguayan girl and selling her as a slave in Rio Grande do Sul – a trial stimulated largely by Uruguayan protests over the incident. Although the girl in question was not on the list, and neither were her parents, Noronha used the list to claim that his Uruguayan slave hunting was legitimate because he had been commissioned to recapture runaway slaves by their Brazilian ex-masters.[11] This list, compiled in 1851, was apparently a response to the 1851 fugitive slave treaty. As noted above, Uruguayan and Brazilian interpretations of this treaty differed, with Uruguayan officials believing that it applied only to slaves who fled Brazil after treaty ratification and many Brazilians thinking it should also apply to those who had fled earlier. The fact that this list was produced so soon after the treaty was signed strongly suggests that the great majority of these fugitives had arrived in Uruguay before the treaty.

Most of those on the list probably had fled from Rio Grande do Sul to Uruguay during or after the ten-year *Farroupilha* civil war between 1835 and 1845, with another wave of fugitives stimulated by the Blanco abolition decree of 1846. However, others probably had been brought to Uruguay earlier by Brazilians with properties there and had subsequently been freed by Uruguayan abolition, which their former owners or their heirs refused to accept, with

---

[10] The term califórnia refers to the California gold rush of the time. Rustling Uruguayan cattle and pillaging ranches were seen as providing gold rush-like opportunities for quick enrichment. Some authors seem to claim that most or all of those captured in Uruguay for enslavement or re-enslavement in Brazil were kidnapped at random by these bandit gangs (Caratti 2013; Grinberg 2016). However, Monsma and Fernandes (2013), in an article based on the first instance trial records of those accused of enslaving or re-enslaving free Uruguayan people in Pelotas, the principal market for slaves of southern Rio Grande do Sul, found that most of the accused were former masters or their heirs, who had refused to accept Uruguayan abolition laws.

[11] Rellação dos Escravos fugidos da Prov^a de R^o Grd^e cujos propietarios me authorizarão por suas cartas de Ordens p^a caturalos, conforme os signaes de cada hum 1851. APERS, Caixa 309, Processo 442, Juízo de Direito da Comarca do Rio Grande em Pelotas, , Maria Duarte Nobre and Manoel Marques Noronha, 1854.

some of them using the services of professional slave catchers like Noronha (Monsma and Fernandes 2013).

This list provides more complete occupational and birthplace information than the probate records analyzed above, although it refers to a more limited period. 246 (91.1%) of the 270 individuals on the list are men. Aside from one eleven-year-old girl, who had probably fled with her mother, all were aged 19 or older, with the oldest being 61. Some had fled several years earlier, and it is not clear if the age noted on the list is the age at which they fled or their current age, but it is likely the latter because it would be of greater value in identifying them. Only about 19% were over 40, and the rest were spread evenly over the ranges 19 to 30 and 31 to 40. Table 2.6 compares the age distribution for the men and women on this list, showing that the two distributions were roughly similar. There may have been a tendency for the women to be somewhat younger, but there are not enough female runaways to confirm this, and the difference observed in the table is not statistically significant. In any case, there is reason to believe that the male slave population, in general, was somewhat older on average than the female because more of the women were born in Brazil.

Table 2.6. Age distributions of male and female runaway slaves on 1851 list.

Ages	Men (%)	Women (%)
11-30	39.7	50.0
31-40	40.9	33.3
Over 40	19.4	16.7
Total	100	100
N	242	24

$\chi^2=1.0$, 2 d.f., nonsignificant
Source: APERS, Caixa 309, Processo 442,
Maria Duarte Nobre e Manoel Marques Noronha, 1854.

Slightly over half of the individuals listed were Africans; about 31% were born in Rio Grande do Sul or listed simply as *crioulos* (Brazilian born) and presumably also from this province. The rest were from other parts of Brazil. The women on this list were somewhat more likely to be born in Brazil than their male counterparts, probably due to the predominance of men among those captured in Africa and sent to Brazil. Fourteen of the 23 women with place of origin identified were from Brazil, whereas more than half of the 238 men were Africans.

Among the men, African captives clearly constituted an older group than the Brazilians. Table 2.7 compares the age distributions of male runaways born in Rio Grande do Sul, other parts of Brazil and Africa. Those from Rio Grande do

Sul are clearly younger, on average, than those imported from Africa or those from the rest of Brazil. Those from Africa appear to be the oldest of all, although there is not a large difference between their age distribution and that of the captives from the rest of Brazil. This probably reflects the birthplace and age composition of the enslaved population in Rio Grande do Sul, due to the interruption of slave imports to the province during the *Farroupilha* War from 1835 to 1845.

Table 2.7. Age distributions of runaway male slaves on 1851 list, by birthplace.

Ages	Birthplace		
	Crioulo/Rio Grande do Sul	Other Brazil	Africa
	%	%	%
19-30	61.6	35.9	30.3
31-40	32.9	46.2	41.0
Over 40	5.5	17.9	28.7
Total	100	100	100
N	73	39	122

$\chi^2=25.1$, 4 d.f., $p<.001$
Source: APERS, Caixa 309, Processo 442,
Maria Duarte Nobre e Manoel Marques Noronha, 1854.

Occupational information for the women on this list is generally absent, and most were presumably engaged in some form of domestic service. Occupation is listed for 213 of the 246 men on the list, and Table 2.8 presents the occupational distribution for the men. Fully 43% were cowboys or horse breakers, categories with easy access to horses and having good riding skills. The great majority of captives in these two occupations also worked on ranches far from the cities and the police, with less supervision than most urban slaves, especially those in the *charqueadas* of Pelotas. They also had employment guaranteed in Uruguay, either on ranches or, more likely, in the Blanco army. Given the low propensity for flight among *charqueada* workers listed in the probate records, the relatively high number of these workers on this list may seem surprising. The *charqueadas* of Pelotas concentrated a large number of slaves, so even with relatively low proportions escaping the absolute number of fugitives from these establishments would be significant. The war also increased opportunities for flight on foot, largely because much of the countryside was controlled by the *Farrapos*, who accepted foot soldiers as well as those who could ride. In addition, some *charqueada* owners, notably Domingos José de Almeida, supported the *Farrapos* and contributed slaves for their army, who could later desert and flee to Uruguay.

Table 2.8. Occupational distribution of male runaway slaves on the 1851 list.

Occupation	Percent	Frequency
Cowboy/Horse breaker	43.2	92
Agricultural labor	9.9	21
Charqueada worker	10.8	23
Artisan/Skilled manual work	22.1	47
Sailor/fisherman/land transport	6.6	14
Unskilled/general work	7.5	16
Total	100	213

Source: APERS, Caixa 309, Processo 442,
Maria Duarte Nobre e Manoel Marques Noronha, 1854.

Not surprisingly, cowboys and horse breakers were more likely to be from Rio Grande do Sul. Table 2.9 shows the occupational distribution of male runaways by birthplace. Over three-quarters of the runaways who had grown up in Rio Grande do Sul were cowboys or horse breakers, whereas only about a quarter of the runaways originally from Africa or other parts of Brazil worked in these occupations. Calculating the percentage in the other direction, about 62% of the runaway cowboys and horse breakers were born in Rio Grande do Sul. This difference is not a consequence of differential age distributions. The differences by birthplace remain when we recalculate Table 2.9 within age categories. Because ranching skills such as riding, roping and castration were best learned by young workers, those who grew up in Rio Grande do Sul were likelier to acquire such abilities. However, some Africans and captives from other parts of Brazil, who probably had been purchased when they were children or adolescents, also became cowboys or horse breakers.

Table 2.9. Occupational distribution of male runaway slaves on the 1851 list by birthplace.

Occupation	Birthplace		
	Crioulo/Rio Grande do Sul	Other Brazil	Africa
	%	%	%
Cowboy/Horse breaker	77.5	24.2	25.2
Agricultural labor	0	6.1	17.5
Salted meat plant worker	2.8	9.1	17.5
Artisan/Skilled manual work	15.5	39.4	21.4
Sailor/fisherman/land transport	2.8	6.1	9.7
Unskilled/general work	1.4	15.2	8.7
Total	100	100	100
N	71	33	103

Source: APERS, Caixa 309, Processo 442,
Maria Duarte Nobre e Manoel Marques Noronha, 1854.

Runaways born in other parts of Brazil were much more likely than others to be artisans or skilled workers, such as masons, carpenters, cabinet makers, tailors, or barbers. Those from Africa were more concentrated than the others among agricultural workers and salted meat plant workers. In fact, 18 of the 20 agricultural workers (90%) and 18 of the 23 salted meat plant workers (78%) among the runaways on this list were Africans.

The other source of information on escapes during the Farroupilha period is a list of fugitive slaves compiled by the government of Rio Grande do Sul in 1850, apparently in preparation for negotiations with Uruguay, Argentina, and Paraguay over the return of fugitive slaves.[12] The cases discussed below are all drawn from this list. Some, but not all, of the runaways on Noronha's list also appear on this list. As in the Noronha list, some of them probably were not escaped slaves but captives who had been taken to Uruguay by their masters and subsequently freed by Uruguayan abolition, whose former masters or their heirs perceived the treaty for the return of fugitive slaves as an opportunity to recover their lost "property". In other cases, the people listed clearly had fled, for the list includes some detail about how they escaped, where they went, and what they did after arriving there. For example, five enslaved sailors from the crew of the schooner Leonidia took the ship's boat in March 1849, crossed the Lagoa Mirim and entered the Jaguarão river, where they disembarked on the Uruguay side and were received by a detachment of troops under the command of Maximo Moreno and taken to the interior of the country. When their owner demanded their return, Moreno, not the most fervent abolitionist, demanded 100 *patacões* (96 *milréis*) apiece for their return.

Most of this list includes less detailed information, often limited to distinguishing physical characteristics of runaways, but if the supposed master knew or had heard something about the destiny of the fugitive, this information was generally included. Like the sailors mentioned above, many had joined Uruguayan military forces, which is not surprising because that country was fighting the civil war known as the *Guerra Grande*, and both the *Blancos* and the *Colorados* were eager for new recruits. Some were no doubt forced into military service in Uruguay. Constantino had fled to Tacuarembó in 1848, where he appeared before the local police chief, who in turn sent him to the front line of the *Blanco* siege of Montevideo. Others volunteered for military service because it provided the best protection from Brazilian slavecatchers. At least three fugitives on this list had presented themselves to the commandant at Fort Santa Teresa, on the Atlantic coast 35 km south of the border. Some of

---

[12] Relação e descrição dos escravos (por proprietários) fugidos da Província para Entre-Rios, Corrientes, Estado Oriental, República do Paraguai e outras províncias brasileiras. Rio Grande do Sul. 1850. Arquivo Histórico do Rio Grande do Sul, Estatística.

the men had served in the *Farroupilha* forces before fleeing to Uruguay, perhaps near the end of the war when it became apparent that *Farroupilha* leaders would betray them and bargain away their promised freedom. The mulatto Raymundo, 38 years old, had served as a sergeant in the *Farroupilha* forces before taking refuge in Uruguay. Mathias, a 28-year-old African, had worked as a carpenter before joining the rebel forces, subsequently fleeing to Uruguay. Vicente, 36, from Bahia, "short, stocky, fat and handsome," had run away sixteen years earlier but had recently been seen in the army of General Servando Gomes in Uruguay.

In some cases appearing on this list, Uruguayans were accused of luring away Brazilian slaves. Captain Pedro Gutierrez of the Blanco army was stationed next to the Quaraí River on the Brazilian border in 1845 or 1846 when he lured away 13- or 14-year-old Antonio, according to the Brazilian who claimed to be Antonio's master. Gutierrez took Antonio to Paysandú, where he served the captain's family until 1848 when the captain took him along to battle as a page. The 24-year-old painter Jacinto had fled to Montevideo four years earlier aboard a packet boat under the protection of Captain Don Pedro Gallego and continued in Gallego's service, thus exchanging captivity for personal dependency.

Uruguayan military officers generally disregarded attempts to reclaim these slaves. Antero, a slave of João Francisco Vieira Braga, fled from Rio Grande in 1846. Later that year, his master discovered that he was working as a police "soldier" in Cerro Largo, but when Vieira Braga asked the departmental commander to return Antero, the response was to send him further into the Uruguayan interior, where his former master could not locate him. Antonio Thomas Correa Vianna had asked *Blanco* leader General Oribe to return three of his slaves, who were serving in the forces of Coronel Juan Barrios in San Carlos, to no avail. The 18-year-old mixed-race cowboy Roque, 30-year-old African Joaquim, from Cabinda, qualified "for general services," and 30-year-old Brazilian-born butcher Laurentino had all apparently fled from Antonio Thomas Correa Vianna in early 1849 and by 1850 were serving in the forces of Coronel Juan Barrios in San Carlos, Uruguay. Vianna had contacted General Manuel Oribe, head of the *Blancos*, to ask for their return, but Oribe ignored the request.

We identified 73 of the runaways on the 1850 list as horse breakers, cowboys, or probable cowboys due to observations such as "very good roper," "excellent horseman," or "has crooked feet from constant horseback riding." Cowboys made good soldiers in the rival armies of Uruguay, both heavily dependent on cavalry, and it is not surprising that many runaways joined the army or were forced into military service. Of the 16 cowboys or horse breakers on this list whose current occupation is identified, 11 were serving in one of the Uruguayan armies. Others worked on Uruguayan cattle ranches or were cattle drivers. Twenty-year-old Zeferino, a pardo with a "strong body," was working on a ranch in Coxilha Grande, Uruguay.

Roughly half of these cowboys and horse breakers were born in Africa, and the rest in Brazil. Many had marks of punishment, especially from whipping, or scars, deformations and impairments caused by their rather hazardous occupation, such as crooked legs or feet, broken arms, legs or toes, scars from cattle horns, or teeth knocked out or lips split by kicks from horses. Several also had smallpox scars. Antero, 27, a "good cowboy and coachman" who had fled from João Francisco Vieira Braga in 1846, suffered from a "broken groin" and enlarged testicles, which caused him to sway as he walked. Some were also said to like drinking and gambling, a sign of their proximity to and interaction with free cowboys. One had learned to read, had "turned bad," and denied being a slave, claiming he had been freed. Some had more than one occupation, especially cowboy and horse breaker. Two of them, apparently from forested regions of Rio Grande do Sul, were both cowboys and sawyers, and one was a cowboy and a mason. One was a cowboy, horsebreaker, and musician. He had fled to the Argentine province of Corrientes, where he was known as *el moreno cantor* (the Black singer). There, he also married a Black Brazilian and "the two of them go around at dances playing music and singing."

Many of those not identified as cowboys also bore the scars of whipping, other violence, work accidents, or smallpox. Joaquim, a partially literate and "very light-colored" *pardo,* talked with a permanently hoarse voice because he had survived an attempt to slit his throat. The *cabra* (mixed-race) Ignacio was missing his front teeth and Adão, 40, mulatto, had a lip split by a kick from a hoof. The 28-year-old sawyer and planer Januario, born in Bahia and "very black" (*muito retinto*), with ax scars on his chest and one foot, had fled six years earlier and was said to be in the department of Paysandú, Uruguay. Benedito, 25, born in Rio Grande do Sul, was "crippled in one hand and one leg." Joaquina, 40, of the Benguela nation, was missing a toe, had a scar on one ear, and marks on one arm and her chest.

In all these cases, the list identifies the country to which the slave had fled. Of the 73 cowboys or horse breakers, four had fled to Argentina, one of them to Entre Rios and the other three to Corrientes. All the other 69 had reportedly gone to Uruguay. It is likely that in several cases, masters assumed that fugitives had headed for the Uruguayan border because this was the logical destination. In many others, however, someone had seen the runaway and reported this to the master, or he had heard from other slaves where the runaway was planning to go. The twenty-year-old horse breaker Benedicto, from Cabinda (Angola coast), had been seen in the *Blanco* forces in Tacuarembó. Another runaway was "well known in the forces of Coronel Manuel Lavalleja as the roping corporal."

Several of the women had fled with male slaves. Carlota, of the Rebolo nation, had fled with José, originally from Mozambique, and the couple was thought to be living in Montevideo. Joanna, of Mozambique, had fled to Uruguay in 1837 with Antonio from Congo. José, 26, and Justina, 30, both Africans from Congo, had fled to Uruguay together in 1848 and were working in the division of Coronel Lamas, Justina in the service of a Major and José, who was deaf, as the personal servant of Lamas himself. Other women had apparently escaped alone. Maria, of the Nagô nation, had fled to Salto, Uruguay and the woman who claimed to own her, the widow Bernardina Maria Ferreira, went to Salto or sent a representative to demand her return, but Maria went to the local Justice of the Peace and said she had been legally freed, at which the Justice said he could only return Maria if the widow produced a receipt of purchase proving ownership. She later presented the document, but Maria went into hiding and was not found.

Conclusion

We focused our analysis largely on enslaved cowboys and others who worked in loosely supervised occupations such as horse breaking. Because they were highly mobile, armed, loosely supervised and lived in a province with two international borders, fleeing was a real option for the enslaved cowboys of Rio Grande do Sul. The ranches and armies of Argentina and, especially Uruguay, provided guaranteed employment for fugitive cowboys, as well as protection from re-enslavement, although military service involved clear hazards and often rigorous discipline, including whipping, and many fugitives were probably drafted into Uruguayan armies against their will. The evidence presented here shows that male slaves, those who worked as cowboys and those born in Brazil were more likely to escape than other captives. The Brazilian-born were probably more likely to escape mainly because more of them rode horses and worked as cowboys. When Africans became cowboys, however, they were even more likely to flee than their Brazilian-born counterparts. Another mobile occupational category, particularly important in Rio Grande do Sul, where all the major nineteenth-century cities were located on navigable waterways, consisted of enslaved sailors. Some of the evidence presented above suggests that this little-researched category may also have been especially prone to flight.

In normal times, slaves tended to flee when masters, administrators, or drivers (*feitores*) did something they felt to be particularly outrageous, especially imposing excessive punishment or punishment the captive considered unjustified (Monsma 2013). In other cases, slaves fled because they had been separated from family members or lovers, because masters planned to send them to Rio de Janeiro or other distant places, or because they disliked specific masters or others who were renting their services.

Cowboys, especially, were valuable slaves, and masters and ranch administrators tried to prevent their flight by treating them better than other slaves, ensuring that they had plenty to eat, warm clothing, maté, tobacco and *cachaça*, allowing them to plant vegetables and raise small animals, and allowing them a certain degree of freedom in everyday life, including, it appears from the criminal court records, permission to hire out their services and to drink and gamble with free cowboys at local general stores (*vendas*) *(ibid)*. Masters and ranch administrators also formed personalized patronage relations with enslaved cowboys, often giving them greater responsibility and privileges in exchange for loyalty. On the other hand, masters imposed cruel punishments on those who fled and sometimes sold them to the owners of establishments with more miserable working conditions, especially the *charqueadas*. With this mixture of rewards for loyal service and severe punishment for unsuccessful escape attempts, most enslaved cowboys did not flee.

However, the *Farroupilha* civil war of 1835 to 1845 in Rio Grande do Sul produced unusual conditions that reduced the risks of flight and stimulated captives to reevaluate their loyalties. The promise of freedom for those who joined *Farroupilha* forces cannot be underestimated as a stimulus to flight. There is emerging evidence, including some presented above, that large numbers of those who escaped to Uruguay during the *Farroupilha* period had first served in the Republican army. The fact that the *Farroupilhas* controlled much of the countryside for long periods also meant that it was more difficult, or at least more dangerous, for masters who supported the monarchy to send employees or others in pursuit of fugitives. This fact, we argue above, also favored fugitives who could not ride horses, such as the many African captives who worked in the *charqueadas*. We have not encountered clear evidence about when the fugitive slaves who joined the *Farrapos* fled again, generally heading for Uruguay, but it is likely that many fled near the end of the war, with the impending Imperial victory and the unwillingness of *Farroupilha* commanders to insist on their freedom in the peace negotiations. Some of them probably fled after hearing about the *Porongos* massacre.

Uruguayans often tried to protect fugitives from re-enslavement, largely because they were valuable soldiers or ranch workers, but in some cases, because they genuinely opposed slavery. Uruguayan government officials and army officers also resented Brazilian disrespect for Uruguayan sovereignty and were little disposed to collaborate with Brazilian slave catchers, whom they viewed as illegal intruders. Yet the Brazilian government and its army often intervened in Uruguayan politics and were able to exercise considerable influence there, especially forcing Uruguay to accept the 1851 extradition treaty, providing for the return of fugitive slaves. Many of those who fled to Uruguay during the *Farroupilha* war were undoubtedly able to live the rest of their lives in relative liberty in their new country, but others were kidnapped by Brazilians and re-enslaved.

Acknowledgements

This research was supported by CNPq – The Brazilian National Council for Scientific and Technological Development. The first author thanks Regina Xavier for encouraging him to look for quantitative evidence regarding the propensity for flight of enslaved cowboys.

References

Unpublished Documents

Arquivo Público do Estado do Rio Grande do Sul, Porto Alegre (APERS)

Caixa 309, Processo 442, Juízo de Direito da Comarca do Rio Grande em Pelotas, 1854.

Caixa 418, Processo 25, Rio Grande, 1852.

Caixa 006.0329, Processo 1033, Pelotas, Tribunal do Júri, 1875.

Arquivo Histórico do Rio Grande do Sul

Estatística. Relação e descrição dos escravos (por proprietários) fugidos da Província para Entre-Rios, Corrientes, Estado Oriental, República do Paraguai e outras províncias brasileiras. Rio Grande do Sul. 1850.

Biblioteca Rio-Grandense, Rio Grande, Arquivo Vieira Braga (BRG-AVB)

Lata 25, Correspondência de 1821.

Lata 26, Correspondência de 1836 a 1840.

Lata 27, Copiador de todas as cartas qᵉ tenho escrito a João Fernandes da Sᵃ Capataz da Estᵃ da Muzica.

Lata 27, Correspondência de 1856 a 1860.

Published Sources

Aladrén, Gabriel. "Experiências de liberdade em tempos de Guerra: escravos e libertos nas Guerras Cisplatinas (1811-1828)." *Estudos Históricos* 22, no. 44 (December 2009): 439-458.

Arquivo Público do Estado do Rio Grande do Sul. *Documentos da escravidão no Rio Grande do Sul. Inventários, o escravo deixado como herança*, 4 vols., edited by Bruno Stelmach Pessi. Porto Alegre: Companhia Rio-grandense de Artes Gráficas, 2010.

Azevedo, Celia Maria Marinho de. *Onda negra, medo branco: O negro no imaginário das elites , século XIX*. Rio de Janeiro: Paz e Terra, 1987.

Bell, Stephen. *Campanha gaúcha: a Brazilian ranching system, 1850-1920*. Stanford, Calif.: Stanford University Press, 1998.

Borucki, Alex; Chagas, Karla; and Stalla, Natalia. *Esclavitud y trabajo: un estudio sobre los afrodescendientes en la frontera uruguaya, 1835-1855*. Montevideo: Mastergraf, 2004.

Caratti, Jônatas Marques. *O solo da liberdade: as trajetórias da preta Faustina e do pardo Anacleto pela fronteira rio-grandense em tempos do processo abolicionista uruguaio (1842-1862)*. Sao Leopoldo: Oikos & Editora Unisinos, 2013.

Carvalho, Daniela Vallandro de. "Fronteiras da liberdade: Experiências escravas de recrutamento, guerra e escravidão (Rio Grande de Sao Pedro, c. 1835-1850)." PhD Dissertation. Universidade Federal do Rio de Janeiro, 2013.

Farinatti, Luís Augusto Ebling. "Um campo de possibilidades: notas sobre as formas de mão-de-obra na pecuária (Rio Grande do Sul, século XIX)." *História UNISINOS* 7, no. 8 (July-December 2003): 253-276.

_____. *Confins meridionais: Famílias de elite e sociedade agrária na fronteira sul do Brasil (1825-1865)*. Santa Maria: Editora UFSM, 2010.

Grinberg, Keila. 2016. "The Two Enslavements of Rufina: Slavery and International Relations on the Southern Border of Nineteenth-Century Brazil." *Hispanic American Historical Review* 96, no. 2 (May 2016): 259-290.

_____. "Illegal Enslavement, International Relations, and International Law on the Southern Border of Brazil." *Law and History Review* 35, no. 1 (Feb 2017): 31-52.

Isola, Ema. *La esclavitud en el Uruguay, desde sus comienzos hasta su extinción (1743-1852)*. Montevideo: Comisión Nacional de Homenaje del Sesquicentenario de los Hechos Históricos de 1825, 1975.

Leitman, Spencer Lewis. *Raízes Socioeconômicas da Guerra dos Farrapos: Um capítulo na história do Brasil do século XIX*. Rio de Janeiro: Edições Graal, 1979.

Lima, Rafael Peter de. "Nacionalidades em disputa: Brasil e Uruguai e a questão das escravizações na fronteira (Séc. XIX)." 4º Encontro Escravidão e Liberdade No Brasil Meridional. Curitiba, 2009.

Machado, Maria Helena P. T. *Crime e escravidão: Trabalho, luta e resistência nas lavouras paulistas, 1830-1888*. Sao Paulo: Editora Brasiliense, 1987.

_____. *O plano e o pânico: Os movimentos sociais na década da abolição*. Rio de Janeiro & Sao Paulo: Editora UFRJ & EDUSP, 1994.

Maestri, Mário. "O cativo, o gaúcho e o peão: considerações sobre a fazenda pastoril rio-grandense (1680-1964)." In *O negro e o gaúcho: estâncias e fazendas no Rio Grande Do Sul, Uruguai e Brasil*, edited by Mário Maestri, 212-300. Passo Fundo: UPF, 2008.

Monsma, Karl. "Esclavos y trabajadores libres en las estancias del siglo XIX. Un estudio comparativo de Rio Grande do Sul y Buenos Aires." In *De la región a la nación: Relaciones de escala para una historia comparada, Brasil-Argentina (s. xix y xx)*, edited by Andrea Reguera and Marluza Marques Harres, 83-119. Tandil, Argentina: Universidad Nacional del Centro de la Provincia de Buenos Aires; CESAL, 2012.

_____. Resistência cotidiana, fugas e a dominação negociada: Os campeiros escravizados do Rio Grande do Sul. *Raízes: Revista de Ciências Sociais e Econômicas*, Campina Grande 33, no.2 (Julho-Dezembro 2013): 29-52.

—— . *A reprodução do racismo: Fazendeiros, negros e imigrantes no oeste paulista, 1880-1914*. Sao Carlos:EdUFSCar, 2016.

Monsma, Karl; and Fernandes, Valéria Dorneles."Fragile Liberty: The enslavement of free people in the borderlands of Brazil and Uruguay, 1846–1866." *Luso-Brazilian Review* 50, no. 1 (June 2013): 7-25.

Osório, Helen. *O império português no sul da América: estancieiros, lavradores e comerciantes*. Porto Alegre: Editora da UFRGS, 2007.

Palermo, Eduardo R. *Tierra esclavizada: El Norte uruguayo en la primera mitad del siglo 19*. Montevideo: Tierradentro, 2013.

Toral, André Amaral de. "A participação dos negros escravos na guerra do Paraguai." *Estudos Avançados*, Sao Paulo 9, no. 24 (Maio-Agosto 1995): 287-296.

Zarth, Paulo Afonso. *Do arcaico ao moderno: o Rio Grande do Sul agrário do século XIX*. Ijuí: Ed. Unijuí, 2002.

CHAPTER THREE

Slavery and Cassava in the Atlantic World: Commercial and Cultural Relationship between Rio de Janeiro and Angola in the Nineteenth Century

Nielson Rosa Bezerra

Universidade do Estado do Rio de Janeiro, Brazil

Abstract

The trade between Rio de Janeiro and Benguela showed an important fluidity since colonial times, gaining great momentum between 1790 and 1830. During this period, it is possible to identify more than 70% of the enslaved who entered Brazil through the port of Rio de Janeiro. This fluidity was due to endogenous and exogenous reasons that occurred in both Atlantic regions, which complemented the interest of the merchants involved in this process. This research is based on the argument that cassava flour had a prominent economic position in the Atlantic markets, especially in the context of the trade of enslaved Africans, who constituted the main workforce that sustained the Brazilian economy during the 19th century.

Keywords: Slavery; cassava flour; Rio de Janeiro; Benguela

***

The African diaspora has been a topic of great relevance in the Brazilian historiography produced by native and foreign historians. This perspective posits that the formation of Brazilian society cannot be understood without close consideration of Brazil's relations with the African coast. Over the period of Portuguese colonization in Brazil, it is estimated that of the 12 million enslaved Africans who were taken to the Americas, 45% were brought to Brazil. In addition, the most recent studies have demonstrated that arguably, the vast majority of African slaves who landed at the port of Rio de Janeiro from central West Africa, particularly Angola, came from ports, cities and places like Luanda, Cabinda, Cassanje and Benguela. The trade between Rio de Janeiro and

Benguela has constantly changed since colonial times, with a great upsurge between 1790 and 1830 (Florentino 1997) when it can be shown that more than 70% of the slaves who entered Brazil through this port were from the Central African region. This flux was due to endogenous and exogenous causes in both Atlantic regions to the mutual benefit of the merchants involved. During the eighteenth century and the beginning of the nineteenth century, many changes occurred in Brazil that strengthened Rio de Janeiro's position as an Atlantic city, which exponentially increased the need for African labor. On the other hand, several regions of what today would be Angola also had an interest in goods produced in Brazil, mainly sugar, tobacco and cachaca (Alencastro 2000).

For a long time, historians believed that tobacco was a commodity almost exclusively produced in Bahia, and normally shipped to several African regions, just as economic relations between Rio de Janeiro and Central West African ports were based on low-quality sugar. Only within the last few decades has historical research pointed to greater economic diversity in these relationships, especially regarding the large quantity of cachaça (jeribita) produced in the Captaincy and then in the Province of Rio de Janeiro and widely used in negotiations between Fluminense and Angolan merchants for the acquisition of slaves. Bilateral ties are being redefined on a daily basis through the latest research, revealing that the Atlantic routes were quite complex. It was common to find large numbers of slaves from West Africa living and working on the streets of Rio de Janeiro. Likewise, recent research has shown that Angolans, although not a majority, were found in places like Maranhão, Bahia and Pernambuco, places that have traditionally been known for their connections with the Yoruba world.

However, even more recent research and reflection have shown that the relationships that involved different interests in the Atlantic world were much more complex than one could imagine. Economic relations between the various African markets were interconnected through commercial networks that crossed borders and promoted constant transformation in several societies. Because of this, it is possible to suggest that historical connections were much broader than imagined until recently and that an important product in the trade was cassava or cassava flour (Demétrio 2008; Soares 2008; Soares 2009; Bezerra 2010).

Mariza Soares (2009) has argued that historians and landowners overlooked cassava flour in the colonial period. When analyzing Frans Prost's paintings during the seventeenth century, the author established an iconographic distinction between sugar mills and so-called flour houses. Through this iconographic research, it was possible to see that cassava flour already played an important role in the set of economic activities of the northeast hitherto known for sugar-production. In that society where distinction and hierarchy established the parameters of social relations, cassava planters were relegated to the background. Even knowing this, there are still few inputs from scholars of colonial economics focused on this issue (Soares 2008).

On another occasion, Mariza Soares states that cassava flour was normally listed as a food item, but that this merchandise was part of the entire Portuguese maritime expansion between the Atlantic and the East. She refers to a hierarchy among products in which sugar would be the most important (Soares 2009). I think it is very interesting to establish a dialogue between the ideas of Mariza Soares and Roquinaldo Ferreira since the latter documents the insertion of fabrics from India into African markets, particularly in Angola, the same region that Mariza Soares emphasizes when reflecting on cassava flour in commercial networks in Africa. Through the work of Roquinaldo Ferreira, an alternative analysis is possible that comments on the position of Brazilian investors in the use of Indian fabrics to achieve success in a certain commercial niche in Angola. For the author, the access to Indian fabrics for the Atlantic market took place through an intra-colonial trade that enjoyed a certain autonomy in relation to Portugal (Ferreira 2003).

Similarly, Mariza Soares also sees a certain autonomy of the Atlantic markets in relation to Portugal. In this sense, the authors do not rule out the influence of Lisbon on the markets of the Portuguese empire. However, their ideas allow us to see that the demands of African markets also influenced the economic dynamics across the Atlantic. According to Soares, sugar, tobacco, and salt were very important products in the Portuguese economy, but the commerce included other key products like cheap fabric, Brazilian cachaça and cassava flour (Soares 2009).

Following the author's reasoning, we can see that cassava flour had an important place in the Atlantic markets from the seventeenth century. This work aims to demonstrate that this importance increased during the eighteenth and nineteenth centuries, considering that cassava flour became one of the commodities that played a role in the valuable Atlantic market and whose function, among others, was its commercialization in complex economic activities led by the African slave trade. Still considering the turn of the seventeenth and eighteenth centuries, Denise Demétrio sought to explain the wide production of cassava flour in the *Reconcavo da Guanabara* mills between 1686 and 1722.

During this period, the processing of cassava flour became increasingly important in relation to sugar mills, given the lower costs of flour production, which fit the situation and needs of settlers in the region during this period. Thus, the author demonstrates that there was a close relationship between the slave trade and the production and trade of cassava flour based on the corresponding fluctuations in the data she analyzed (Demétrio 2008).

According to Maurício de Abreu, in 1582, the city of Rio de Janeiro was destitute since all the inhabitants, including Governor Salvador Corrêa, were very poor; however, in 1584, it was shown that the captaincy experienced a sudden bout of progress; reflected in three sugar mills and more than 150 households. Interestingly, among these three *engenhos*, Abreu identified two in *Reconcavo da Guanabara*. The historian also shows connections between parishes in Rio de Janeiro and overseas interests, particularly in Angola, where a governor of Angola maintained productive and commercial connections between the still rare sugar mills of the Reconcavo,[1] which contributed to the development of the city of Rio de Janeiro. In 1610, Rio de Janeiro had more than two thousand households, being considered a rich city at that time (Abreu 2010).

The importance of cassava flour is highlighted by Cristóvão Ambrósio Brandão, who pointed out that ships sailing from the Rio to Angola carried flour, which was sold at a high price (Fernandes 1960).

The seventeenth century saw the development of the slave trade between Brazil and Africa. However, it was not only the African slave trade that developed during this period but also the products that served as a bargaining chip, including cassava. It is important to highlight that this did not mean the absence of sugar activity; on the contrary, during this period, there was a sudden increase in the number of sugar cane mills in the Reconcavo, highlighting that cassava flour did not replace sugar but that both activities coexisted, each serving important economic functions in the colonizing activities of the city of Rio de Janeiro and the area surrounding the Guanabara Bay (Abreu 2010).

Luís Felipe de Alencastro also mentioned the importance of cassava flour as an economic activity in Rio de Janeiro and its connections with the African market, explaining that ships from Lisbon would stop for cassava in Rio de Janeiro and the captaincy of Sao Vicente (today Sao Paulo state), before heading to African ports. Around 680 tons of cassava flour were sent annually from Guanabara Bay to Angola in the first decade of the seventeenth century. In Luanda, for example, the period saw an increase in the trade of slaves and the consumption of products like Brazilian cassava flour. Alencastro argues that

---

[1] N.E. Reconcavo is the geographic are of land located at recessed coastal area that directly connects to a larger main body of water, such as an ocean. It is the same as a bay. In this case, it would be the Guanabara Bay, however, the region popular known as the Guanabara Bay is usually the portion of the bay where the city of Rio de Janeiro is located. In fact, the Guanabara Bay incorporates five municipalities, with an area of almost 160 sq miles. Because this article examines a portion of the bay outside the city of Rio de Janeiro, it refers to the area as *Reconcavo da Guanabara* or Guanabara *Reconcavo*.

cassava exports made a decisive contribution to opening Rio de Janeiro to the Atlantic economy, with lower production costs freeing up capital for the purchase of African slaves. Cassava was also an important source of food for sailors and slaves during those trips, which also made freight costs between Brazil and African ports cheaper (Alencastro 2001).

At the end of the eighteenth century and the beginning of the nineteenth century, the production and trade of cassava flour were the main activities practiced in the *Reconcavo da Guanabara*. Cassava flour was processed on almost all agricultural properties in the parishes of the *Reconcavo*, on some properties for consumption only, but on other farms, large flour houses produced merchandize to supply Rio de Janeiro and for trade in the Atlantic markets (Bezerra 2010).

Rio de Janeiro and Benguela: connected histories

On August 3, 1821, the newspaper *Diário do Rio de Janeiro* announced various products offered for sale, from several sellers, including textiles from Benguela, English riding saddles, tobacco boxes made in Lisbon, and carriage harnesses made of Indian metal. Ads also included the sale of the *Bergantim Saudade do Sul*, emphasizing that the vessel was "covered in copper, suitable for the slave trade".[2] The same newspaper regularly published ads for the sale and rental of slaves, such as one from July 6, 1821: "whoever intended to buy a Black rower from the Benguela nation" should look for Felizardo José da Malta in the Ordinance of the Comptroller of the Navy.[3]

Since the eighteenth century, Rio de Janeiro had become the main Atlantic city of the Portuguese Empire. At the beginning of the nineteenth century, this position was consolidated with the transfer of the Portuguese Court, which transformed all aspects of Rio de Janeiro. The capital was a slave city, but more than that, Rio de Janeiro was the main gateway for African slaves to Brazil during the eighteenth and nineteenth centuries, playing an important role in the distribution of Africans throughout south-central Brazil. However, the Atlantic dynamic of Rio de Janeiro was not limited to the slave trade but included several other international products, as shown in the pages of the newspaper.

The information in the Diário de Rio de Janeiro represents what Sanjay Subrahmanyam called a "connected stories" perspective, as he considered various historical events and cultural experiences, relating events that took place in the interior to major international events. By taking this perspective

---

[2] *Diário do Rio de Janeiro*, 3 de agosto de 1821. Biblioteca Nacional, Rio de Janeiro.

[3] *Diário do Rio de Janeiro*, 6 de julho de 1821. Biblioteca Nacional, Rio de Janeiro.

into consideration, it is possible to reinvent global geographic interpretations, considering the transformations that took place through their connected histories, a view that is also present in Silvia Lara's analysis of the straight connection between slave trading in Africa and the political history of Portuguese America. (Subrahmanyan 1997; Lara 2005).

Traditional models, considered fixed paradigms, have been systematically redefined through studies based on hypotheses that, until recently, were ignored by scholars in the human and social sciences, including history. An example of this break is John Thornton's (2004) work on Atlantic history. The author examines the participation of marginalized social agents in the social, economic, and cultural formation of the Atlantic, contributing to the review of imbalances in historiography constructed through approaches that exacerbated Eurocentric perspectives of the Atlantic. Thus, a new space can be built for Africans in the history of Africa and the Americas, allowing them a more prominent role than is usual. For Thornton, Africans participated effectively in the transformations in the society in which they lived, given that they were connected from the interior to the coast through their many possible interactions throughout the Atlantic complex (Thornton 2004).

Every year, thousands of vessels left the Brazilian coast for African coasts. It would be nothing new to claim that, like the thousands of other brigantines, there were galleys, boats, and others sailing to Africa in search of lucrative deals in the transatlantic African slave trade. It is also no longer news that many Brazilian goods were successfully distributed in several African markets, as in the case of cachaça, also called jeribita, and tobacco. As could only be the case, the brigantine *Mercurio* left Rio de Janeiro for Benguela loaded with cachaça and tobacco. In addition to these goods that we have already looked at, on that brigantine, there was also a large amount of food, in principle to feed the crew.

The Atlantic connections between Rio de Janeiro and southern Angola, more precisely Benguela, have been confirmed through several studies of the Atlantic trade and the African diaspora in Rio de Janeiro. According to Mary Karasch, Benguela was one of the other main African embarkation ports for Rio de Janeiro. During part of the nineteenth century, "the Benguelas had flooded the city and became one of its greatest nations. The name came from the port of Benguela, the most important slave trade center in southern Angola" (Karasch 2000, 57). Manolo Florentino identified Central Atlantic Africa as the main exporter of humans to Rio, pointing out that the volume of slaves from this region tripled in absolute terms from 1811 (Florentino 1997), while Flávio Gomes identified Benguelas among the Africans living in the city of Rio de Janeiro and its surroundings in the same period. In more recent research on boatmen and sailors employed in Guanabara Bay, although the Cabindans were considered the "best Africans" for these activities, the Benguelans were the majority among those from the West Coast, second only to those from Mozambique (Gomes, Farias, and Soares 2005).

There are many studies on Africans imported into Rio de Janeiro. However, there is little information on trade other than on slaves from Africa to Brazil. Likewise, in addition to those already known - tobacco, jeribita, etc - a more systematic investigation is still needed of the Brazilian goods supplied to African markets. By drawing attention to the trading of cassava flour, I intend to offer a new look at old questions about the Atlantic connections between Rio de Janeiro and Benguela.

Benguela was one of the most important transatlantic ports. Founded in 1617 between the Katumbela and Kapondo rivers, Benguela has always been a stopover on Portuguese routes for repairing vessels and obtaining supplies – water in particular – even before it became an important slave exporting port. Only Ajudá (Ouidah), Luanda and Bonny surpassed Benguela in the general calculation of the export of slaves to the Americas. Mariana Cândido explored the connection points between the slave trade, the movement of borders and the formation of identity in Benguela, seeking to analyze the impacts of the Atlantic slave trade in the region in order to understand the close relations between Portuguese, Africans and Creole slaves in the process of making slaves available to meet Atlantic demands, the social reconfiguration implied by these relations, as well as the impact of the Atlantic slave trade on Benguela society. Cândido also stresses the commercial relations between the coast and the interior of southeastern Angola, identifying salt, jeribita and Asian fabrics, among others, as the preferred goods for the acquisition of slaves in African markets (Candido 2006).

During the 1700s, Benguela acquired increased importance in Portuguese occupation south of the river Kwanza. Located in a region of several kingdoms that maintained antagonistic relations, Benguela gained importance in the trading of slaves (as a result of the war between those kingdoms); there, great quantities of slaves could be acquired in markets and passed on to foreign traders. There is no doubt that Benguela was one of the main sources of slaves sent to the southeast of Brazil. According to Joseph Miller, Brazilians began exporting slaves from Angola on a large scale from 1710, when there was an increase of two thousand slaves until 1730, reaching a peak of eight or nine thousand around 1784-1795 (Miller 1999; Silva 1999). Brazilian demand for enslaved labour, the sea currents and geographical proximity to the port of Rio, allied with the availability of slaves in markets of the Kwanza River and the commercial value of goods from Rio de Janeiro, can explain such a network.

According to Mariana Cândido, Brazilians dominated the trade in slaves and other goods in Benguela and were a common sight at the port of Benguela, which led to intense traffic between Brazil and that region. The presence of

Brazilian traders stimulated the ventures of *sertanejos* and *pombeiros* who organized caravans to the interior of Central Africa, where they acquired slaves from, among other places, the open markets from where the majority of the slaves sold in Benguela and destined to Brazilian ports came (Candido 2006).

Mariza de Carvalho argues that since the colonial period, "the flour of wood," a type of cassava flour made in Brazil, was traded in the markets of Luanda and Benguela. According to her, the commerce in cassava flour and cachaça coexisted, favoring a complex service network in which slaves were exchanged for cachaça and fed with the cassava flour on their long journey, emphasizing the importance of flour produced in Rio de Janeiro in sustaining the trade and in developing the complex network that involved enslaved Africans on both sides of the Atlantic (Soares 2009).

Besides, having consolidated its position among slave shipping ports for the Americas, Benguela supplied ships with sailors who enjoyed a good reputation as the most experienced workers on voyages transporting slaves across the Atlantic. In 1777, Captain Felix José da Costa received instructions from the Royal Junta do Comércio to hire men from Benguela to continue his journey, including some to be employed as nurses as well (Candido 2010).

At the end of the eighteenth century, Benguela experienced a food supply crisis, resulting from the lack of rain and reduced movement of vessels from Rio de Janeiro, that led local authorities to appeal to the colonial administration to guarantee goods like cassava flour, beans, and corn from Rio de Janeiro to supply that region. The correspondence between authorities shows that the aid was to feed not only slaves but also the general population.

In January 1800, Diogo Ignácio de Pina Manique, representative of the Portuguese Crown, wrote a letter to Rodrigo de Souza Coutinho, asking him to "encourage the growing of cassava so that some flour can be sent to the kingdom".[4] In February of the same year, Rodrigo de Souza Coutinho issued a warning to Francisco da Cunha e Menezes, ordering him "To promote the cultivation of cassava and the manufacture of its flour, commonly called pau".[5] During the entire colonization of the city of Rio de Janeiro and its surroundings, cassava flour also emerged as an important commodity in internal supply. It can be said that cassava flour crossed the Atlantic as the main source of food for the ships' crews and to supply the needs of other regions of the Portuguese Empire, as was the case in Benguela.

---

[4] Biblioteca Nacional, Rio de Janeiro. Seção de Manuscritos. II-30, 34, 016, 003. Lisboa, 01 de janeiro de 1800.

[5] Biblioteca Nacional, Rio de Janeiro. Seção de Manuscritos. I-31, 30, 104. Mafra, 07 de fevereiro de 1800.

Benguela was one of the main suppliers of slave labor to Rio de Janeiro, with enslaved people from Benguela predominant among those held on the small estates and by the small slaveholders in the parishes of the *Reconcavo*, who produced mainly cassava flour. At the same time, the Portuguese colony in southern Angola demanded Portuguese intervention to guarantee the supply of products from the port of Rio de Janeiro. Thus, it is possible to connect the cassava flour from the *Reconcavo da Guanabara* to the Atlantic Slave Trade, offering a new perspective on relations between Rio de Janeiro and Benguela.

The *Reconcavo*: a place of cassava flour production

The Portuguese presence in the parishes of the Guanabara region dates back to the end of the 16th century, when the Portuguese Empire, in partnership with the Catholic Church, promoted occupation of the area around the bay, ensuring Portuguese sovereignty in Rio de Janeiro. The occupation began with the distribution of allotments, the construction of chapels, the creation of parishes, and the setting up of mills and farms combining ecclesiastical power and economic exploitation. This information can be found in eighteenth-century reports of pastoral visits. Monsenhor Pizarro speaks of the creation of several parishes, such as Sao João de Trairaponga (1647), Santo Antônio da Jacutinga (1657), Nossa Senhora da Piedade de Magé (1657), Sao Nicolau do Suruí (1683), Nossa Senhora da Piedade de Inhomirim (1696), Nossa Senhora do Pilar (1717), Nossa Senhora da Guia de Pacobaíba (1722), Nossa Senhora da Conceição de Marapicu (1737), and Nossa Senhora da Piedade do Iguaçu (1759). Parishes were the first administrative institutions of the Portuguese State through the reinvention of the staff of the Catholic Church. The need to occupy space and to extend an administrative arm through ecclesiastical control seems to be a combination that allowed for the foundations of a secular colonizing action (Pizarro e Araújo 1945).

There were close ties between the *Reconcavo* and the city, either through the presence of the church, through commercial ties, or through kinship ties between families installed there and other family branches resident in the city. The Portuguese colonization process in the *Reconcavo da Guanabara* was supported by an administrative establishment founded on control of the population through religion. Ecclesiastical records were the documentary basis for population control, recording baptisms, marriages, deaths and wills, among others. In addition to the religious bureaucracy that was intertwined with lay life, the masses were also the main cultural references originating in Europe that influenced everyday life. Masses, processions, funerals and other religious ceremonies were not only acts of devotion but also spaces for the exercise of sociability. Nor can we fail to consider the religious brotherhoods where free men and slaves were brought together and organized for several purposes (Reis

1995; Soares 2004). The Catholic Church thus legitimized Portuguese colonial occupation through the parishes, which maintained an important presence among European colonists, natives and African slaves.

This colonial occupation also followed the natural hydrography of the region, where the first agents of Portuguese colonization in the region needed to control the constant flooding and swamps. Waterways were, therefore, important references for centers of colonial occupation, marked by a rural economy and ecclesiastical administration through the formation of parishes. The rivers also compensated for the reduced agricultural capacity of the wetlands with the easy flow of goods through the river ports that were established. During this period, the Iguaçu, Sarapuí, Pilar, Inhomirim, Suruí and Saracuruna rivers, among others, as well as being transport routes, were also the natural landmarks delimiting properties and parishes founded in the region. According to the memoirs of Monsignor Pizarro, along the rivers that cut through the parishes of Iguaçu, Inhomirim, Jacutinga, Marapicu, Meriti and Pilar, there were 37 river ports, indicating the importance of combining the flow of agricultural production and the circulation of people (Pizarro e Araújo 1945). Thus, their strategic function can be seen as vital from an economic point of view, for the disposal of goods, as well as from a social, for the movement of people, information, cultural traditions, artistic expressions, etc. These perspectives reference the reflections of Joseph Miller, who affirmed that the Atlantic crossing not only provided labor, but that the slave trade also allowed the displacement of cultural traditions, habits and customs that were reactivated in America (Miller 1988).

According to historical sources, during the eighteenth century, compared to the Bahian *Reconcavo*, the Guanabara *Reconcavo* was composed primarily of small and medium-sized properties, with modest sugar and cachaça production but with a preponderance of food production. In addition, the number of slaves employed in each property was also small, with the exception of the 200 slaves from Morgadio dos Ramos in the parish of *Nossa Senhora da Conceição do Marapicu*.

Table 3.1. Agricultural production in *Reconcavo* (1769-1779).

Goods	Quantity	Unit of measurement
Sugar	464	Box
Cane liquor	257	Cask
Cassava Flour	45,920	Bags
Rice	20,990	Bags
Beans	1,560	Bags
Corn	1,315	Bags

Source: Relatório do Marquês do Lavradio ao Vice-rei Luís de Vasconcelos (1769-1779). Revista do IHGB. Tomo 76 (1913), p. 327-328.

Table 3.1 shows that at the end of the eighteenth century, food production predominated in the *Reconcavo* of Rio de Janeiro. While the survey recorded a meager production of sugar (464 boxes) and cachaça (257 barrels), there was an annual production of 69,785 bags of food products, 65.8% of which was cassava flour. We need to emphasize that cassava flour, like sugar, was a product processed in mills. Thus, we can argue that in that period the *Reconcavo da Guanabara* was supported by food production, especially cassava flour, which ensured the region's insertion in the Atlantic economy in combination with the African slave trade.

On March 7, 1797, in the parish of *Nossa Senhora de Iguaçu*, Gracia Maria, a Black woman born in Guinea and a widow of Manoel Torres, was buried in the cemetery of the *Confraria de Nossa Senhora do Rosário* [Brotherhood of Our Lady of Rosary]. She was shrouded in the habit of St. Anthony, according to her desire expressed in her will, along with other concerns about her soul after death, including ordering masses for the welfare of her soul. She also declared she was up to date with the annuities to be paid to the Brotherhood and, therefore, wanted to be accompanied by the brothers until the end of her burial.[6]

The will of the African woman Gracia Maria raises some questions. She claimed to have come from Guinea, a complex concept until the eighteenth century, representing a set of ports, localities and ethnicities with which many of the Africans who worked in Rio de Janeiro identified. Mariza Soares (2001) recognizes the importance of Brotherhoods as a space of identity and sociability for Africans from Costa da Mina. The document also shows that Gracia Maria had a few slaves and that she was part of a network of freed people, including some Africans whom she herself had freed. Among her declared assets were a fully equipped flour mill and the farmland with the cassava fields. It is not clear if Gracia Maria was ever enslaved. She claimed to be a widow with no other social classification. However, we can show that Gracia Maria maintained and expanded her capital through the production of and trade in cassava flour. This idea is reinforced when she leaves the farm, the flour house, and the fields for her two slaves, Antônio and Lucrécia, to work for a year after her death. Her intentions are even more explicit in the case of Lucrécia, who would have the right to work another year and a half in the fields to accumulate enough money to pay for her manumission. The property would ultimately go to João Gomes da Conceição, a free man who lived in Rio de

---

[6] Arquivo da Cúria Diocesana de Nova Iguaçu, RJ. Livro de Assentos de Óbitos e Testamentos de Livres. Número 11. Microfilme 1. Freguesia de Nossa Senhora da Piedade de Iguaçu (1777-1798).

Janeiro. We know nothing of this man other than that he was formerly a slave of Gracia Maria.[7]

The type of slavery in the *Reconcavo* led to the construction of a social identity that involved individuals from different African regions living in proximity. Most of the properties in the Rio de Janeiro region were small or medium-sized, usually with no more than 30 slaves, making for a close relationship between actors from different social strata, even between masters and slaves (Bezerra 2010; Soares and Bezerra 2011).

Analysis of the cultivation of cassava in the *Reconcavo da Guanabara*, neglected by historiography and colonial society, represented a factor in social mobility, with the possibility of a rise from slave to master. Not to mention that in the case of the woman described, it was the cassava planted on her farm and the flour processed in her small mill that guaranteed her the respect of the Brotherhood to which she was affiliated and in other sectors of the slave society in which she lived.

The production of cassava flour was not a prerogative only of freed slaves. Many planters in Iguaçu maintained production and trade networks that revolved around cassava flour. This was the case of Alberto Pinheiro, a widowed native of Porto, who died in 1779. In his will, he reveals a network of *compadrio* by leaving "alms" for some godchildren and for his sister-in-law and *comadre* Joana de Brito, to whom he left the "black slave Gracia". In addition, he left two other slaves, David and João, to his granddaughter, Izabel Felizarda. He also declared that he had another Creole slave named Alberto, whom he freed in his will. As a member of the *Irmandade do Santíssimo Sacramento* [Brotherhood of the Holy Sacrament], his concern for the slaves was expressed through Catholic ritual, as he ordered twelve masses for their souls. In addition, he claimed to have 412 square meters of land in addition to cassava fields, eight field slaves and three infant slaves.[8]

The documents examined above present evidence that the well-being of slaves was taken into consideration by their masters. The will of Gracia Maria da Conceição Magalhães, drawn up in 1797, demonstrates that slaves were able to negotiate manumission and that the mistress was careful to order masses for their souls, which could have many interpretations. However, I would like to emphasize that human relations between masters and slaves were asymmetrical,

---

[7] Ibid.

[8] Arquivo da Cúria Diocesana de Nova Iguaçu. Livro de Assentos de Óbitos e Testamentos de Livres. Número 11. Microfilme 1. Freguesia de Nossa Senhora da Piedade de Iguaçu (1777-1798).

especially in a society characterized by the presence of individuals of diverse origins and status.

José Pereira Pinto had his will registered on December 9, 1787, also in the parish of *Nossa Senhora da Piedade do Iguaçu*. As a free man, he also had a network established through the Church, as demonstrated by the alms he had left for his godchildren. However, his testament stands out for a gesture that involved the relationship between flour and slavery that we are dealing with in this work: he left all his personal belongs, like wooden cupboards and clothes, for his slaves, as well as the flour mill and all its assets, including all the tools.[9]

The case shows asymmetry in the relations between masters and African enslaved, especially when it came to the production of cassava flour. Perhaps this can be explained by the lack of social prestige that it implied about the gentlemen of the flour house in relation to the powerful gentlemen of the sugar mill, who had enjoyed public recognition from the colonial period. After death, it is possible that the production of flour was seen as slave service or even a property worthy of freed slaves. Despite the absence of any sign of social prestige, the cassava economy ensured the sustenance and expansion of capital in the region and many freedoms of enslaved Africans.

According to the classic book by Stuart Schwartz (1986) on the Bahian region, food production predominated, but sugar, tobacco and leather were exported through the port of Salvador. In that region, there was a hierarchy of crops. The best lands were reserved for planting sugar cane and tobacco. The southernmost lands of the Bahian *Reconcavo* were reserved for subsistence agriculture, while the production of sugar in Bahia was surpassed only by Pernambuco. When that captaincy was dominated by the Dutch (1630-1654), Bahia became the number one sugar producer, a position it held for more than a century. (Schwartz 1986). A similar logic in the Portuguese strategies of colonial occupation would be seen in Rio de Janeiro's *Baia de Guanabara* or *Reconcavo da Guanabara*. Clearly, the Portuguese sought to move from the coast towards the interior, exploring the natural resources and possibilities of both regions. However, there is a clear turnabout in the goods produced in Bahia in comparison to those grown around Guanabara Bay. Where sugar production was primary in the Bahian *Reconcavo*, in the *Reconcavo da Guanabara* the volume produced was well below the volume of food, with the emphasis on cassava flour.

Apart from food production, Denise Demétrio refers to the frequent purchasing and resale of mills in the Rio de Janeiro region at the end of the seventeenth

---

[9] Ibid.

century, a process that certainly guarantees part of the economic sustainability of the local elite through credit and real estate deals. She found that even after the sale of land, the same owners remained in the region, "baptizing and marrying their slaves," reaffirming the economic importance of the production of food, including cassava flour, in the captaincy of Rio de Janeiro, a fact emphasized by the Marquês do Lavradio in a report to the colonial administration on the economy of the parish of Jacutinga, at the end of the eighteenth century. Sugar production was, therefore, not the main product of the region (Demétrio 2008, 74-75).

Throughout the process of colonization, the parishes of Rio de Janeiro's *Reconcavo* established themselves as important food producers. While I acknowledge the importance of the production of sugar and cachaça, goods recognized by traditional historiography as the main sources of colonial wealth, regional differences must be considered. The Rio de Janeiro sugar economy employed slaves acquired in other parts of the captaincy of Rio de Janeiro, such as Campos and Paraty. The production of cassava flour was a key factor in the South Atlantic trade, as much as for internal subsistence (Soares 2008; Soares 2009).

I reject the idea that Rio de Janeiro's *Reconcavo* occupied a secondary space in the affairs of the captaincy and that slavery there was minor and unimportant, not justifying a more detailed investigation. On the contrary, I believe that the slaves employed in areas other than export activities took on greater importance and deserve closer attention from historians from the point of view of economic, social, and cultural history. In addition, food production supported the internal logic of the colonial economy. Analysis of 45 inventories of slave owners who lived and had business in the Reconcavo and in the city of Rio de Janeiro showed that 73% of the properties in the parishes located around Guanabara Bay systematically produced cassava flour in quantities that far exceeded levels of family consumption (Bezerra 2010).

It is also important to highlight that all agricultural production in the Reconcavo da Guanabara used the rivers and paths that cut through the region as a means of transport, connecting the coast and the interior of Rio de Janeiro. The Iguaçu, Sarapuí, Magé, Pilar, Iriri and Suruí rivers, among others, served as outlets for the *Reconcavo's* and the city of Rio de Janeiro's produce.

Evidence was revealed in the Court of Appeal of 1811, where Captain José Vaz de Sousa filed a lawsuit against his neighbors Francisco da Silva Barros, Bento Cabral, Miguel Barros and Florêncio da Costa, among others. According to the plaintiff, the said persons repeatedly crossed his property at *Quifonge* farm, located in Suruí, on the edge of the village of Magé. More precisely, these neighbors, many of whom were free mulattoes, passed behind his villa where his slaves worked, holding up that work by talking to the captives. When the authorities asked the claimant if he knew why outsiders used the path across his farm, the captain replied that they did so to transport their produce to the port on the Suruí River to be shipped to the city of Rio de Janeiro. The complainant alleged that the said neighbors could either use the *Caminho do Cosme* (Cosme's Road) or cut a path across his property and save time. To defray the costs of upkeep of the path, Captain José Vaz demanded a toll of two hundred *milréis* each time they crossed his farm.[10]

This dispute appears in a lawsuit found in the National Archives as part of Mr. Bento Cabral's inventory, although he is mentioned only as one of the defendants in the lawsuit. The defense is set out by the free mulatto Francisco da Silva Barros, as will be seen below. At first, Francisco Barros justifies his not immediately appearing with a defense, arguing he did not think his neighbor's threats would create a legal problem since he himself had reasons to sue his neighbor but had not done so. He also argued that even though he had been summoned three times, he had been in Rio de Janeiro on important business where the delay could have caused far greater losses than would a dispute between neighbors.[11]

In his own defense, Francisco Barros claimed that he had been living on his own land where he produced food in the parish of *Sao Nicolau de Suruí* for over 16 years. Since he had bought the place, he and his neighbors had used a wide path crossing lands that belonged to Dr. João Roiz to reach the port of embarkation. Captain Francisco Vaz had recently acquired those lands, but he, Barros, and the neighbors had continued to use this shorter path, seeing no problem because the path had been used since time immemorial.

In a kind of reply, Captain José Vaz reaffirmed his complaints and added further accusations against his neighbors, especially Francisco Barros. According to him, the use of a private path through his backyard was a problem since products from his farm were prepared there, his slaves could be distracted from their work, and his large family was put at risk. Vaz ordered his slaves to attack the mulatto when he refused to pay the tax charged. But he still had not paid, and had shipped his goods to Rio de Janeiro, and filed a complaint full of false accusations.[12]

Apparently, Francisco de Barros's defense employed the legal artifice of mounting several appeals, prolonging the trial as long as possible. The several documents read similarly, following the argument that the public had the right

---

[10] Arquivo Nacional. Inventários: Juízo de Fora. Processo 1824. Caixa 585. Bento Cabral, 1811.
[11] Ibid.
[12] Ibid.

to use the path. Although the case was not resolved, it shows that the production of and commerce in cassava flour had a direct influence on the opening of roads in the region.

Cassava flour in the Atlantic world

In 1807, José Reginaldo de Mello e Velho was a widowed father of four children, owner of "some lands" located in the parish of *Nossa Senhora da Piedade de Magé*, whose seat was the village of Magé, located right in the so-called "bottom" of the bay. Like most producers in the *Reconcavo*, Reginaldo de Mello e Velho produced, among other foodstuffs, cassava flour. That year, he decided to diversify his business. He joined Manoel Antônio Coelho, a merchant based in the main square of Rio de Janeiro, and two other partners. The daring business aimed at selling the food he produced, along with other goods, in several Atlantic ports beyond Guanabara Bay. This was a family story that involved the merchant Manoel Antônio Coelho, his partner and fellow traveller of Reginaldo de Mello e Velho, sergeant and merchant Manoel Lopes Ribeiro (Reginaldo's father-in-law), and his three sons, Manoel, Luíza and José. From the documentation seen, there was a well-defined plan to make a "round trip" along the African coast, selling their goods in exchange for slaves. Starting in 1808, the trip went well until the stretch between the ports of Calabar and Benguela when Senhor Reginaldo de Mello e Velho suddenly died. His personal tragedy did not interrupt the trip, let alone business. Back at the port of Rio de Janeiro, the slaves they had acquired were handed over to the consignees and payment was received. Upon receiving the share of his late son-in-law, on behalf of his grandchildren, Manoel Lopes Ribeiro alleged a loss of profit and filed a lawsuit against the partners of Reginaldo de Mello and Velho in favor of his grandchildren.[13]

Four years later, sergeant Manoel Lopes Ribeiro, grandfather of Reginaldo's children, took Manoel Antônio Coelho to court "asking for a certain amount from the company" put together for the trips of the brigantine *Sao José Diligente*, claiming that the amounts paid by Manoel Antonio Coelho to his grandchildren were less than they were entitled to. According to him, his late son-in-law was entitled to 25% of the business profits from the trip from which he did not return. In addition to this percentage, he also demanded compensation for the death of his son-in-law so that the orphans had capital to finance new investments. Finally, he declared that he feared the end of the company,

---

[13] Arquivo Nacional. Inventários: Juízo de órfãos. José Reginaldo de Mello e Velho. Caixa 1122. Processo 346. Magé, 1811-1830, p. 14.

claiming that without it all the farmers who had joined his son-in-law in expectation of good business were at risk.[14]

It is, therefore, clear that Reginaldo would have been the head of a group of farmers from the *Reconcavo* (then also called the "sertão", a former colonial designation for settlements located away from main cities) who came together to do business with the larger traders in the centre of Rio de Janeiro. His father concurred, with the objective of marketing flour on the African coast, in particular at the port of Calabar. Reginaldo, being the son-in-law of a prestigious man (his father-in-law was a merchant and a military man), his neighboring farmers would certainly see him as having the necessary connections for the success of the enterprise. In his petition, Manoel Lopes Ribeiro stated that his son-in-law's partners returned to Rio de Janeiro with the proceeds from the sale of food in Calabar and sold all the cargo of the brigantine, that is, the slaves they had acquired, and accused the merchant Manoel Antônio Coelho of deceiving his grandchildren over the amounts received.

In his defense, Antônio Manoel Coelho presented new information about the case. According to him, when the brigantine returned from Calabar, the officers made an inventory of all goods on board and distributed copies of this to interested parties, including the representatives of the deceased partner. According to the accused, the fourth part of the expected profits made available on that occasion amounted to 900,000 *réis*. From it was deducted the debt that the deceased had accumulated with the company, leaving a balance of 1:600,000 (one *conto* and six hundred thousand *réis*), which was not charged to the heirs due to the misfortune they were going through. He also declared that as soon as he arrived at the port of Rio de Janeiro, he informed Manoel Lopes Ribeiro of the facts and accounts of the brigantine, as he knew that he was responsible to the heirs of his partner, who were minors. At that time, according to his claim, he proposed sharing the slaves so that each was sold at the convenience of each owner; however, Mr. Ribeiro did not accept. He then sold some slaves for money and others in installments. Mr. Coelho ended his defense by declaring that the accusations that he was manipulating the estate of the company or that he had taken advantage of the death of the partner were unfair.[15]

The cases narrated above confirm that small farms producing flour in the Guanabara *Reconcavo* had their place in the Atlantic world. This documentation shows, at a level of detail not seen in any previous material, the effective

---

[14] Ibid.
[15] Ibid.

participation of a farmer from the *Reconcavo* in the broader markets formed by relations between Brazil and Africa. The tensions and disputes between neighbors for the right of access to a road that facilitated the flow of supplies to Rio de Janeiro did not end with the consumption of these supplies by residents of the city. They also crossed the bay and the ocean to Africa and were directly associated with the slave trade in Africa.

The defense of Mr. Antônio Manoel Coelho, an experienced trader, resident in the city of Rio de Janeiro, shows the level of diversification of investments made in these trips. Certainly, the size of the profits obtained was possible due to the low level of investments required, as seen in the networking by José Reginaldo de Mello e Velho with the many small farmers who produced cassava flour in the Reconcavo. Some of the elite of the Reconcavo of Rio de Janeiro, in addition to slave laborers, also had porters and boatmen responsible for transporting the goods they produced to Rio de Janeiro. Their homes and commercial houses show that these people profited at all stages of the production of cassava flour and other supplies. The case of Mr. José Reginaldo de Mello e Velho goes beyond these limits because, in addition to being a farmer, he goes beyond the borders of local commerce and tries his luck on the other side of the Atlantic. Moreover, the process illuminates the way José Reginaldo related to the traders of Calabar, indicating his previous knowledge of this port and its business dealings.

According to Luís Felipe de Alencastro, in the seventeenth century, the Guanabara *Reconcavo* supplied around 680 tonnes of cassava flour annually to Angola, and as the demand for slaves increased, as did the consumption of food in Luanda, the cassava flour trade between them grew. Therefore, cassava flour constituted one of the key pieces of the South Atlantic economy, whether it was to feed the crews of the slave ships, to feed the slaves who were in African ports waiting to be shipped, or as a supply for the troops involved in the "long Brazilian wars" in Angola (Alencastro 2001).

Another argument that may support the hypothesis that Rio de Janeiro was, for many years, a distribution center for cassava flour produced in Brazil for the Atlantic markets stems from the information that surplus flour was sent from the Salvador market to Rio de Janeiro. According to Barickman, in the 1820s, many vessels from the flour-producing villages in the south of the Bahian *Reconcavo* were sent to Rio de Janeiro and Pernambuco (Barickman, 2003). Ships laden with cassava flour from Bahia entered the port of Rio de Janeiro, carrying as well as cargoes from various regions of the south of the province, such as Ilha Grande, Angra dos Reis and provinces like Santa Catarina. João Fragoso analyzes the growing importance of the port of Rio de Janeiro in the commercial network built around the Atlantic within the scope of the

Portuguese empire, emphasizing that the captaincy became a crossroads for domestic and international trade routes after the 1700s.

Among these products was cassava flour produced in the Guanabara *Reconcavo*. The case of Mr. José Reginaldo de Mello e Velho was not an exceptional one. The "paths" of the cassava flour from the *Reconcavo*, traversed by boatmen and drovers, extended beyond the interior of Minas Gerais or the streets of Rio de Janeiro as seed capital for business with the other side of the Atlantic.

I have no doubt that the most profitable activity of the round trip carried out on board the *Sao José Diligente* was the slave trade. As much as there was diversity in the economic frameworks of the Atlantic, no business was more important and significant than the trade in souls. However, at the opposite end of the business, there is a small trade, difficult to evaluate: the sale of other goods from the fields and mills of the Guanabara region in African ports; in addition, they listed cassava flour in the inventory along with sugar cane, tobacco, sugar and rice, among others (Bezerra 2010).

Final considerations

There are many studies on slavery, the Atlantic trade, and the African diaspora. Many issues I raise here have been examined by renowned historians in Brazil and abroad. We conceived the Atlantic trade firstly by the extraordinary amount of people sold into slavery between Africa and several regions of the Americas. Just as African markets supplied the Americas with enslaved labor, these markets also received various goods from American colonies, giving rise to a complex dynamic of interests. In addition, it is important to link economic thinking with the cultural transformations that this process imposed on the formation of American colonial societies, such as Brazil.

The importance of cassava flour was not restricted to domestic markets and consumption on vessels. It is true that African markets consumed cassava flour and used African slaves to access these goods, just as they were used to gain access to tobacco, cachaça and sugar. In Rio de Janeiro, cassava flour was produced, consumed and traded from early colonial times. There are records showing that by the end of the sixteenth century, the Portuguese were already exploring this culture in the lands of the *Reconcavo da Guanabara*. Cassava flour was already being exported to African markets, especially on the South Atlantic routes, reaching places like Luanda and Benguela at the beginning of the seventeenth century. This perspective rethinks the peripheral position of the *Reconcavo da Guanabara* in Rio de Janeiro's historiography over the years. The surrounding regions of Rio de Janeiro had a place in the complex commercial networks of the Atlantic, given that African labor was employed on the properties that produced cassava flour on a large scale, in addition to sugar and cachaça in smaller proportions, but also with Atlantic pretensions.

Studies of the economy of cassava flour as an important commodity in the colonial economy make it possible to arrive at new perspectives on African slavery in the *Reconcavo da Guanabara*. The profile of slavery in this region also demonstrates some characteristics that allow us to identify connections previously unnoticed in earlier research. In the parishes of the *Reconcavo*, there was a concentration of African-born slaves. This is not new, as this group represented about 70% of the slave population in the city of Rio de Janeiro. However, when considering that the *Reconcavo da Guanabara* is characterized by small properties ranging between 1 to 30 slaves employed in food production, we can conclude that the extent of trafficking included the most remote regions of the Captaincy of Rio de Janeiro.

I would still like to highlight the work dynamics of many landowners and slaves in the *Reconcavo da Guanabara*. Some important figures of the Portuguese colonial administration, such as the Correia de Sá family, worked with cassava flour in the *Reconcavo*. However, some freed Africans were also able to maintain small flour-producing properties. In the latter case, the production of cassava flour had a certain autonomy negotiated around the farm. This certainly represented the possibility of accumulation of savings to buy manumission and maintain some productive activity. Even though it was not a large-scale activity, these possibilities allowed mobility for some freed Africans who achieved the status of owners of property and of slaves. In the case of the most powerful families, another peculiarity needs to be highlighted. Many maintained properties in the *Reconcavo*, and in the city, some had slave ships employed in the traffic and there are cases of people who maintained properties even in Angola. In this way, the elite of the *Reconcavo* were not subject to economic, political and social isolation. Among the property owners of that region, there were many men who diversified their interests, favoring connections with several places, including regions in Africa.

In a region of small properties, slavery was characterized by asymmetric social relations influenced by the proximity between various actors. There is nothing new in the fact of a master leaving goods for one or more slaves to enjoy after his death. However, masters leaving the entire productive part of their lands to their slaves is a situation that deserves some consideration. When the master left the farm, the flour house and the cassava fields for his slaves, in practice, he left the entire "productive company" that guaranteed his livelihood throughout his life. This was not a common situation and can be explained by the asymmetries present in everyday social relations in places of the kinds we have analyzed here.

On the other side of the Atlantic, Benguela emerged as an important port of embarkation for slaves and a place that offered markets for colonial goods from Brazil. That Angolan city was an important connection on the South Atlantic routes in which Bahia and Rio de Janeiro, for example, also participated. Evidence presented here aimed to prove that cassava flour was a desired commodity in southern Angola. At the end of the eighteenth century, a supply crisis arose in Benguela because no vessels were carrying cassava flour, leading the local authorities to mobilize to get the colonial power to intervene. It is possible that this intervention had some success since, in the first decades of the nineteenth century, the number of African slaves from Benguela increased exponentially in the slave population of Rio de Janeiro.

References

Abreu, Maurício de Almeida. *Geografia Histórica do Rio de Janeiro (1502-1700)*. Vol 2. Rio de Janeiro: Andreia Jakobson Estúdio, 2010.

Alencastro, Luís Felipe de. *O trato dos viventes: formação do Brasil no Atlântico Sul*. Sao Paulo: Companhia das Letras, 2001.

Araújo, José de Souza A. Pizarro e. *Memórias Históricas do Rio de Janeiro*. Vol. 3. Rio de Janeiro: Imprensa Nacional, 1945.

Barickman, B. J. *Um contraponto baiano: açúcar, fumo, mandioca e escravidão no Reconcavo baiano, 1780-1860*. Rio de Janeiro: Civilização Brasileira, 2003.

Bezerra, Nielson Rosa. As chaves da liberdade: confluências da escravidão no Reconcavo do Rio de Janeiro, 1833-1888. Niterói: EdUFF, 2008.

_____. Mosaicos da Escravidão: identidades africanas e conexões atlânticas do Reconcavo da Guanabara, 1780-1840. Tese de Doutorado em História. Niterói: UFF, 2010.

Candido, Mariana Pinho. "Enslaving Frontiers: Slavery, Trade and Identity in Benguela, 1780- 1850". PhD Dissertation. York University, CA, 2006.

_____. "Different Slave Jorneys: Enslaved African Seamen on Board of Portuguese Ships, 1760-1820." *Slavery and Abolition* 31 (September 2010): 395-409.

Demétrio, Denise. Famílias Escravas no Reconcavo da Guanabara. Séculos XVII-XVIII. Master's Dissertation in History. Niterói: Universidade Federal Fluminense, 2008.

Fernandes, Ambrósio Brandão. *Diálogos das grandezas do Brasil (1618)*. 2 edição integral. Recife: Imprensa Universitária, 1960.

Ferreira, Roquinaldo Amaral. Transforming Atlantic Slaving: Trade, Warfare and Territorial Control in Angola, 1650-1800. PhD Dissertation. Los Angeles: UCLA, 2003.

Florentino, Manolo. *Em costas negras: uma história do tráfico de escravos entre a África e o Rio de Janeiro*. Sao Paulo: Companhia das Letras, 1997.

Fragoso, João. "A noção de economia colonial tardia no Rio de Janeiro e as conexões econômicas do Império Português: 1790-1820". In *O Antigo Regime nos trópicos: a dinâmica imperial portuguesa (séculos XVI-XVIII)*, edited by

João Fragoso, Maria Fernanda Batista Bicalho e Maria de Fátima Gouvêa, 29-72. Rio de Janeiro: Civilização Brasileira, 2001.

Karasch, Mary. *A vida escrava no Rio de Janeiro, 1808-1850*. Sao Paulo: Companhia das Letras, 2000.

Gomes, Flavio dos Santos; Faria, Juliana Barreto; Soares, Carlos Eugênio L. *No Labirinto das nações: africanos e identidades no Rio de Janeiro, século XIX*. Rio de Janeiro: Arquivo Nacional, 2005.

Lara, Silvia Hunold. "Conectando historiografias: a escravidão africana e o Antigo Regime na América Portuguesa. In *Modos de Governar: idéias e práticas políticas no Império Português*, edited by Maria Fernanda Bicalho e Vera Lúcia Amaral Ferlini. Sao Paulo: Alameda, 2005.

Miller, J.C. *Way of Death: Merchant Capitalism and the Angolan Slave Trade (1730- 1830)*. Madison: University of Wisconsin Press, 1988.

Miller, Joseph. "A economia política do tráfico angolano de escravos no século XVIII". In *Angola e Brasil: nas rotas do Atlântico Sul*, edited by Selma Pantoja e José Flávio Sobra Saraiva, 21-38. Rio de Janeiro: Bertrand Brasil, 1999.

Pinto, Leonardo Aguiar Rocha. *Fregueses e Freguesias: ação do Estado Português ao longo das vias de comunicação entre o Rio de Janeiro e Minas Gerais*. Rio de Janeiro: Stampa, 2007.

Reis, João José. *A morte é uma festa: ritos fúnebres e revolta popular no Brasil do século XIX*. Sao Paulo: Companhia das Letras, 1995.

Schwartz, Stuart B. *Segredos Internos: engenhos e escravos na sociedade colonial*. Sao Paulo: Companhia das Letras, 1986.

Silva, Rosa Cruz e. "Benguela e o Brasil no final do século XVIII: relações comerciais e políticas". In *Angola e Brasil: nas rotas do Atlântico Sul*, edited by Selma Pantoja e José Flávio Sobra Saraiva, 51-68. Rio de Janeiro: Bertrand Brasil, 1999.

Soares, Mariza de Carvalho. *Devotos da cor: Identidade étnica, religiosidade e escravidão no Rio de Janeiro, século XVIII*. Rio de Janeiro: Civilização Brasileira, 2000.

——— . "O vinho e a farinha, 'zonas de sombra' na economia atlântica no século XVII." In *A Companhia e as relações econômicas de Portugal com o Brasil, a Inglaterra e a Rússia*, edited by Fernando de Sousa, 215-232. Lisboa, CEPESE/ Afrontamento, 2008.

——— . "Engenho sim, de açúcar não: o engenho de farinha de Frans Post". *Varia Historia* 25, no. 41(Jan-Jun 2009): 61-83.

Soares, Mariza de Carvalho; Bezerra, Nielson Rosa (Orgs.). *Escravidão Africana no Reconcavo da Guanabara, séculos XVII-XIX*. Niterói: EdUFF, 2011.

Subrahmanyam, Sanjay. "Connected Histories: notes towards a Reconfiguration of Early Modern Eurasia". In: *Modern Asian Studies* 31, no. 3, (1997): 735-762.

Thorton, John. *A África e os africanos na formação do Mundo Atlântico (1400-1800)*. Rio de Janeiro: Campus, 2004.

PART II

BLACK AGENCY IN THE POST ABOLITION

CHAPTER FOUR

The Great Migration in Brazil: Blacks Families and Households. Rio de Janeiro, (1888-1940)

Carlos Eduardo Coutinho da Costa
Universidade Federal Rural do Rio de Janeiro, Brazil

Abstract

This article aims to analyse the process of Black migration in Brazil, from Vale do Paraíba to the city of Rio de Janeiro, after abolition. It tries to illuminate this process beyond the dual explanations normally given for such migrations: attraction vs. expulsion. The usual explanation of black migration after the abolition of slavery was based on widespread alarming newspaper articles, as well as the liberal ideology of modernisation. Thus, the emergence of the favelas and ghettoes in the outskirts of Rio de Janeiro is still connected with Black migration from the Vale do Paraiba after the Lei Aurea. Based on this assumption, it is important to review the historiography, which only sees black migration as one of family disorganisation, a problem of underemployment and unhealthy housing conditions. They undertook migration as a conscious act with its own significance and not just as a reaction to material loss. In order to achieve this objective, qualitative, quantitative, demographic and geographic reference analyses of this experience were employed. The main object of this article is to illuminate the experiences of black migrants in their formation of families, their occupations and the areas they chose to live.

Keywords: Migration, abolition, Black family, Labor, Brazil

***

Brazilian historiography, for years, understood the post-abolition migration as a process of loss on the part of former captives. The formation of slums, ghettos and the periphery in the city of Rio de Janeiro was still explained as resulting from the migration of those freed by the Abolition Law of 1888, many coming from the Paraiba Valley – a region that saw the greatest concentration of slaves in the second half of the nineteenth century. The historiography, based on the ills of the 'inheritance of slavery' and the 'social anomie' of the former captives and their descendants, was in part responsible for the creation of a negative image of these trajectories in the post-abolition period— perpetuated until today (Carvalho 1987; Rios and Mattos 2005; Nascimento 2005). In contrast to this view, I emphasize the importance to be accorded the agency of former captives and their descendants in this process. They took to migration as a conscious act of itself. Thus, this article proposes to analyze — through examination of civil registers of births and deaths in the municipality of Nova Iguaçu and through interviews, studies of individual trajectories and secondary bibliography — the collective trajectories of migrants as agents of this process. The aim is to highlight the quantitative (demographic) and qualitative aspects, such as fears, violence, hopes and goals, that explain migration and to redefine it in this new context (Grossman 1989).

The Great Migration

Historians from Jamaica, Cuba and the United States acknowledge the importance of the post emancipation period, when freed men and women and their descendants migrated in order to experience freedom. In certain locations, such as Alabama, in the early post-abolition years, a good number of former slaves left the plantations, using their right to come and go to travel initially between several localities with no apparent destination. In the first months after 1865, in the southern United States, many newspapers reported a seemingly disordered population movement and not just, as was expected, to the north. After all, having the right to travel wherever one wanted during a certain period was considered a source of pride and excitement for former slaves. However, nothing seems to have influenced the migration more than the search for reunion with separated relatives sold during slavery (Foner 1988).

In addition to exercising their freedom, many sought greater independence from the power of landowners through the acquiring of land and control of the pace and form of work. In the case of Jamaica, for example, it was believed that the freed persons would tend to buy cheap, unproductive land for subsistence, far from large properties. Nevertheless, what was actually seen was a movement to the contrary: according to Holt, they were able to buy small properties, migrating to areas close to urban centers and agro-exporting areas. In this way, they sought on their farms to combine subsistence production with surpluses for sale in local markets, just as they wanted to sell their labor to large farmhouses. That is, from this survival strategy, they could obtain three distinct sources of survival, expanding their independence (Holt 1992).

In the Cuban case, the eastern side of the island attracted potential migrants. According to the data analyzed by Rebecca Scott, between the censuses of 1862 and 1899, a new pattern could be distinguished in the population distribution of Blacks, now located in the East. This region offered greater access to land because of the following factors: part was mountainous, not conducive to large-scale sugar production; and after the Ten Years War, this land was distributed by the government to be occupied and revitalized. At the same time, migration to the cities was limited since, according to Scott, "the proportion of the black population of the island resident in Havana Province, for example, did not increase sharply during the period of emancipation" (Scott 1991, 252). Similarly, after an analysis of statistical data, the author states that the figures "do not seem to portray a mass migration to the cities" (ibid). In other words, people found in the 1899 census of the cities were probably descendants of urban Black residents, not migrants from the old sugar plantations.

In the United States, part of the migration to urban centers occurred due to the search for Black social institutions such as churches, schools and mutual aid societies, as well as organizations, such as Freedman's Bureau, to help against the violence so common in this period. In Foner's view, in some places, the consequences of migration to the cities were disastrous: due to the lack of work and money, these migrants moved to the suburbs, where hygiene was poor and disease proliferated. However, among all the experiences of the post-abolition population of former slaves and their descendants, Foner identified that the most common decision in the early years in the south of the United States was to stay on the plantations, now working under different conditions (Foner 1988). The Great Migration, as the migration of the population of free Blacks towards the north of the United States was usually called, only began in the twentieth century, in 1910, with the apex in 1920, and not in the early years of post-emancipation (Gregory 1995). There is an entire North American bibliography that looks at southern migrations towards the north under various themes: political, social, economic, non-economic, racial and cultural.

In the Brazilian case, the first studies on the theme of post-abolition Black migration emphasized negative experiences. The most widespread and usually reproduced explanation of the trajectory of former slaves in the post-abolition period was based on alarming news in newspapers and on the liberal logic of modernizing the country. The theory of the liberation of labor from the countryside to cities, that is, the expulsion — to construct a reserve army that would lead to the future industrialization of Brazil and its calamitous social consequences such as segregation and the creation of slum districts — was one of the most popular across the word and was no different here.

When analyzing the city of Rio Claro, Warren Dean realized that, in the competition for work between immigrants and nationals, Blacks lost room. With the impossibility of social insertion through work on farms in the interior of Sao Paulo, the former captives were expelled and forced to migrate to cities on the rise, in this case, the port city of Santos (Dean 1977). For José Murilo de Carvalho, for example, abolition markedly transformed the characteristics of Rio de Janeiro since "the population of the capital has changed in terms of number of inhabitants, ethnic composition, occupational structure" (Carvalho 1987). Such growth created a shortage of housing in the city center, a preferred area. For many, the city's hills remained an option, forming what we currently call *favelas* (Lopes 1992, 3). That is, after 1888, the Federal Capital became the center of attraction for the unemployed labor of the Southeast, finding itself in a production crisis.

For the previously mentioned authors, from an economic view of the process, only the segregation of labor remained for the migrants. According to Carvalho, "abolition launched the rest of slave labor into the free labor market and broadened the contingent of underemployed and unemployed" in Rio de Janeiro city (Carvalho 1987, 16). In other words, in the unfair contest of these migrant workers with residents of Rio de Janeiro city and immigrants, the result was racial, social and spatial segregation. Thus, for these authors, the negative post-abolition trajectory of Blacks would be mostly linked to economic conditioning, not taking cultural aspects, among them violence, into account.

However, more recent works have challenged the hypothesis of spatial segregation as the "legacy of slavery" and of "victimization," some arguing that Black people did not fit in with the modernity being created at the time since they were only spectators of new situations, thus neglecting the agency of former slaves, their desires and life projects. (Rios and Mattos 2005; Nascimento 2005). In other words, migration should not be seen as a result of slavery and its subsequent dissolution but rather through the lens of the agency of Black men in the post-abolition period.

Even from this new perspective, it should be noted that in fact, the population of Rio de Janeiro city increased significantly after 1890. According to Brazil's demographic censuses, while in 1872, there were 274,972 people in the Federal Capital, including slaves and free people, this number increased to 522,651 in 1890, reaching 1,157,873 inhabitants in 1920. In other words, only superficial analysis would attribute these figures to a migratory movement to this city, which apparently did not occur in the immediate post-abolition period but rather throughout the 1920s. However, in the censuses consulted, there are no references to the origins of these people, much less to their motivation, which reinforces the need for research into other sources that could inform these data, such as interviews and civil registers of births and deaths.

In interviews with direct descendants of former slaves, Mattos came across three types of life trajectories after the liberation of slaves in 1888. In the first, she found stories of great stability. During the last years of slavery in Brazil, in the region of the Paraiba Valley, several landowners managed to keep the freed persons on the farms by freeing them in large numbers, trying to build "bonds of gratitude" with the workers, in order to organize a true "army" of Black workers (Mattos 1997). Many of these groups stayed on the farms for many years and came to form what today *Fundação Palmares* recognizes as surviving *quilombola* communities located in the valley. In addition, there were those who somehow bought small properties and settled there, working as sharecroppers, partners, or on contract, obtaining part of their livelihood through small farms. In short, in the immediate post-abolition period, the largest part of this population remained in the Paraiba Valley. (Mattos 2005; Guimarães 2009).

The interviews also revealed the trajectories of those who could not achieve stability: they migrated from farm to farm in search of temporary jobs and rarely secured any kind of social mobility because of their intense movement. Their life stories are marked by violence, instability, poverty, and lack of extensive family ties (Rios and Mattos 2005). Finally, there were those who definitely migrated to the rising centers. This last group, consisting mostly of children and grandchildren, direct descendants of former slaves, migrated only in the 1920s when the social and financial condition of their parents could no longer be reproduced. For those who lived in the countryside, soil erosion, pests and lower employment due to the devaluation of coffee affected the workers in Paraiba Valley much earlier. Probably to survive, they had to give up their last asset, the land. Eventually, the entire worn-out area started to be used as pasture for cattle, which was becoming the most economically viable alternative for the region (Fragoso 2013).

Little or no attention was paid to the social and cultural characteristics of this process. Studies show that nothing encouraged migration more than the desire of many former slaves to reunite families long separated by the scourge of slavery (Fraga 2006, 314). A second factor encouraging migration may also have been the search for greater and better access to education. Following their period of slavery, many slaves recorded, in their manumission papers, the desire to exchange captivity for long years of compulsory service if their master agreed to assist them in case of illness and, above all, to educate their children (Lima 2005). There has been little study of access by the Black and brown population to basic education in the Paraiba Valley, but in peripheral regions, such as *Baixada Fluminense* (a region in Rio de Janeiro state), there exist studies demonstrating the entry of Black teachers and students into schools (Bezerra 2012). It is quite possible that a good number of young people chose to migrate in pursuit of greater access to education, likely seeing it as an avenue for social mobility.

In the same way, one can also point to violence as a stimulus for migration. In an interview with Ana Lugão Rios, Cornélio Cansino said that as a child, his family members were forced to move to the Sao José farm in the town of Juiz de Fora, Minas Gerais state. His father worked a small field on the Sao Lourenço farm and, having to hoe the area, he ended up missing his workday on the owner's fields. To teach him a lesson, the owner forced the former slave to open the gate to his fields and let the oxen in to eat his crops. His uncle, worried about the situation, invited them to live with him on the Sao José Farm.[1] Although this example of violence does not directly demonstrate any racial connotation, in the interior of Sao Paulo, there were cases of murders very similar to those in the southern United States during the same period (Henri 1975; Tolna 1992; Tolnay and Beck, 1995; Woofter 1928; Tolnay 2003). Analyzing the correspondence between the chief of police and the local delegate in the town of Sao Carlos (Sao Paulo state), Karl Monsma came across cases of lynching (Monsma 2009; 2005). According to one of the letters found, a month and a half after the abolition, 400 people broke into the police station and shot and killed 'freed John,' who had broken into a local house two days before. After killing him, the gathering hanged him in the city's main square. Monsma concluded that when such cases of violence occurred, Black populations migrated out of fear. (Monsma 2009).

In the same way, Lucia Helena Silva, analyzing the records of the House of Detention of Rio de Janeiro City, was able to identify the migration of this population to the then Federal Capital between 1890 and 1920. According to her, migration from the interior of Sao Paulo state was linked to the following factors: escaping unfair competition for jobs with European immigrants, lack of land and racism (Silva 2001).

With the decrease in European immigration, partly due to the First World War, there was an increase in the need for labor in the capital and peripheries, and soon, newspapers would spread information about job opportunities in the city of Rio de Janeiro and its surroundings. In several places in the pages of the newspaper *O Correio da Lavoura*, there is a concern about the farm workers of Paraiba Valley, as well as several notices from the Ministry of Agriculture inviting them to come to work (Nascimento 2013). In Rio de Janeiro, employment opportunities increased as regions around the city expanded their production, partly to supply the city with food and partly for agricultural products for export — as was the case of the orange groves in Nova Iguaçu, Campo Grande, Madureira and Cascadura — in addition to industries, especially the factories in Bangu. It is still unknown if the newspaper was also read in Vale do Paraiba; however, its pages show a clear relationship between

---

[1] Interview of Cornélio Cansino to Ana Lugão Rios, in 1994. Memórias do Cativeiro Collection (AMC), LABHOI (Laboratorio de HIstória Oral e Imagem), Universidade Federal Fluminense. Electronic version available at http://www.labhoi.uff.br/narrativas/depoimentos.

the two regions. They also received news from the Capital through migrant relatives and friends.

In the case of Nova Iguaçu, a metropolitan region of Rio de Janeiro, in the first decades of orange production, workers were called up on only two occasions — during planting and for the harvest — meaning they migrated seasonally to this region, returning home at the end of the activity (Souza 1992). It is interesting to consider how the news about job opportunities or the availability of free land reached areas far from the capital. The story of Dionísio offers some clues to this mystery. His grandson, Manoel Seabra, a resident of the Sao José Community, said that his grandfather used to walk for six days from the village of Nova Iguaçu to their home, outside the village of Santa Isabel do Rio Preto, district of Valença, also in the Valley. On his trips, besides bringing gifts, he used to tell the relatives about the events and opportunities in Nova Iguaçu.[2] This practice of exchanging information between relatives, especially information on new work opportunities and free land, was common among peasants (Martins 1996).

Also key in the spreading of such news were the railroad workers. The railway lines cut through the coffee farms of the valley crossed Baixada Fluminense, and ended downtown in Rio de Janeiro. José Gomes de Moraes, better known as Seu Juca, a resident of Barra do Piraí, worked for 40 years in the train station *Central do Brasil*, in downtown Rio de Janeiro, returning home every day.[3] Railway workers, on returning to their homes, used to tell relatives and friends all the information they obtained on the route, increasing interest among future migrants. In the same way, this transportation network contributed to emigration from Paraiba Valley. The railroad, after all, since the last quarter of the nineteenth century, transported passengers and goods between the capitals of Sao Paulo and Rio de Janeiro.

Among the interviews recorded as part of the project, "Memórias do Cativeiro Collection," one can find stories of descendants of former slaves who chose to emigrate to Rio de Janeiro. People like Cornélio Cansino, born in 1913 in Juiz de Fora, Minas Gerais state, who migrated to Sao Paulo state as a youngster and years later moved back to Rio de Janeiro, where he met his two brothers, Ricardo and Geraldo. They all went to live in the center of the city. Cornélio got a small house on Frei Caneca Street, central area, while Ricardo

---

[2] Interview with Manoel Seabra in 2003. Memórias do Cativeiro Collection, LABHOI (Laboratoio de HIstória Oral e Imagem), Universidade Federal Fluminense. Electronic version available at http://www.labhoi.uff.br/narrativas/depoimentos .

[3] Seu Juca's Interview, 2006. Acervo Universidade Federal Fluminense/Petrobras Cultural Memory and Black Music Collection, LABHOI.

and Geraldo were not so lucky, living on Catumbi Hill, on Sao Carlos Street, now the Sao Carlos slum.[4]

Although these examples demonstrate the possibility of housing very close to large urban centers, most migrants who were direct or indirect descendants of former slaves seem to have lived in peripheral regions. In Bahia, for example, Walter Fraga Filho managed to join a migration of freedmen to the Metropolitan Region of Salvador but did not prosper, finding few opportunities (Fraga 2006). In other regions, such as Paraná, according to Leonardo Marques (2009), former slaves migrated to nearby cities that were still marked by a mixture of rural areas and growing urbanization. Based on these experiences, we can conclude that even if the destination were the urban center, this first generation of migrants probably settled in the surrounding areas of their destinations, working in farming and cattle raising. They had been familiar with manual labor in the countryside and might have found their first jobs there.

I argue that the demographic and economic growth of the outskirts of Rio de Janeiro, and in particular of the region called *Baixada Fluminense*, must be rethought as not a direct result of the expulsion of the poor population from the center of the federal capital, as José Murilo de Carvalho (1987) stated. Rafael Mattoso (2009), for instance, demonstrated that the growth of these regions was connected to their own dynamic of attraction and not just as a result of the expulsion of people from downtown Rio de Janeiro. The neighborhood of *Madureira*, for example, attracted the population's interest because of its varied commerce, while *Bangu* grew demographically because of the nascent industry. (Martins 2009).

The Great Migration in Rio de Janeiro

Following the procedure of investigating the trajectories of direct descendants of former slaves from Vale do Paraiba, the information from 16 interviews filed in the Laboratory of Oral History and Image of Universidade Federal do Rio de Janeiro, carried out between 1994 and 2001 by Ana Lugão Rios, was analyzed. The research looked at everyone mentioned in the reports, except those who died in childhood or adolescence, considering as migrants only those who established residence away from where their slave ancestor had lived. The testimonies were collected in several municipalities of Paraiba Valley and surrounding towns — Valença, Paraiba do Sul, Bananal, Juiz de Fora and Bias Fortes. Of the 466 people born between 1850 and 1959, 137 (29.4%) migrated

---

[4] Interview with Seu Cornélio Cansino, 1995. Memórias do Cativeiro Collection, LABHOI (Laboratoio de HIstória Oral e Imagem), Universidade Federal Fluminense.

from their origin, as opposed to those who opted to stay: 329 (70.6%). Although the pursuit of stability was the norm among those who experienced the transition from slavery to freedom, according to the interviews, a good many of those born between 1850 and 1869 undertook some migration. In this first section, it was noted that most of them were men, probably single, who fit Ana Rios' first typology; therefore, they migrated within the state, from farm to farm. (Rios 2005).

The definitive migration to metropolitan and peripheral regions of Rio de Janeiro city was more often found in the life paths of those born after 1888. According to the testimonies collected, this phenomenon began in the mid-1920s, reaching its peak in 1930, and ended in mid-1940. Most migrants were male, and at the peak of the migration process, 1930, they were between 10 and 30 years old. This means that men born between 1900 and 1919 probably did not find the same living conditions as their ancestors on the coffee farms while still young and so opted for the strategy of definitive migration, as Ana Rios pointed out earlier. Migrant women, on the other hand, are more common among those born in 1910-19 and 1920-29. Many of them, like Leonor, another one interviewed by the author, migrated following relatives.[5] Thus, despite the larger number of men migrating, it is assumed at first glance that women also migrated after spouses and/or male relatives had become settled.

Baixada Fluminense, Rio de Janeiro's Metropolitan Region, appears as the preferred destination for children and grandchildren of former slaves of Paraiba Valley. According to the interviews previously mentioned, 39.4% of the people who had some experience of displacement in their trajectory did not have a specific destination, spreading out almost always through centers on the rise, such as the town of Juiz de Fora in Minas Gerais; however, the remaining 60.6% headed for Baixada Fluminense.

Taking once again the 1930s as the apex of migration to this region, among the elderly, born between 1850 and 1879, who probably experienced slavery, 100% of those with any experience of migration went to Baixada Fluminense. Dionisio and his wife, Zeferina, followed a similar trajectory. After their children settled in Cabuçu — a neighborhood in the town of Nova Iguaçu — they moved to Baixada Fluminense at an advanced age because, as their grandchildren point out, there were facilities generated by urban growth, such as the Iguassú Hospital.[6] However, it is the migration of young people that attracts the greatest

---

[5] Interview with Izaquiel Inácio in 1995. Memórias do Cativeiro Collection, LABHOI (Laboratoio de HIstória Oral e Imagem), Universidade Federal Fluminense.

[6] Interview with Florentina Seabra in 1995. Memórias do Cativeiro Collection, LABHOI (Laboratoio de HIstória Oral e Imagem), Universidade Federal Fluminense.

attention. It was those born between 1900 and 1929 who most often chose to live in Baixada Fluminense. As people most often migrated when they were either in late adolescence or, more commonly, around the age of 20, we can say that those born between 1890 and 1929 increased the migration to Baixada Fluminense between 1910-1949, with a significant drop in this movement in the 1950s and 1960s among those born between 1930 and 1949.

If, during the first decades of the recently inaugurated Republic, the young descendants of slaves from Paraiba Valley found it difficult to obtain jobs in that region due to the devaluation of coffee on the international market and the massive opening of cattle raising and eucalyptus plantations, which demand less labor at the same time, Baixada Fluminense began to export oranges. The production of citrus fruit on small farms began quietly in the 1920s, peaking at the end of 1940 (Pereira 1977). Due to urban growth, connected to government initiatives in sanitation policy and export incentives, it became necessary to co-opt labor to ensure the survival of this venture (Souza 1992).

At the end of the First Republic, there was a mass migration to the Nova Iguaçu region. Compared to the municipalities of the Paraiba Valley, the demographic growth of *Baixada Fluminense* was huge. According to the 1872 census, there were 31,251 people in the region; in 1920, the population was 33,396. However, in the Rio de Janeiro State Economic and Financial Statistics Report for the year 1931, the population of Nova Iguaçu had reached 42,408 inhabitants (Souza 1992). The biggest leap occurred in the following decade, in the 1940 census, which showed population growth of over 300% in just 20 years.

Graph 4.1. Population per year according to the census for the towns of Paraiba do Sul, Valença, Vassouras and Iguassú.

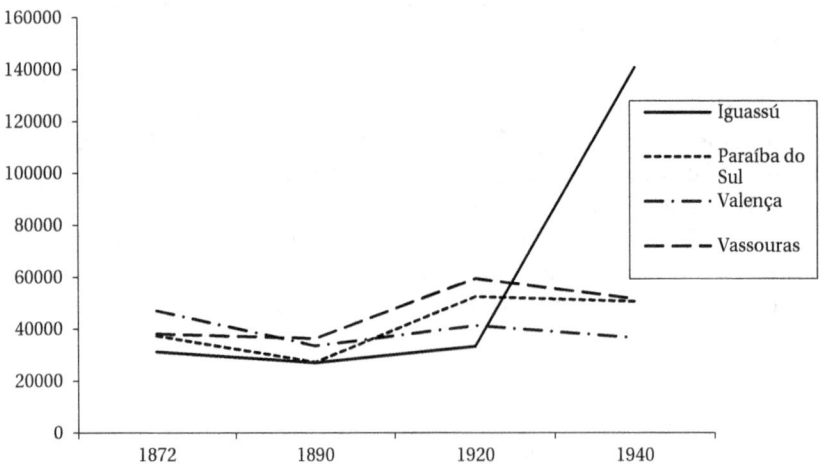

Source: Brazilian Institute of Geography and Statistics. IBGE.
Censuses of 1872, 1890, 1920 and 1940.

The demographic growth is confirmed by the official records of birth and death for the decade of 1920. Despite the existence of under-registration, birth registration in the town of Nova Iguaçu increased from 1914 onwards.

Graph 4.2. Civil records of births and deaths in absolute numbers. Town of Nova Iguaçu, 1889-1939.

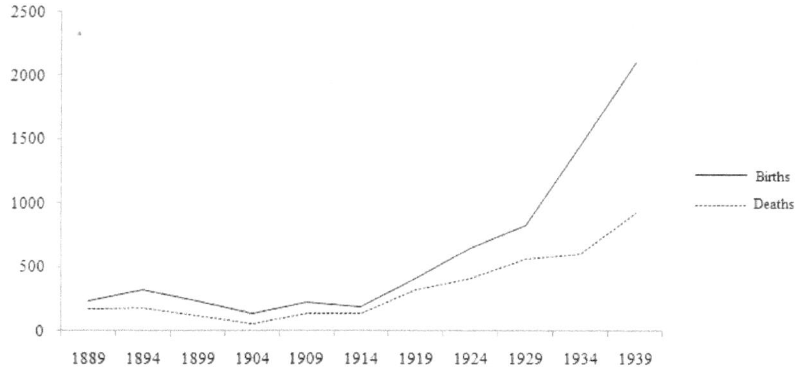

Source: 1st Civil Registry Office of Natural Persons of the Town of Nova Iguaçu.

On February 18, 1931, a federal decree made birth registration obligatory and free of payment. In 1939, another decree enforced the previous demand for registration; that year alone, 1,187 late registrations were made. Three types of birth records were surveyed. The first were those registered within the period stipulated by law, that is, up to 60 days from the birth of the child (Castro 2006, II). The second relates to the late registration of children, encouraged by new legislation that annulled fines levied for delay. And finally, the registrations of people who, during adolescence or adulthood, spontaneously approached the notary office and declared their birth. Although it is not possible to affirm whether the color of skin was declared by themselves or decided by the notary, the variety of details of the second and third types of records is greater than that of the first since they provide, in addition to the precise place of birth, addresses and professions. Because of these features, in this article, the "self-declared" make up the sample that allowed for analysis of the migration of black and brown workers.

According to those records, persons classified as white and brown came mainly, in this order, from municipalities in the Paraiba Valley, from the Northeast states, and Rio de Janeiro city, followed by other localities in the interior of Rio de Janeiro state. The immigrants, identified as Black, originate from municipalities in Paraiba Valley, other localities of Rio de Janeiro state, and Minas Gerais state. Overall, migratory flows to the Baixada Fluminense were predominantly from the Paraiba Valley and from the Northeast states.

It is important to note the determination of Blacks and Browns to seek legal recognition of themselves and their family through the official registry. On registering, in most cases as adults, most declarants were residents of the region and had contracted a marriage, which represented a certain stability. Alexandre Gonçalves Barboza Júnior, for example, a farmer married to Adalgiza Travassos Barboza, a native of the town Mar de Espanha in the state of Minas Gerais (also in the Paraiba Valley), registered his three children on September 14, 1934: José Maria Barboza (born on September 26, 1917), Geraldo Travassos Barboza (born on December 5, 1918) and Margarida Maria Barboza (born on September 02, 1919). Apparently, he first migrated alone and only later brought his wife and children, registering all on the same day.[7] Given that the civil registry of birth demonstrates a person's stability in the region, it is reasonable to assume that they arrived months or even years before the registration.

I was able to follow several cases, from birth in the Paraiba Valley to registration in Baixada Fluminense. I found, for example, adult males, probably single, who migrated to Baixada Fluminense between 1934 and 1939, like Gil. On December 14, 1917, Agostinho Alves de Amorim and his wife, Brígida Alves de Amorim, baptized their son, Gil, in the church of Santa Isabel do Rio Preto, district of Valença, Rio de Janeiro state, declaring that the child was born on September 17 of the same year.[8] Gil probably migrated to Baixada Fluminense at a young age, as he went to the Civil Registry of Nova Iguaçu to declare his birth. He gave his name as Gildo Alves de Amorim, Black, and gave the names of his paternal grandparents, Álvaro de Amorim and Eliza de Amorim, and maternal grandparents: Pedro Américo de Amorim and Maria da Conceição.[9]

Cross-checking this experience with other civil records shows that, at first, there was a predominance of men among migrants to Baixada Fluminense. In 1934, women accounted for only 15% of the national immigrant population, and in 1939, 32%. Despite a greater number of men migrating and their being pioneers in migration, it should be noted that women also participated in this movement. They did not always migrate in the company of or in accordance with their spouses and their migration had its own characteristics, not always associated with the developmental process of a region.

---

[7] Civil Registry of Birth of Nova Iguaçu (RCN), book 49, reg. 6222, 6223 and 6224, of 9/14/1934.

[8] Ecclesiastical Archive of the Church of Santa Isabel do Rio Preto, book: s/n, seat, 226, p. 185, 1917.

[9] Civil Registry of Birth of Nova Iguaçu, book 60, reg. 14.880, 1939.

Households

In the process of identifying internal migration to Rio de Janeiro city and its surroundings, I used the method called "geoprocessing." Ian Gregory, to indicate the use of geographic information systems applied to studies in history, coined the term Historical Geographic Information Systems (HGIS) (Gregory 2007), adding the "when" to the "what" and "where" questions that characterize non-historical Geographic Information Systems (GIS). GIS has allowed some innovations, such as the automatic comparison of historical maps with aerial satellite databases and images or old maps, intensifying the production of new data (Gil 2013; Valencia 2016). In all the documents analyzed, there are references to the place of residence of migrants. With these, it was possible to build a large map, over time, of the spaces occupied by migrants from the 1890s to 1940s.

Between 1889 and 1939, the population of the municipality of Nova Iguaçu tended to concentrate in several specific regions. First of all, it is worthwhile mentioning the large internal population displacement that occurred after 1914 in which Whites, Browns and Blacks seem to have abandoned the old town center, located near the Iguassú River. Local historians and academics had already pointed to a change during the transition from the nineteenth century to the twentieth in Baixada Fluminense without being able to prove it numerically (Souza 2002; Souza 1992; Torres 2004; Pereira 1977; Barros 1993). The economic decline of the old town center, caused mainly by the coffee crisis and by the silting up of the rivers, which served to reduce production in the countryside, as well as several epidemics followed by *choleras morbus*, a motivated departure from the old village of Iguassú. The region of Maxambomba, in that same period, arose as a new regional economic axis due both to the construction of the railroad and to the new orange plantations. Soon, the new town center had a concentration of businesses, including doctors, an apothecary and pharmacists. Because of these factors, in 1916, the region was elevated to town status and became known as "Nova Iguaçu."

From 1919, an increasing number of Whites, Browns and Blacks abandoned localities in the interior of the country and dispersed to several areas, looking for a better life. With the massive arrival of workers from various regions of the country, property value in Nova Iguaçu rose, leaving few families able to afford housing in town. Only White people were now able to stay and a significant proportion of brown people left for the interior of the municipality, where the properties were cheaper. The experience of those registered as Blacks was quite different, having never completely left the rural area of the municipality.

In the 1930s, we became aware of the growth of towns whose economy was centered on orange production. In towns like Miguel Couto, Brejo and Morro

Agudo, Brown and Black migrants were predominant. No other town seems to have attracted more migrants than Mesquita among the recently emancipated. In conclusion, Black and Brown migrants did not concentrate in the towns but remained scattered in their outskirts, where there was a possibility of combining paid work with access to property ownership, finally achieving their ancestors' project of freedom.

Chart 4.3. Division by color in the regions of residence of the self-declared (%). Municipality of Nova Iguaçu, 1929-1939.

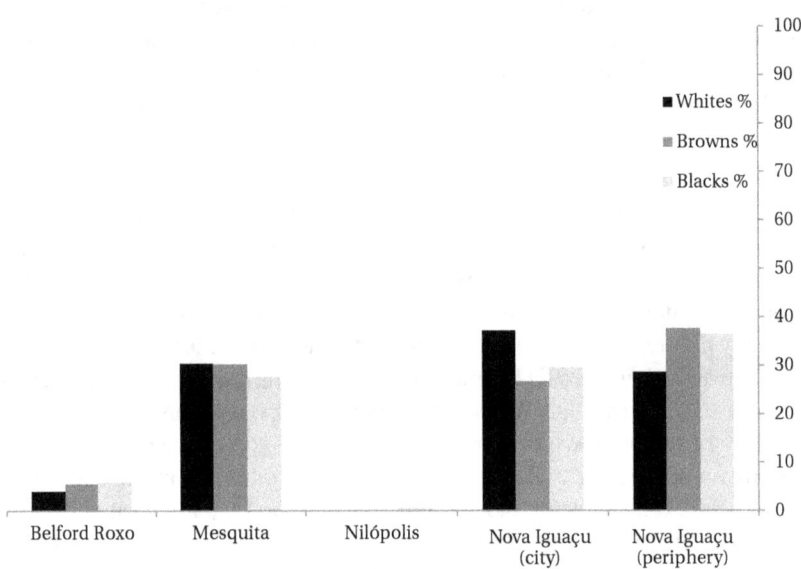

Source: Civil Birth Records from the first Nova Iguaçu Natural People's Registry.

This data shows that although Nova Iguaçu was clearly a region where whites were in the majority, other groups had access to property. Thus, no segregation by color had occurred. If, until 1939, white migrants were in the majority in the central region of Baixada Fluminense, there was no clear exclusion from the living space, as Brown and Black made up, at various times, 40% of the population, even if concentrated in the outskirts.

Nevertheless, one of the most interesting areas of data refers to Black migrants. They were not concentrated in any single part of the metropolitan region and, on the contrary, were dispersed across all regions. It appears they were not hindered in their mobility, nor was there any kind of spatial segregation. Even though they lived far from the city centre, some managed to have access to health and education, as these localities at the time already had quicker access to the capital.

If there were no impediments to mobility and the choice of places to live, why did Blacks and Browns choose to live on the outskirts of the Nova Iguaçu City Hall? In the period after abolition, from 1889 to 1939, they did not migrate to Rio de Janeiro City as expected; on the contrary, they remained, and the family continued to reside, in the places where their parents and grandparents had been slaves. With the migration reaching its apex in 1920, they were able to improve their livelihoods, acquiring ownership, opening small businesses, or working in the orange plantations. They found in Nova Iguaçu more favorable conditions for success.

Conclusion

The mass migration did not occur in the immediate post-abolition period. According to the analysis of civil birth records, most migrants arrived in the late 1930s. By cross-checking this information with life stories, it is possible to confirm that the definitive migration from the Paraiba Valley to the Metropolitan Region of Rio de Janeiro city took place between the 1920s and 1940s and was undertaken by young people, mostly single men born in the years following abolition. Taking migration as an active life improvement strategy rather than a consequence of family breakdown, it is possible to define another configuration in this process experienced by direct descendants, or not, of former slaves: they chose to live on the outskirts of Rio de Janeiro city, especially in the metropolitan area known as Baixada Fluminense - a region on the rise where it was possible to combine work on the farms with other important factors in social mobility, such as schools.

The evidence presented so far suggests that Blacks and Browns have managed to accomplish the peasant project and sustain it over the years. That is, in a region where large-scale orange production was not fully directed towards export, much less based on large properties, Blacks and Browns, with or without a history of passage through slavery, migrated to Baixada Fluminense. Little is known about the conditions under which they did so: when were they able to buy land? What were the working conditions? Only a more refined study using other sources can complement this analysis.

Finally, the spread throughout the region of Baixada Fluminense after the 1930s may explain the absence of large Black communities.

References

Barros, Ney Alberto Gonçalves de. *Um pouco da história de Iguassu a Iguaçu*. Nova Iguaçu: Colégio Leopoldo Machado, 1993.

Bezerra, Nielson. *A cor da Baixada: escravidão, liberdade e pós-abolição no Reconcavo da Guanabara*. Duque de Caxias, RJ: APPH-CLIO, 2012.

Carvalho, José Murilo de. *Os bestializados: o Rio de Janeiro e a República que não foi*. Sao Paulo: Companhia das Letras, 1987.

Dean, Warren. *Rio Claro: um sistema brasileiro de grande lavoura, 1820-1920*. Rio de Janeiro: Paz e Terra, 1977.

Foner, Eric. O significado da liberdade. *Revista Brasileira de História* 8, no.16 (1988):9-36.

Fraga, Walter Fraga. *Encruzilhadas da liberdade*: histórias de escravos e libertos na Bahia (1870-1910). Campinas: Unicamp, 2006.

Fragoso, João. *Barões do café e sistema agrário escravista*: Paraiba do Sul/Rio de Janeiro (1830-1888). Rio de Janeiro: 7 Letras, 2013.

Gil, Tiago, *Cartografia digital para historiadores: algumas noções básicas*. Fortaleza: Expressao Gráfica Editora, 2013.

Gregory, I. N.; ELL, P. S. *Historical GIS: Technologies, Methodologies, and Scholarship*. New York: Cambridge University Press, 2007.

Gregory, James N. The southern diaspora and the urban dispossessed: demonstrating the census public use microdata samples. *The Journal of American History* 82, no. 2 (1995): 111-134.

———. *The southern diaspora: how the great migrations of black and white southerners transformed America*. Chapel Hill: University of North Carolina Press, 2005.

Grossman, James R. *Land of hope: Chicago, Black southerners, and the great migration*. Chicago, IL: University of Chicago Press, 1989.

Guimarães, Eliose Silva. *Terra de preto: usos e ocupação da terra por escravos e libertos (Vale do Paraiba Mineiro, 1850-1920)*. Niterói: EdUFF, 2009.

Henri, F. *Black migration: movement north, 1900-1920*. Garden City, NY: Anchor, 1975;

Holt, Thomas. *The problem of freedom: race, labor, and politics in Jamaica and Britain, 1832-1938*. Baltimore: Johns Hopkins University Press, 1992.

Lemann, Nicholas. *The promised land: the great migration and how it changed America*. New York: Knopf, 1991.

Lieberson, Stanley and Wilkinson Christy. A comparison between northern and southern blacks residing in the north. *Demography*, no. 13 (1976):199-224.

Lima, Henrique Espada. Sob domínio da precariedade: escravidão e os significados da liberdade de trabalho no século XIX. *Topoi* 6, no. 11 (July-December 2005): 289-326.

Lopes, Nei. *O negro no Rio de Janeiro e sua tradição musical: partido-alto, calango, chula e outras cantorias*. Rio de Janeiro: Pallas, 1992.

Marques, Leonardo. *Por aí e por muito longe: dívidas, migrações e os libertos de 1888*. Rio de Janeiro: Apicuri, 2009.

Martins, J. S. O tempo da fronteira: retorno à controvérsia sobre o tempo histórico da frente de expanSao e da frente pioneira. *Tempo Social* 8, n. 1 (May 1996): 25-70.

Martins, Ronaldo Luiz. *Mercadão de Madureira: caminhos do comércio*. Rio de Janeiro: Condomínio do Entreposto Mercado do Rio de Janeiro, 2009.

Matoso, Rafael. *Echos de resistência suburbana: uma análise comparativa das contradições socioespaciais cariocas a partir das experiências dos moradores da Freguesia de Inhaúma (1900-1903)*. Dissertation (Master's Degree), Federal University of Rio de Janeiro, Rio de Janeiro, 2009.

Mattos, Hebe. *Das cores do silêncio: significados da liberdade no Brasil escravista*. Rio de Janeiro: Nova Fronteira, 1997.

_____. Novos quilombos: ressignificações da memória do cativeiro entre descendentes da última geração de escravos. In *Memórias do cativeiro: família, trabalho e cidadania no pós-abolição*, edited by Ana Lugão and Hebe Mattos, 232-255. Rio de Janeiro: Civilização Brasileira, 2005.

Monsma, Karl. Histórias de violência: inquéritos policiais e processos criminais como fontes para o estudo de relações interétnicas. In *Estudos migratórios: perspectivas metodológicas*, edited by Zeila Demartini and Oswaldo Truzzi, 159-221. São Carlos: EDUFSCar, 2005.

_____. Linchamentos raciais depois da abolição: quatro casos do interior paulista. In: Anais do Congresso Internacional da Latin American Studies Association, XXVIII. Rio de Janeiro: Lasa, 2009.

Nascimento, Álvaro. 13 de Maio: memória da escravidão e educação nas páginas do *Correio da Lavoura* (Nova Iguaçu, RJ, 1917-1950). In *Cruzando fronteiras: novos olhares sobre a história do trabalho*, edited by Alexandre Fortes, 205-228. Sao Paulo: Fundação Perseu Abramo, 2013.

_____. Qual a condição social dos negros no Brasil depois do fim da escravidão? O Pós-abolição no ensino de história. In *A República e a questão do negro no Brasil*, edited by Maria Aparecida Salgueiro. Rio de Janeiro: Museu da República, 2005.

Pereira, Waldick, *A Mudança da Vila (História Iguaçuana)*. Nova Iguaçu: Artesgráfica, 1970.

_____. *Cana, Café e Laranja: História econômica de Nova Iguaçu*. Rio de Janeiro: FGV/SEEC, 1977.

Rios, Ana Lugão and Hebe Mattos. *Memórias do cativeiro: família, trabalho e cidadania no pós-abolição*. Rio de Janeiro: Civilização Brasileira, 2005.

Scott, Rebecca. Defining the boundaries of freedom in the world of cane: Cuba, Brazil, and Louisiana after emancipation. *The American Historical Review* 99, no. 1 (February 1994): 70-102.

_____. *Emancipação escrava em Cuba: a transição para o trabalho livre, 1860-1889*. Rio de Janeiro: Paz e Terra; Campinas: Unicamp, 1991.

Senra, Nelson de Castro. *História das estatísticas brasileiras*. Rio de Janeiro: IBGE, 2006. v. 2.

Silva, Lucia Helena Oliveira. "Construindo uma nova vida: migrantes paulistas afrodescendentes na cidade do Rio de Janeiro no pós-abolição (1888-1926)". PhD Dissertation. Unicamp, 2001.

Souza, Marlúcia dos Santos. "Economia e sociedade iguaçuana." Master's Thesis. Universidade Federal Fluminense, Niterói, 2000.

Souza, Sonali Maria de. "Da laranja ao lote: transformações sociais em Nova Iguaçu". Master's Thesis. National Museum/Federal University of Rio de Janeiro, 1992.

Tolnay, Stewart E. Migration experience and family patterns in the 'promised land'. *Journal of Family History*, no. 23 (1998): 68-89.

———. The great migration and changes in the northern black family, 1940 to 1990. *Social Forces* 75, no.4 (June 1997): 1213-1238.

———. The great migration gets underway: a comparison of black southern migrants and non-migrants in the north, 1920. *Social Science Quarterly* 82, no. 2 (2001): 235-252.

———. The African American 'great migration' and beyond. *Annual Review of Sociology* 29 (2003): 209-232.

Tolnay, Stewart E.; Beck, E. M. *A festival of violence: an analysis of southern lynchings, 1882-1930*. Urbana, IL: University of Illinois Press, 1995.

———. Racial violence and black migration in the South, 1910 to 1930. *American Sociological Review* 57, no. 1 (February 1992): 103-116.

Torres, Gênesis (Org.). *Baixada fluminense: a construção de uma história: sociedade, economia, política*. Sao João de Meriti-RJ: IPAHB Ed., 2004.

Trotter Jr., Joe William. *The great migration in historical perspective: new dimensions of race, class & gender*. Bloomington and Indianapolis: Indiana University Press, 1991.

Valencia Villa, C. E. *Ao Longo Daquelas Ruas. A economia dos negros livres em Richmond e Rio de Janeiro, 1840-1860*, Paco Editorial, Sao Paulo, 2016.

CHAPTER FIVE

Life after Slavery: Migration, Work and Culture in Brazil 1900-1929

Lúcia Helena Oliveira Silva

Universidade Estadual Paulista, Brasil

Abstract

This article seeks to discuss some life experiences of freedmen and their descendants that were engendered by the processes of displacement or migration within the country in the first decades of post-abolition. Large cities such as Rio de Janeiro and São Paulo received a large population of freed migrants, a mixture of different ethnicities since the times of slavery. Since a good part of the workers and workers were enslaved, the work experience was a determinant and continuing or running away from it was a guide to re-signifying freedom. From sources such as records of prisoners made at the *Casa de Detenção* in the city of Rio de Janeiro, oral testimonies of descendants of freedmen and literature of the time, we will seek to present the meanings of migration in the lives of some freedmen and women in São Paulo and Rio de Janeiro.

Keywords: Post-abolition, criminalisation, freedom, migration, Rio de Janeiro

***

Slavery is one of the great themes that characterize the history of Brazil. The long prevalence of this socio-economic system defined economic policies, and the process that led to the ending of slavery is equally important. Indeed, if slavery ended in 1888, two years later, the imperial regime also came to an end. In the historical context that coincided with the right to freedom for all the slaves and the change in the political regime in the country, many free men and their descendants migrated. Moving long distances or short, some of the freedmen sought to discover and conquer other spaces, enjoying their new autonomy. In this essay, I reflect on the several ways explored in those processes of moving inside the country.

When I talk about the migration of freedmen, one cannot avoid thinking about the most famous migration process that occurred in the United States of America, called the Great Migration. The Great Migration, occurring between 1900 and 1930, involved around six million people who left the south for the North, searching for better jobs and escaping the violence committed by racist organizations (Tolnay and Beck 2009; Grossman 1989). Although the historical context was different in the USA (internal war and the reconstruction periods), the movement of freedmen, starting with the end of slavery in 1888 until the first decades of the twentieth century to several parts of the country was also a constant process, inspired mainly by the search for good living conditions, yet very little is known about the motivations and directions.

The internal migration processes throughout the history of Brazil have been defined as a consequence of the development of export-focused economic structures, such as the gold, sugar cane, and coffee cycles. In fact, from the seventeenth to the nineteenth centuries, economic development that demanded an enslaved labor force also attracted the free population. That population often moved around the country in search of better living conditions. They were also motivated by the search for unoccupied land, many times because of expulsion from occupied lands by rich farmers and to avoid forced enlistment in armies involved in internal conflicts.

Carlos Eduardo Costa (2015) explained that part of the historiography of the first half of the twentieth century viewed migration as a negative characteristic resulting from poor conditions inherited from slavery. This was also the position of Warren Dean, who studied the Rio Claro – Sao Paulo region. For him the competition for jobs between free men and immigrants was to the disadvantage of the former due to the preferences of the farmers. In this case, the choice to migrate was a consequence of a lack of jobs. In the view of Florestan Fernandes (1978), the lack of jobs and the consequent movement of ex-slaves were due to their unpreparedness and the survival of a state of anomie within a society that was being industrialized. Such conditions, as well as the unpreparedness, were problematized years later by Andrews (1998). In his studies, when Andrews compared immigrants with free men, he found that both had experience only in fields and not in factories. The choice for labor in Sao Paulo was, therefore, based on racial bias and not a matter of ability. These studies shed light on the approaches to the formation of the labor market, as well as showing the interference of racialist ideas in economic policies. In these analyses, we can see the importance of economic issues in the decisions to seek out places with better living conditions. The years after abolition were marked by the rise of hired labor, interest in the maintenance of control, and the inequalities in labor relations for the hegemonic groups.

However, besides the economic influences, new research has analyzed the force of the agency of free men in the migration process. As Carlos Eduardo Costa stated, migration is "a conscious act and with its own meaning, not only a consequence of material laws" (Costa 2015, 102). This author, in a study on the migration of ex-slaves in the Vale do Paraiba to Rio de Janeiro and the metropolitan area, found that personal expectations directed the internal migrations as much as did the economic aspects. In this context, Edinelia Souza (2008) studied Black migration in the *Reconcavo* Baiano[1] during the post-abolition period. Souza noticed that mobility was one means of securing a hard-won autonomy that was not always definitive. The *Reconcavo* movement was considered a strategy to escape the adverse conditions created by the occasional droughts in the region. As soon as weather conditions improved, the migrants returned, demonstrating other than economic conditioning. She argues that the migration was not mechanistic but rather was an experience that involved volition and historical context.

Those aspects are particularly important in reflecting on some migrations that have been researched. They concern migrants, most of them children of freedmen, who were arrested and registered in the jailhouse of Rio de Janeiro city at the end of the nineteenth century, more precisely in 1890. The collection of documents, previously called *Casa de Detenção da Corte* (The Court's Jailhouse), comprises police records consisting of registration books for prisoners, with a file on each person arrested. Each book registered 250 cases of imprisonment, addresses, and dates of arrest and release. That is, there is much data that gives us information on people who were arrested and taken to the city prison. The jailhouse was used to house prisoners held for offenses and awaiting trial, as well as those already tried and sentenced, and all the people arrested in the streets of Rio de Janeiro. The files contain very important data and though they were not always precisely filled in, they are still a very valuable source in understanding a part of the population of the city.

My interest was in finding Afro-descendant migrants who lived in Rio de Janeiro city between 1888 and 1920, that is, in the years following abolition. That period was one of adaptation for such people as well as for the society and each created a point of view regarding the Afro-descendant population in the city. We must bear in mind that the chosen period was one of intense changes in the country and in the world. It coincided with the period of colonialism in Africa and in Asia and the circulation of ideas on Social Darwinism and scientific racism that promoted negative perspectives on the intellectual contribution of people with African or Asian ancestry. Studies based on these

---

[1] N.E. Reconcavo is the geographic are of land located at recessed coastal area that directly connects to a larger main body of water, such as an ocean. It is the same as a bay.

assumptions were carried out by Raymundo Nina Rodrigues (1957) and Oliveira Vianna (1938), deeply influencing the views of Brazilians at a time when the formation of the republican nation and national identity were being discussed. In this view, miscegenation could provide the desirable whitening, bringing the nation closer to Europe, considered the model for civilization and modernity. The fact that the country had, for centuries, depended so much on slave labor, and that its population was predominantly Afro descendants, constituted a biological and social problem in the view of the doctor and anthropologist Nina Rodrigues. The solution to this dilemma was to 'whiten' the population by bringing European immigrants to serve as laborers on the great coffee plantations and who would colonize the sparsely populated areas.

Meanwhile, the formerly enslaved looked for work and better living conditions. Focusing on the migrations as one of the ways of shaping life in liberty, I believe that many ex-captives stayed in the same places where they had been slaves. Some farmers, anticipating abolition, bought the permanence of workers through a system of partnership, offering land to plant and a small remuneration, which kept some of them on the same farms. Other workers moved from farm to farm in search of more acceptable conditions, and others went to the urban centers, abandoning life on the farms. The choice of the Afro-descendant migrants who went to the urban centers motivated me because migration is a challenging process that demands breaking with a known life and established bonds and constructing a new life in other places. With few resources and precarious travelling conditions, which could involve walking part of the route and the ever-present risk of having their freedom taken away by some authority, an increasing number of people moved from place to place during the last quarter of the 1800s.

In the survey of those made prisoners in Rio de Janeiro city, we find that cases of imprisonment rose in festive seasons such as carnival, Christmas, and other holidays, mainly because of fights and drunkenness. That also applied to women imprisoned for drunkenness, prostitution and fighting in public. Prostitution was heavily criticized in newspapers and the sentence in case of suspicion was imprisonment, with judges, in cases of recidivism, doubling the number of days in jail. Data also show that most men detained by the police were under the age of 30 (Silva 2016), which confirms the studies of other researchers, such as Carlos Costa (2015) and Ney Lopes (1992), pointing to an enormous flow of children and young men into the city after slavery. I collected data from a police record book that listed all prisoners born outside Rio de Janeiro. The book, numbered 5628, covering June to September of 1894, identified 48 immigrants among 250 prisoners, or 19.2% of the prison population. The distribution is seen in Table 5.1 below:

Table 5.1. Birthplace (states) of migrant prisoners in 1894.

Birthplace	Quantity
Bahia	14
Ceará	01
Rio Grande do Sul	05
Pernambuco	04
Minas Gerais	04
Rio Grande do Norte	02
Maranhão	01
Sergipe	02
Cabo Verde	05
Ilha de Sao Tomé	01
Africa	02
Sao Paulo	07
Total	48

Source: Public Archives of the Rio de Janeiro State, Jailhouse [Fundo Casa de Detenção], book number 5628, year 1894.

As seen in the sample, there were people from several parts of Brazil, predominantly from Bahia (*baianos*). This predominance of *baianos* among immigrants arriving in Rio de Janeiro city was repeated in other registers. Indeed, the presence of *baianos* among the population of Rio de Janeiro city was common since the second half of the nineteenth century, having affected the culture of the city, whether through the cooking of Bahian women who sold food in the streets or through social gatherings in their homes with music and religious meetings. The network of *baianos* in Rio is at the root of street carnival and samba schools, as well as of the provision of support to newcomers from the same state. According to Roberto Moura:

> Apart from the Africans, generally bantus, brought to Rio de Janeiro during the slave trade, Blacks people from other ethnic groups joined those traded in the Northeast during the gold and later coffee cycles, ending up in the city making up the population of working class neighborhoods through intermarriage. There, the free *baianos* migrated out of choice constituted an elite among the population and extrapolating from the information on their survivors and descendants, we can suppose that they were predominantly "nagôs" (Yorubas). (Moura 1995, 120).

There was a regular presence of free *baianos* in Rio de Janeiro after slavery and it explains a certain status that they had in relation to other migrants. People from Rio de Janeiro pejoratively called those from the North and Northeast states, such as Maranhão, Pará, Sergipe, Pernambuco, Alagoas, and Piauí, "Paraiba*s*." Unlike them, there was a certain respect among the workers for the *baianos*, whose importance was also acknowledged in popular cultural life. Afro-Brazilian religious life was influenced by people from Bahia in the form of candomblé symbolized by the participation of the "*quituteiras*" (women who sold food in the streets) and who were members of the religion. The most famous woman of that period was Tia Ciata. Born Hilária Batista de Almeida in Salvador, Bahia, in 1854, she came to Rio in 1876 and went to live near Alfandega Street among other *baianos*, according to Moura. As a priestess of candomblé she welcomed other migrants from Bahia to her house in well-known gatherings, parties, and religious ceremonies (Moura 1995). The example of Ciata as someone from another city who received migrants from her hometown was repeated all over the city, with such women being well-known and respected entrepreneurs, with "tia" (aunt) used both as a term of endearment and as a mark of respect. Besides this, sponsorship by women from Bahia contributed to the development of samba and Black music in Rio de Janeiro.

Besides the *baianos*, people from other provinces (called states after 1891), such as Sao Paulo were listed among the prisoners. The presence of migrants from Sao Paulo, the "*paulistas*", could seem strange at first since they came from a place that was constantly seeking workers. However, in Sao Paulo, a policy favoring European migration had been initiated from the 1880s. Around 1890 there were about one million European immigrants working on plantations as well as in urban centers. This competition left Afro-descendants with menial and low-paid jobs, including seasonal work such as harvests and clearing forests in new areas, heavy work with many risks and often badly paid. Migrants from the North and Northeast areas were motivated by the long droughts, conflict with local rich farmers, and the lack of opportunities for ownership. As well, the former slaves were only too willing to leave places marked by negative experiences of oppression.

In addition to the national migrants found in the records, there were eight Africans: five from Cape Verde, one from Sao Tomé and two listed simply as Africans. The two from Cape Verde were the youngest, 22 and 34 years old, and the migrant from Sao Tomé, 45. The two said to be simply Africans, Jerônimo Lemos and Miguel Guilherme, were older, 66 and 76 years, with Miguel described as an incorrigible thief and Jerônimo as drunken and rowdy. That information, on the other hand, also indicated that they lived in the city to the point that they were known to the authorities.

Prisoners were also identified by skin color, such as black, *pardo* (brown) and *fula* (Black person with lighter skin). Rio de Janeiro city was a place where Africans could easily mix with a population that was more than half Black, whereas mingling with the local population was more difficult for Africans and

Life after Slavery

Afro-Brazilians living in small and medium towns where their identity was attached to their former owners even after emancipation.

Another condition common to all the registered prisoners is their marital status: all claimed to be single. Being single did not mean they lived alone but rather perhaps without official matrimonial bonds, something that might facilitate their mobility. As we saw in the history of Tia Ciata – who, by the way, was married – it is possible that they tried to live near people with whom they had something in common, such as origin, place of work or profession, and of course family ties. This hypothesis explains why most of them lived in central areas where there were cheaper tenement houses and where they were nearer workplaces such as the port.

There is a great variety in the professions, including specialized crafts. The table below compares prisoners for whom there is birthplace, age, profession and skin color data.

Table 5.2. Data on migrants arrested between June and September of 1894.

Name	Birthplace	Age	Profession	Skin Color
João G. Pereira	Bahia	24	brick layer	black
João F. Oliveira	Bahia	50	Cook	fula
Victorino Dias	Sao Thome Island	45	Caulker	black
Alfredo S. Pires	Rio G. Sul	22	carpenter	parda
Pompeo J. A. Magalhães	Rio G. Sul	20	Baker	black
Pedro Taveira	Ceará	28	Painter	parda
João A. Pereira	Pernambuco	22	blacksmith	parda
Casimiro Monteiro	Cabo Verde	34	Worker	fula
Manoel Prissio (Manoel Veríssimo)	Cabo Verde	26	Docker	parda
João B. Oliveira	Bahia	28	Worker	black
Manoel A. Brito	Minas Gerais	23	Worker	nothing
Irineo Andrade	Bahia		Worker	black
Francisco Fernandes	Pernambuco	48	carpenter	black
Luis Lima	Santos-SP	22	carpenter	pardo
Francisco J. Nascimento	Rio G. Norte	27	Worker	fula
Victor Santos	Sao Paulo	24	Cook	black
Raymundo F. Silva	Maranhão	25	Worker	parda
José Valentim	Cabo Verde		Docker	fula
Casimiro A. Alves	Sao Paulo	21	Caulker	black
Antonio P. Alegre	Rio G. Sul	32	Sailor	fula
Antonio Alves	Minas Gerais	22	carter assistant	fula
João G. Lopes	Pernambuco	32	Sailor	black
José F. Frutuoso	Bahia	32	Docker	black
Manoel J. Silva	Pernambuco	34	Docker	black
José J. O. Maracanã	Sergipe	28	Docker	parda

Braz I. Santos	Bahia	29	Worker	black
Luiz A. Rufino	Sao Paulo	75	Coachman	black
Benigno G. Santos	Sao Paulo	24	music teacher	parda
Eduardo G. Pinto	Cabo Verde	30	Sailor	black
Aureliano F. Almeida	Sao Paulo	21	Worker	parda
José A. O. Mendes	Sao Paulo	23	Cook	black
João B. Cordeiro	Rio G. Norte	48	Worker	parda
Graciliano C. Silva	Bahia	25	Tailor	parda
Candido F. Castro	Bahia	25	Carrier	black
Christovão F. Telles	Sergipe	50	Worker	black
Antonio L. Evangelista	Cabo Verde	38	Worker	fula
José G. Oliveira	Minas Gerais	23	Barber	fula
Libanio A. Candido	Bahia	63	Salesman	black
Camilo J. Lima	Bahia	30	bricklayer	fula
Pedro de Oliveira	Rio G. Sul	18	Butler	fula
Cleto E. Ribeiro	Bahia	30	without data	black
Francisco A. Pereira	Bahia	22	Worker	parda
Miguel Guilherme	Africa	76	Baker	black
Antonio Gonçalves	Minas Gerais	23	police officer	fula
Ireneo A. Silva	Bahia	52	Docker	preta
Jeronimo C. Lemos	Africa	66	shopkeeper	black
Pompeu A. Souza	Rio Grande do Sul	44	coachman	black
Julio A. Reis	Bahia	no data	Cook	black

Source: Public Archives of Rio de Janeiro State. Book n. 5628, Jailhouse, year 1894.

Everyone listed in the document gave surnames that could have belonged to their parents, been adopted from former owners, or been invented where the prisoners had no surnames and there was no official rule on surnames. Looking at the table, two professions stand out: a prisoner who was a policeman and another one who was a music teacher. Both were qualified which meant they had had the opportunity for specialized training for their roles. Other declared professions were related to the learning of a craft and working in urban areas: carter, baker, coachman, carrier, shopkeeper, etc. There were also jobs connected with the port: shipwrights, sailors, and proper occupations for a coastal city.

It is possible that those migrants did not represent all the migrants to that city, but they were a representative sample of the people who went there. On the other hand, if the ability of Afro-descendent migrants in the city to mix with those already living there provided anonymity and an opportunity to create new identities, their arrests also indicated that there was repression. The movement of ex-slaves was under constant surveillance, mainly in the city. After the *Lei Aurea*, restrictions on the Black presence in the streets continued with the same rigor. The construction of a new society, while giving preference to white workers, marginalized the Afro-descendant population as paid workers.

However, Blacks and mulattoes resisted the oppression and discipline imposed, constructing autonomous forms of living and socialization, defying those created by government policies.

As part of the modernization process of the republican nation, new rules replaced the laws of the imperial period. The *Código Penal* (Criminal Code) was created in 1890, where two chapters were dedicated to dealing with the presence of the poor in the streets, specifically about beggars, drunks, vagabonds and *capoeiras*. The idea behind the law was to replace unwanted people with "useful citizen workers," even if that meant confining the unwanted in asylums for the poor. The Criminal Code regulated crimes and misdemeanors and the penalties for each infringement, but to be punished, there first had to be a trial. Yet, we see in the examples of arrests that there was a systematic application of penalties without trial. That is, it seems there were criteria applied by police authorities that did not always follow the legal process, and that certainly depended on the police chief and other officials such as the policeman, clerk and other people connected with the jailhouse. Behind those criteria were the ideas of public order and discipline, demanding strict control of the Black and poor presence in the city's streets. Thus, many inhabitants of Rio de Janeiro city, even those who had never been arrested, could be considered vagabonds and idlers. Such a situation arose not only there but across the whole of Brazil. Marina Carvalho points out that this imposition of discipline aimed to control people considered idlers or potential criminals before they could break the rules (Carvalho 2006).

With the oppression represented by the application of the new Criminal Code, the question is: Why did people migrate to urban centers, in this special case, to Rio de Janeiro? One of the clues could lie in the population increase in Rio de Janeiro that had been a common feature since the beginning of the nineteenth century, especially after the arrival of the Portuguese Royal Family (Corte Portuguesa) in 1808. As the headquarters of the Portuguese Kingdom, the city became the administrative and economic center with the port that received more Africans in the transatlantic trade with America. It is worth pointing out that the urbanization process and the creation of cultural institutions such as libraries, museums, schools, newspapers and theaters among others, energized cultural life in the city. Many more ex-slaves were needed for the new urban jobs, according to Mary Karash (2000). Many of the occupations of slaves, when slavery ended, remained jobs relegated to the Black community. That profusion of Black people allowed an Afro-descendent migrant to blend in, besides having more workspaces reserved for the community, such as the port. Those who came to Rio de Janeiro probably knew or had heard comments about those conditions. In addition, the presence of free workers was part of a community with deep roots in the urban center.

Sidney Chalhoub (1990) called it "the Black city," a term originally applied to the period before abolition, designating the geographical and social space where Black people (enslaved and free) maintained their customs and established social ties, away from the gaze of owners and the police (Chalhoub 1990). Such social activity did not end with abolition, continuing to be a feature of communities and neighborhoods marked by the Black presence, which attracted newcomer Afro-descendants in the first years of the new regime.

Those conditions were very attractive for those who came from small cities where their identity was still connected with former owners and those who wanted to start a new life free of the past. Ney Lopes, studying the Afro-Brazilian cultural contribution in Rio de Janeiro, confirms the increase in population after the abolition of slavery. Many groups came to Rio de Janeiro in the post-abolition period, such as migrants from the Paraiba valley, veterans from the Paraguay War, those affected by drought in the Northeast region, and ex-slaves from all parts of the country (Lopes 1992). According to Sylvia Damazio (1996), the population of Rio de Janeiro increased by 95.8% between 1872 and 1890 and by 56.30% up to 1906, causing problems such as a housing shortage. The increase resulted from both internal and external migrations, given that, because of several epidemics, deaths in that period exceeded births. We must also remember that the port of Rio de Janeiro attracted people from other parts of the country, as well as foreign immigrants such as Africans born in Cabo Verde and Sao Tomé, as the police records indicated.

It is noticeable that most Black people were arrested for minor offenses such as drinking, fighting or unacceptable behavior in the streets more than for real crimes, probably related less to criminal culpability clearly defined and more to a need to discipline the presence of Blacks in the street. In addition, the arrests indicated a life extrapolated from principles of modesty, morality and what was considered honest behavior, and of acceptable hours for going out and staying in the streets. It is important to point out that the clerks' views of the men and women arrested, as shown in the descriptions in the documents of the jailhouse, were marked by the racial and social prejudice of that time.

In this sense, the ideas of morality and the control of the popular groups were heavily influenced by the eugenic ideals common in that period. According to Maria Stella Bresciani (1987), the transformations in European cities at the end of the nineteenth century brought a new definition of the urban space that tried to prohibit and discipline the working classes. Urban reforms originating in England influenced the French, who, between 1853 and 1870, undertook a program of demolition and construction to beautify Paris with many parks and wide avenues following the example of London.

The entire process dismantled traditional working-class neighborhoods seen potentially as a focus for rebellion. The engineer Pereira Passos, who studied in

France at the École Polytechnique and was appointed mayor of Rio de Janeiro, initiated the urban reforms that took place in the first years of the twentieth century. His plans were heavily influenced by the movement in Europe and had the support of the federal government. Passos authorized the demolition of old buildings and old tenements occupied by the lower class as he opened new avenues and parks. His goal was to make the city equal to European capitals, as a "civilized place." Many of those displaced from the central areas went to live on the hills of the city, creating what was called *favelas*.

In legal terms, the concern was not only in defining idleness but also in ending it. Initiatives such as alms houses and re-education for work, imported from Europe, were adapted in Brazil, allowing for the construction of the *Colônia Correcional Dois Córregos* and prisons in urban and rural areas, and also of asylums. According to Magali Engel (1995), Brazilian asylums emerged with the republic, with the first appearing at the end of the imperial regime. The *Hospício D. Pedro II*, for example, was mandated to accept destitute slaves of penniless owners, destitute merchant seamen and the mentally unwell who had no resources to pay for their treatment. From the first republican reform, the hospice started to receive all the people who, from acquired or congenital mental conditions, disturbed the public peace, offended good moral custom, and tried to kill other people or themselves.

For more than three centuries, because of the society's basis in slavery, there had been a devaluation of physical labour as the work of enslaved or Black people. Only lighter and specialized work should be considered as activities for the more affluent groups. However, in the republic, work began to be seen as a moral instrument, leading to racial discrimination and criminalization of those considered lazy and dangerous, such as the poor working population of Afro-descendant origin.

Final considerations

The end of slavery is marked by the struggle of Black men and women on multiple fronts for citizenship. Among the various avenues employed by the freedmen and their descendants, migrating to other spaces was one of the bridges they crossed in the reconstruction of a different life. In doing so, they created new bonds of friendship, seeking out places of leisure and even engendering new conflicts. Despite the difficulties, new barriers were broken, such as the processes of discipline, the maintenance of differentiated treatment, the influences of ideas of scientific racism, and restraints on religious liberty and on mobility that were legally prescribed in the Criminal Code. However, the process of resistance by the local and migrant Afro-descendant populations continued and grew, creating indelible marks in the culture, evidence present among the local migrant Afro-descendant population across the city. In other words, the repression of the Afro-descendants was massive and continuous, but equally so were the dynamics of resistance of the group who created a Black city within the city of Rio de Janeiro, who not only maintained it but created several identities to become one of the most vibrant and representative characteristics of Rio de Janeiro.

Primary Source

Arquivo Estadual do Rio de Janeiro. Livro no. 5628. Fundo Casa de Detenção. Ano 1894.

References

Andrews, George R. *Negros e brancos em Sao Paulo, 1888-1988*. Bauru, SP: Edusc, 1998.

Bresciani, Maria S. *Londres e Paris no século XIX: o espetáculo da pobreza*. 4ª ed.. Sao Paulo: Brasiliense, 1987.

Chalhoub, Sidney. *Visões da Liberdade: uma história das últimas décadas da escravidão na Corte*. Sao Paulo: Cia das Letras, 1990.

Carvalho, Marina. "Vadiagem e criminalização: a formação da marginalidade social do Rio de Janeiro: 1888-1902". Presented at the XII Encontro de História Regional Anpuh: Usos do Passado, Niteroi, RJ, August 14-18, 2006, 11p. http://www.snh2011.anpuh.org/resources/rj/Anais/2006/conferencias/Marina%20Vieira%20de%20Carvalho.pdf

Costa, Carlos E. C. Migrações negras no pós-abolição do sudeste cafeeiro (1888-1940). *Topoi* 16, no. 30 (June 2015): 101-126.

Damazio, Sylvia. *Retrato Social do Rio de Janeiro na virada do século* Rio de Janeiro: Eduerj, 1996.

Dean, Warren. *Rio Claro: um sistema brasileiro de grande lavoura, 1820-1920*. Rio de Janeiro: Paz e Terra, 1977.

Engel, Magali. "A loucura na cidade do Rio de Janeiro: ideias e vivências (1830-1930)." PhD Dissertation, IFCH/U district of Valença nicamp, 1995.

Fernandes, Florestan. *A Integração do Negro na Sociedade de Classes*. 3ª ed. Sao Paulo: Ática, 1978.

Grossman, James R. *Land of hope: Chicago, black southerners, and the great migration*. Chicago, IL: University of Chicago Press, 1989.

Hebe, Mattos M. *Das cores dos silêncio: os significados da liberdade no sudeste escravista Brasil, século XIX*, 2ªed., Rio de Janeiro: Nova Fronteira, 1998.

Karasch, Mary C. *A Vida dos Escravos no Rio de Janeiro*, Sao Paulo: Companhia das Letras., 2000.

Lopes, Nei. *O negro no Rio de Janeiro e sua tradição musical: partido-alto, calango, chula e outras cantorias*. Rio de Janeiro: Pallas, 1992.

Moura, Roberto. *Tia Ciata e a Pequena África* no Rio de Janeiro. 2ª edition, Rio de Janeiro: Secretaria Municipal de Cultura, 1995.

Piragibe, Vicente. *Diccionário de Jurisprudência Penal do Brasil*, 2º vol., Sao Paulo: Livraria Acadêmica, 1931.

Rocha, Oswaldo P. *A Era das Demolições: cidade do Rio de Janeiro: 1870-1920.* Rio de Janeiro: Secretaria Municipal da Cultura, 1986.

Rodrigues, Raimundo Nina. *As raças humanas e a responsabilidade penal no Brasil.* Salvador: Progresso, 1957.

Soares, Carlos E. L. *A negregada instituição: os capoeiras no Rio de Janeiro.* Rio de Janeiro: Secretaria Municipal de Cultura, 1994.

Souza, Edinelia M. O. "Pós-abolição na Bahia. Hierarquias, lealdades e tensões sociais em trajetórias de negros e mestiços de Nazaré das Farinhas e Santo Antonio de Jesus (1888/1930)". PhD Dissertation, Universidade Federal do Rio de Janeiro, 2012.

Tolnay, Stewart E. and Beck, E. M. Black Flight: Lethal Violence and the Great Migration, 1900-1930. *Social Science History* 14, no. 3 (Autumn, 1990): 347-370.

Vianna, Francisco José de Oliveira. *Raça e Assimilação.* São Paulo: Companhia Editora Nacional, 1938.

Wissenbach, Maria C. Da escravidão a liberdade: dimensões de uma privacidade possível. In *História da vida privada no Brasil,* edited by Fernando Novais, v.2, 49-130. Sao Paulo: Cia das Letras, 1999.

CHAPTER SIX

Historical Aspects of Forced and Free Black Migrations in the ABC Islands

Marco A. Schaumloeffel

University of British Columbia, Canada

Abstract

This article aims to study two different historical periods that involve forced and free migration to and from the Aruba, Bonaire and Curaçao. The first period analysed is the singular role Curaçao played in the transatlantic slave trade and its implication in the forced migrations of Africans to and within the Americas when the island operated as an *entrepôt*. The second period covers the more recent and free migrations from and to the ABC Islands from around the 1920s, the period of the opening of the Panama Canal and the establishment of an oil refinery, until the 2000s, when the population declined.

Keywords: Caribbean migrations, Panama Canal, Aruba, Curaçao, Bonaire

***

Introduction

The history of the ABC Islands, Aruba, Bonaire and Curaçao, during colonial times, has unique characteristics, especially the history of Curaçao, compared to other islands in the Caribbean and the Latin American territories. Unlike most colonized areas to which enslaved Africans were taken as their final destination, most of Curaçao's forced migration was destined not to the ABC Islands themselves but to the Spanish colonies on the Latin American mainland and other Caribbean islands. Curaçao did not function under a typical colonial plantation system dedicated to the production of sugar or any other export commodity. Due to climatic conditions, Curaçao had only a few plantations for the production of food staples and from the beginning of its colonial history, the economy focused on international commercial transactions. The island, therefore, functioned as an *entrepôt* for enslaved Africans, and the slave traders operated there as "middlemen" in the lucrative business of human trafficking. This is the first historical period that will be briefly analysed here to understand how forced migration took place and was operationalised and managed in the ABC Islands.

The second period to be discussed in this article roughly encompasses the last century and a few decades prior to it, and it is characterised by the free movement of Afro-Caribbean populations from and to the ABC Islands. The most recent migratory movements of the last decade are also briefly examined at the end of this article. These free movements of people can sometimes be characterised more as a "semi-free" movement than completely free since it often involved or still involves economic factors that end up, if not explicitly forcing then pushing migration, leaving Afro-Caribbean peoples with a restricted range of choices when deciding whether to immigrate or not.

Forced migration caused by the slave trade

The Caiquetíos, a branch of the Arawak Amerindians, were the first inhabitants of Curaçao. It is believed that they settled in Curaçao around 4,500 B.P. (Benjamin 2002). They were Amerindians of the same ethnic group as found on Venezuelan coasts and established regular trade and even a "kind of political bond, a primitive political organization, at the head of which stood the *cacique* of the peninsula of Paraguaná (Venezuela)" (Hartog 1979). In 1499, the Spanish sailor Alonso de Ojeda arrived with an expedition, establishing the first registered European contact with Curaçao. Most of the Curaçaoan Caiquetíos were enslaved and sent to the island of Hispaniola in 1513 to work in the copper mines. In fact, the enslavement and transportation of Caiquetíos by the Spaniards to the island of Hispaniola was the first known forced migratory movement in the history of the ABC Islands.

As there was no gold on the ABC Islands, in 1513, the Spanish viceroy Diego Columbus declared them *islas inútiles* or *useless islands* (Goslinga 1979, 14). The type of soil and low rainfall did not support the establishment of a plantation system with high yields from sugar, and Spaniards, therefore, ignored and abandoned Curaçao. When the Dutch occupied Curaçao in 1634, about 400 Amerindians were left. All but seventy-five of them were deported to the Venezuelan coast, and by 1795, only five "full-blooded" Indians could be found on Curaçao (*ibidem*, 6). In this context, the Dutch met no major resistance during the occupation of Curaçao:

> (...) Dutch conquest of Curaçao in 1634 was not resisted strongly by the Spanish, who had little incentive to retain Curaçao. The reasons the Dutch, unlike the Spanish, were interested in Curaçao were based on salt and shipping. The Dutch herring industry – an important segment of the Dutch economy – had lost its source of salt when Portugal and Spain became allied in opposition to the Dutch. Portuguese colonies no

longer would export salt to the Dutch, and attempts to procure salt elsewhere were thwarted (Benjamin 2002, 56).

The Atlantic Slave Trade and the commercial ties between Africa and the Americas are well known. As an instrument for their maritime activities, Dutch merchants founded the Dutch West Indian Company (DWIC) in 1621, which had jurisdiction over the Caribbean, North America, Brazil and the African slave trade. The DWIC granted the rights to a trade monopoly for the West Indies and became fully operational in 1628 (Friedman 1999); certainly succeeded in its main objective:

> By the 1640s, the Dutch had overtaken the Portuguese as the leading slave traders in West Africa. Although the Portuguese had traded for a number of other goods in addition to slaves, the Dutch concentrated almost solely on the slave trade. By 1705, a Dutch official in Africa reported that local rulers had abandoned trade in other items, such as gold and ivory, and instead focused exclusively on the trade in slaves because of the volume and the perceived high profits (Falola and Warnock 2007, 148).

Elmina Castle, the main Portuguese slave-trading post on the Gold Coast (modern Ghana), was captured by the Dutch in 1642. It is estimated that the Dutch transported around 5,000 slaves per year and some 900,000 to the Western Hemisphere during the entire period of their operations (Falola and Warnock 2007, 149).

Hartog also confirms that enslaved Africans were taken by the Dutch to Curaçao from areas that were former Portuguese strongholds: Arguin, in the North of present Dakar, Senegal; Sao Jorge da Mina, today Elmina, in Ghana; Ndongo, renamed Angola by the Portuguese; and the Congo. He underlines that "the so-called Mina slaves [taken to Curaçao], i.e., the negroes shipped from Sao Jorge da Mina, mainly came from Upper Guinea" (Hartog 1968, 170).

Jacobs points to another link in the history of the slave trade, namely the link established by the DWIC between Curaçao and Upper Guinea. Dutch slave traders were very active in Upper Guinea, especially on Cape Verde and in the Gorée region, where the DWIC had its bases:

> (...) profiting from the demise of Portuguese control, the Dutch would for approximately five decades become the leading trade nation in the Cape Verde region with Gorée as a thriving center from where slavery and other trading activities along the Upper Guinea Coast were developed, connecting this region to the Spanish Americas in general and to Curaçao in particular (Jacobs 2009, 356).

Over time, the natural harbour of today's Willemstad, located in the Schottegat inlet, was transformed into a port hub for trade between the Netherlands and the colonies of New Holland (Dutch Brazil in Pernambuco) and New Amsterdam (current New York), as well as for intra-Caribbean trade. The Dutch West India Company transformed Curaçao into a centre of the Atlantic slave trade, becoming an *entrepôt* of enslaved Africans sold under the *Asiento*, an agreement signed with the Spanish to supply their colonies in South America and the Caribbean with regular shipments of enslaved Africans. Zuurzak and St. Joris were the largest slave-camps on Curaçao. Hartog points to the reason for the existence of those camps:

> Many of the slaves died en-route or arrived in very poor health. Consequently, Curaçao slave-camps came into existence to restore their health and to act as lay-over places before reshipment. (...) From 1648 onward the slave-trade constantly expanded, reaching its climax between 1685 and 1713, after which it gradually fell off. The last slave-ship presumably docked here in 1778 (Hartog 197917).

Most enslaved Africans were held in these camps and later sold to colonies on the South American continent and French and English territories in the Caribbean. Only a few remained in Curaçao to work in plantations or as house servants (Munteanu 1996).

In 1678, Amsterdam became the centre for linen trade and, consequently, Curaçao, an emporium for European products of every description. Due to the harsh and arid conditions, Curaçao never developed a typical colonial plantation society. Farms were more for internal subsistence than for export and trade and were never able to supply local needs. Trans-shipment of legal and, in some periods, illegal goods naturally became the main source of income for Curaçao (Hartog 1979). The DWIC was dissolved in 1791, and its stock was bought by the Dutch government.

It is also interesting to note a factor in forced Black migration that is largely ignored in history: Sephardic Jews started to migrate from Brazil to Curaçao after the Portuguese expelled the Dutch from the Northeast of Brazil in 1654. They either returned to the Netherlands or went to Dutch colonies and other territories in the Caribbean; a small group of 23 also settled in New Amsterdam, modern New York (Hershkowitz 2004). Curaçao, as a Dutch colony, was by then one of the safe havens for the Sephardi. The end of Dutch Brazil, therefore, was a milestone in Sephardic settlement in Curaçao, and not exclusively for Jews fleeing the Portuguese in Brazil: "... the Dutch loss of Pernambuco to the Portuguese indirectly brought a new group of settlers to Curaçao: Jews fleeing from the Spanish and Portuguese Inquisitions" (Benjamin 2002, 56). The Sephardic Jews immigrated, sometimes directly and sometimes via Amsterdam, into

Curaçao and took with them an unknown number of enslaved Africans and Afro-Brazilians. The only certainty is that they did not arrive alone in Curaçao but with their servants. Joubert and Perl state that "the Sephardic exiles from Brazil reached Curaçao via Amsterdam and apparently did not take with them many slaves due to logistical constraints." (Joubert and Pearl 2007), whereas Goodman mentions Jews coming from Brazil taking "slaves along as well, and there is reason to believe that they were also accompanied by Brazilian mistresses and wives" (van Dantzig 1968, 77 *apud* Goodman 1987, 368). Apart from establishing a Brazilian connection, the Sephardic Jews were also present in trade in Cape Verde, Upper Guinea and other parts of West Africa: There were "ties between the Dutch and the Upper Guinea Sephardim as well as (…) their network stretching to Curaçao, it should be emphasised that contrary to popular belief, the Upper Guinea Sephardim's main objective seems to have been trade rather than religion" (*ibidem*, 364). Martinus also makes observations about the presence of the same Sephardic Portuguese names active in the slave trade on both sides of the Atlantic, especially in Cacheu, Cape Verde and Curaçao (Martinus 2004). He also mentions van Dantzig, who describes the business involving the DWIC and the Company of Cacheu. "The Portuguese licensed Company of Cacheu, founded in 1692 mainly for the slave trade, had intimate links with the Portuguese Jews of Amsterdam and had its own office in Curaçao" (van Dantzig 1968 *apud* Martinus 2004,145).

In Curaçao, enslaved Africans also naturally resisted and fought for their freedom and rights. There were two revolts, a short one in 1750 at Hato Plantation and another in 1795, involving about 4,000 Africans in a rebellion that lasted a month. It was led by slaves known by the names Tula Rigaud and Bastiaan Carpata (Rodriguez 2007); both revolts were crushed by the Dutch and the leaders of the uprisings were killed.

The first mention of the African presence in Bonaire dates back to March 1636, when the Dutch occupied the neighbouring islands of Aruba and Bonaire with the aim of safeguarding Curaçao, an island that had been secured just two years earlier. According to Hartog, in Bonaire, the Dutch erected a "stronghold garrisoned by 40 whites, 13 negroes and seven Indians" (Hartog 1975, 19). For a long time, the total number of enslaved Blacks there remained low. By 1700, there were no more than 97 Africans, but soon after 1700, the number increased when the production of salt became the main source of income for Bonaire. To further increase the number of enslaved workers, the colonizers settled all enslaved Blacks in a village called Rincón and "by allowing all the slaves to live together, they called into being what was termed 'a breeding-place' of slaves" (Hartog 1975, 25).

Black enslavement started as late as 1715 in Aruba, mainly due to local climatic and soil conditions and the pattern of colonization of the island. This first attempt lasted only four years, when an attempt by the DWIC to cultivate maize failed and the 20 enslaved Blacks taken there from Curaçao were returned (UNESCO 2007). Later, when the island was opened for colonization, enslaved Blacks were brought back, but not to work on large plantations. The men were employed in growing ground provisions for their masters or as craftsmen, whereas the women were exploited as house servants and shop workers. However, in Aruba, the number of "enslaved never exceeded 21% of the total population. In 1849, 596 slaves were living in Aruba." Emancipation in 1863 brought freedom to the remaining 496 enslaved Blacks. Farm workers were given lands for provisions and became peasants, house servants and craftsmen kept on doing the same work, whereas some other emancipated Blacks joined the police force or even became successful merchants (Hartog 1975).

About the origin of the enslaved Africans taken to the ABC Islands, one can only presume that the percentages must have been similar to those known for the DWIC, i.e., most would have come from West Africa, especially from the Slave Coast, current Togo, Benin and Nigeria, (45.4%) and the Gold Coast, current Ghana, (21.6%), and a just over a quarter from the Congo and Angola regions.

From 1799 to 1815, Curaçao changed hands several times between the French, British and Dutch. In 1816, Dutch rule was finally restored by the Treaty of Paris, signed at the end of 1815 following Napoleon's defeat. Slavery was finally abolished in 1863.

Free Migration after Emancipation and in the Last Century

Free migration from and to the ABC Islands started soon after slavery was abolished in 1863. The main influences on free migration were always the economic factors that impacted the islands. A lack of jobs and economic opportunities, the factors triggering migration, more severely affected the Black male work force. Still, there was throughout the history of the islands a migration of the Black female work force to other parts of the Caribbean looking for better job opportunities or as *yaya* (the Papiamento word for "nanny") or housemaids serving the richer local families that migrated elsewhere. The most significant movements between emancipation and the beginning of the twentieth century are of Black people leaving Curaçao for Latin America and other parts of the Caribbean, starting a steady intra-Caribbean migratory flow. To the best of my knowledge, no large movement of people migrating to the ABC Islands is registered in the first post-emancipation years.

Afro-Curaçaoans went to work on railway projects in Costa Rica, on the construction of the Panama Canal, and in agriculture and other economic areas in Venezuela, Colombia, Surinam, the Dominican Republic, Puerto Rico and Cuba (Marks 1976; Allen 2006). In the case of labour migration to Cuba, it was primarily to work in sugar production from 1917 until 1921, when a production crisis generated a stream of Afro-Curaçaoans in the opposite direction, taking them back to their homeland (Allen 2006).

Apart from the prospect of earning more money, Allen points to another important factor that many times motivated Caribbean intra-regional migration, namely, kinship relationships stimulating migration intended to reunite families previously separated by either forced migration before emancipation or by free migration on economic grounds (Allen 2006). Family reunification more often affected women and children who moved to reunite with their partners and fathers who had migrated earlier.

As already mentioned, the wave of migration out of Curaçao at the beginning of the twentieth century was due to a lack of economic opportunities and progress. The exodus was significant and by 1919 amounted to around 3,000 people, at the time the equivalent of 10% of the Curaçaoan population or, more impressively, around half of the active work force (Hartog 1961). This certainly had a significant impact on the local economy. On the other hand, this mass migration also had a positive economic impact, as migrants sent foreign exchange to their families remaining in Curaçao.

One of the most relevant factors in the twentieth-century migration to Curaçao and Aruba was the discovery of oil in the Maracaibo Basin. Consequently, Royal Dutch Shell and Esso/Exxon established fairly large oil refineries in Curaçao and in Aruba respectively, creating jobs and attracting immigrants from the Netherlands and, above all, from surrounding Spanish speaking countries, especially from Venezuela and Colombia. A significant migratory influx is evident during that time, as described by Hartog:

> ... the revolution brought about on Aruba by the advent of the oil-industry, is – making allowance for certain minor differences – also applicable to Curaçao, though the growth of the population was less marked here (Aruba from 9,000 in 1926 to 59,858 by January 1965; Curaçao from 33,000 in 1916 to 134,250 by January 1965) (Hartog 1968, 324).

The new economic opportunities generated in all sectors by the oil refineries, especially in the services sector, also caused many Arubans, Curaçaoans and their descendants born abroad, to migrate back to Aruba and Curaçao during this period of general progress and growth. Another group that migrated to Aruba and Curaçao during this period of good economic times was composed of Black British West Indians, who suffered residential and social segregation once established in Aruba and Curaçao. When they "came to live there, [they] were separated from the 'native' Black and Euro-mestizo Indian populations" (Sharpe 2005, 298-299). Thomas-Hope, for example, also mentions that "movements from St. Vincent in the early decades of the twentieth century were chiefly to the oil companies active in the Netherlands Antilles of Aruba and Curaçao" (Thomas-Hope 2002, 59), as well as Barbadians who "likewise actively engaged in the movements to the oil industry located in the southern Caribbean" (*ibidem*, 38), a movement that did not exclusively include Aruba and Curaçao, but migration to Trinidad as well. Afro-Caribbean women from the Eastern Caribbean also went to Aruba to work as domestic workers and formed a distinct minority that was itself very diverse, as pointed out by Aymer, who affirms that "the domestics on Aruba are a microcosm of ethnic minorities created cross-culturally through labor migrations" (Aymer 1997, 125). In fact, and contrary to general assumptions, a census carried out in 1960 revealed that "the number of female Caribbean immigrants to Curaçao slightly exceeded that of men by the ratio of 2,491: 2,281" (Phillips *apud* Allen 2006, 90). This shows that the importance of the migration of Black female domestic workers can by no means be ignored in the migratory history, the composition of the social fabric and, consequently, their contribution to the society and the economy of Curaçao.

The establishment of the Shell Isla oil refinery in Curaçao in 1918 and the Esso/Exxon oil plant Lago Oil and Transport Company Ltd. in Aruba in 1929 also caused a so-called "internal migration" from Bonaire to the other two islands. Hartog mentions that in 1926, Bonaire reached its peak of 7,521 inhabitants, but soon after, "many Bonaireans found employment on the tankers. Hundreds, and before long thousands of Bonaireans left their island" ((Hartog 1975, 71) *ibidem*) and migrated to Curaçao and Aruba.

In the last decades of the century, a significant number of Afro-Curaçaoans and, to a lesser extent, Afro-Arubans migrated to the Netherlands. As is repeatedly the case, the most important factor causing this migration wave to Europe was also the economic situation at home. Oostindie compares immigration to the Netherlands from Surinam and the Dutch Antilles, consisting mostly of Curaçaoans, showing that the migration between Curaçao and the Netherlands is two-directional and made up mainly of a first generation, whereas the Surinam migration is one-way only traffic to the Netherlands and is made up of three generations. In 1998, the Surinamese community in the Netherlands was over 275,000, while the Antillean community, a majority of whom were Curaçaoans, stood at 90,000 (Oostindie 1998, 136). Currently, the numbers are around 356,000 for the Surinamese community and about 166,000 from the former so-called Dutch Antilles. It is interesting to note the remarkable case of Surinam; half of its population emigrated to the Netherlands just prior to its declaration of independence in 1975. Aruba and Curaçao, after their refineries closed down operations in 1985, also faced mass emigration of their citizens to the Netherlands, composed mainly of "poor and working class people" (Sharpe 2005, 291). This is also corroborated by Allen when she states that the dismantling of the refineries "caused about a third of its [Curaçao´s] young people under the age of forty-five to migrate to the Netherlands for employment and better social security" (Allen 2006, 80). This migratory movement obviously had an economic, social and cultural impact on Aruba and Curaçao, causing a significant shift in local population patterns.

Currently, Aruba and Curaçao are politically independent from the Netherlands but are constituent countries of the Kingdom of the Netherlands, and Bonaire is a special municipality of the Netherlands.

The data available on migration from and to Aruba indicates, as previously mentioned, that there was a sharp increase in population after the Lago oil refinery was established in the second decade of the last century. According to Aruba Demographics, a website dedicated to demographics in Aruba, "in 1960, 23% of the population of Aruba consisted of foreign-born individuals," and when dismantling of the refinery started in the 1980s, there was a sharp decline in population, with people searching for opportunities elsewhere. In the 1990s and the following decade, Aruba experienced a boom in the tourism industry, which caused net migration to the island based on the new job opportunities this favourable moment created in several areas of the services sector. For some time, the net increase in population reached peaks of more than 5,000 people moving to Aruba every year. Whereas after the decline caused by the closing of the oil refinery in 1981, only 18.5% of the population in Aruba was foreign-born; by 2010, that amount peaked at 34%, i.e., more than one-third of its population was not born on the island. Out of the total population, in 2010, Colombians were by far the biggest group of foreign-born with 9.1%, followed by Dutch 4.3%, Dominicans 4.1%, Venezuelans 3.2%, Curaçaoans 2.2%, Haitians 1.5%, Surinamese 1.2%, Peruvians and Chinese each 1.1% and others 6.2%. However, these numbers changed more recently, with Venezuelans being responsible for over 40% of the total official immigrants arriving in Aruba in 2017, with illegal immigration not being taken into account, which certainly would have increased those numbers. According to the *Quarterly Demographic Bulletin 2020* of the Central Bureau of Statistics of Aruba, the total population in the second quarter of 2020 stood at 112,269 persons, with 65.3% being born in Aruba and the former Netherlands Antilles, 9.6% in Colombia, 4.8% in Venezuela and 4.6% in the Netherlands. The same dataset shows that there are consistently more Aruban residents and citizens of the former Netherlands Antilles leaving rather than arriving in Aruba, as well as consistently more Colombians and Venezuelans arriving than departing, whereas the numbers of Dutch citizens arriving and leaving are more balanced, with a slight advantage in arrivals over departures.

Among the reasons for people to immigrate to Aruba are the lower standards of living in neighbouring countries, the economic and political crises in Venezuela, lack of safety and healthcare in their home countries, the specific need for labor in the Aruba economy due to an aging population and the demands of the tourism industry, people using the territory as a springboard to enter Europe, and the climate, in the specific case of the so-called snowbirds escaping the winter in the Northern hemisphere for a milder climate, and persons choosing the island as their place of retirement. Black people, especially Afro-Latinos, are certainly more impacted by the several economic causes of migration to Aruba than by the latter two factors. As for the reasons to emigrate from Aruba, one can surely affirm that the most frequent is the search for a better standard of living and reunions with family members who emigrated previously. According to the UN Department of Economic and Social Affairs, in 2013, amongst the five top countries or areas of destination for over 12,000 persons migrating from Aruba, the United States of America was the number one destination for 5,455 persons, followed by the Netherlands with 3,489, Curaçao with 1,674, the Dutch part of Sint Maarten with 1,273 and the remainder to the Caribbean Netherlands totalling 732 persons.

Curaçao also experienced an influx of migrants between the end of the last century and the beginning of the 2000s, most of it intra-regional Caribbean migration of Afro-Caribbean people. The figures show that there was "a large increase of immigrants from Caribbean islands such as Haiti, the Dominican Republic, and Jamaica, as well as Guyana and Colombia in South America" (Allen 2006, 84). The most recent numbers relating to emigration and immigration made available by the Central Bureau Statistics of Curaçao show that between 2014 and 2019, a total of 29,651 people migrated from Curaçao to other places. The vast majority, 23,423 (about 79%), went to the Netherlands, followed by other territories of the former Dutch Antilles - Bonaire, Aruba and Sint Maarten, respectively, with a not-so-significant emigration to other places like the USA, Colombia, China, India and Canada, among others. On the other hand, the patterns of immigration to Curaçao are slightly different: Between 2014 and 2019, a total of 29,043 migrants arrived in Curaçao, with 16,991 (about 59%) coming from the Netherlands. Due to geographical proximity and the political and economic crises of the last years, Venezuelan immigrants now occupy second place, with a total of 1,809 immigrants (6.2%), and continuing the trend that started about two decades ago, with some notable immigration also from the Dominican Republic (1,306 persons) and Colombia (951 persons). Interestingly, there were more immigrants from China (777 persons) between 2014 and 2019 than from Bonaire (743), Sint Maarten (585) or Aruba (557). A total of 382 persons immigrated from Surinam, also a former Dutch colony and a developing country long facing economic problems. The migration data for Curaçao suggest that currently, there is a balance in the movement of people, with a slight shift of more Curaçaoans moving to the Netherlands than people moving from the Netherlands to Curaçao, and with that difference being balanced by immigration from elsewhere, especially from Spanish-speaking countries from the wider Caribbean macro-region. Amongst the factors triggering migration from those Spanish-speaking countries to Curaçao are certainly the relatively worse economic situation back home, geographical proximity, and that, given the many lexical similarities with Papiamentu, the primary national language, most Curaçaoans can understand and speak Spanish, so that language is not a major barrier to adapting and living in Curaçao.

Final remarks

As seen above, migratory movements of Black people affecting Aruba, Bonaire, and Curaçao can be divided into forced and free migration, with Emancipation in July of 1863 the milestone separating these two types of migration. Prior to emancipation, Black people were taken to the ABC islands as slaves and would either stay and be exploited as farm workers, domestic workers, or work in service industries or would, in their vast majority, be sold to other parts of the Caribbean and Latin America, where the DWIC held *asiento* rights. Free movements of Afro-Caribbean people started soon after emancipation and were mainly due to the search for better economic prospects or for family reunions. Since then, there has been a constant influx and efflux of Afro-Caribbean peoples in the ABC Islands, with the larger movements provoked by re-emerging local and regional economic crises, the establishment of oil refineries in Aruba and Curaçao and the local boom of tourism services experienced in recent decades.

Another fact that becomes clear around free migration affecting the ABC Islands is that after emancipation, intra-Caribbean migration played a more significant role than migration from and to other areas of the world, impacting the cultural identity of the region.

Lastly, a new migratory wave might happen soon as a result of the recent COVID-19 pandemic. Currently, Aruba, Curaçao and Sint Maarten find themselves obliged to take up massive interest-free loans from the Netherlands at the price of conforming to certain imposed conditions. These loans are not seen as money for investment in infrastructure or for the development of the territories but mainly as urgently needed monies to finance the ordinary expenses of respective governments, for example, payment of public workers´ salaries. Already, friends there are talking of "activating their plan B" within the next months if economic conditions do not improve soon. "Activating their plan B" almost always means migrating to the Netherlands. They also speak of people they know who migrated within the first six months following the COVID-19 outbreak in March 2020. The future will show whether this pandemic, with worldwide health and economic impacts, will also be responsible for triggering yet another new and large migratory wave affecting the ABC Islands. As seen in this article, that would not be a new departure for the islands, merely a continuation, just another chapter of their recurrent migratory history.

Primary Sources Digital Repositories consulted

Central Bureau of Statistics Aruba: Recent Immigrants in Our Society. 2018. https://cbs.aw/wp/wp-content/uploads/2018/09/AMIS16-Article-1.pdf (accessed 31 Aug 2020).

Central Bureau of Statistics: The foreign-born population of Aruba. https://arubademographics.com/wp-content/uploads/2016/01/The-foreign-born-population-of-Aruba.pdf (accessed on August 31, 2020).Christiaan G. C. *A Short History of the Netherlands Antilles and Surinam.* The Hague: M. Nijhoff, 1979.

Migration in Aruba. Sociaal Economische Raad. https://ser.cw/files/2019/05/Presentatie-Migration-in-Aruba-Final-version.pdf (accessed August 31, 2020).

Quarterly Demographic Bulletin. Central Bureau of Statistics. https://cbs.aw/wp/index.php/2020/06/15/quarterly-demographic-bulletin-2019-2/ (accessed August 31, 2020).

StatLine. http://opendata.cbs.nl/statline/#/CBS/nl/dataset/37325/table?fromstatweb (accessed on August 06, 2020).

UN Department of Economic and Social Affairs: Migration Profiles. https://esa.un.org/miggmgprofiles/indicators/files/Aruba.pdf (accessed August 31, 2020).

UNESCO Places of Memory of the Slave Route in the Latin Caribbean. LACULT. Last modified 2007. http://www.lacult.unesco.org/sitios_memoria/Lineamientos.php?lan=en

References

Allen, Rose-Marie. Regionalization of Identity in Curaçao: Migration and Diaspora. In *Caribbean Transnationalism: Migration, Pluralization, and Social Cohesion*, ed. R. Gowricharn, 79-89. Lanham: Lexington Books, 2006.

Aymer, Paula L. *Uprooted Women: Migrant Domestics in the Caribbean.* Westport, Connecticut/London: Praeger, 1997.

Benjamin, Alan F. *Jews of the Dutch Caribbean: Exploring Ethnic Identity on Curaçao.* London/New York: Routledge, 2002

Dantzig Van. *Het Nederlandse aandeel in de slavenhandel.* Bussem: Van Dishoeck, 1968.

Falola Toyin, and Amanda Warnock *Encyclopedia of the Middle Passage.* Westport: Greenwood Publishing Group, 2007.

Friedman, Saul S. *Jews and the American Slave Trade.* New Brunswick/London: Transaction Publishers, 1999.

Goodman, M. The Portuguese Element in the American Creoles. In *Pidgin and Creole Languages: Essays in Memory of John E. Reinecke*, edited by Glenn Gilbert, 361-405. Honolulu: University of Hawaii Press, 1987.

Hartog, Johannes. A *short History of Bonaire*. Bonaire: Island Territory of Bonaire, 1975.

____. *Curaçao: Short History*. Aruba: De Wit, 1979.

____. *Curaçao from Colonial Dependence to Autonomy*. Aruba: De Wit, 1968.

____. *Geschiedenis van de Nederlandse Antillen*. Vol. 3 *raçao van Kolonie tot Autonomie*. Arub: De Wit, 1961.

Hershkowitz, Leo. By Chance or Choice: Jews in New Amsterdam 1654. *De Halve Maen.American Jewish Archives Journal* 77, no. 2 (2004): 1–13.

Jacobs, Bart. The Upper Guinea Origins of Papiamentu Linguistic and Historical Evidence. *Diachronica* 26, no.3 (2009): 319–79.

Joubert, Sidney., and Matthias Perl. The Portuguese Language on Curacao and Its Role in the Formation of Papiamentu. *Journal of Caribbean Literatures* 5, no. 1 (2007): 43–60.

Marks. A. F. *Male and Female in the Afro-Curaçaoan Household*. The Hague: Martinus Nijhoff, 1976.

Martinus, rank. *The Kiss of a Slave: Papiamentu's West-African Connections*. 3rd ed. Amsterdam: Universiteit van Amsterdam, 2004.

Munteanu, Dan. *El Papiamentu, Lengua Criolla Hispánica*. Madrid: Gredos, 1996.

Oostindie, G. J. The Delusive Continuities of the Dutch Caribbean Diaspora. in *Caribbean Migration. Globalised Identities*, 127-147. London: Routledge, 1998.

Rodriguez, Junius P. *Encyclopedia of Slave Resistance and Rebellion*. Volume 1: A-N. Westport/London: Greenwood Publishing Group, 2007.

Sharpe, Michael. Globalization and Migration: Post-Colonial Dutch Antillean and Aruban Immigrant Political Incorporation in the Netherlands. *Dialectical Anthropology* 29, no. 3-4 (2005): 291–314.

Thomas-Hope, Elizabeth. *Caribbean Migration*. Barbados/Jamaica/Trinidad and Tobago: University of the West Indies Press, 2002.

PART III

UNWANTED PEOPLE WITH DANGEROUS IDEAS

CHAPTER SEVEN

The Antillean Immigration in Cuba: Labor and the Politics of Race

Kátia Couto

Universidade Federal do Amazonas, Brazil

Abstract

This paper examines the Haitian immigration that arrived in Cuba in the first decades of the 20th century, influencing the political perspective of the country and promoting a new stage in the discussions of national and racial issues. The research focused on the speeches published in Cuban newspapers and magazines, the reception and performance of Haitians in the labor and party movements, and their relationship with the first black party in Cuba. The objective is to discuss the process of incorporation of immigrants from the Antilles in Cuba, focusing especially on workers who came from Haiti. We analyse arguments presented by the press and its contribution to the construction of a negative image of Haitian workers, the repatriation of these and other workers from the neighboring islands to Cuba and the organisation of an association to educate the descendants in the ideal of culture and national identity of Haiti.

Keywords: Migration, Repatriation, Association

***

The presence of Jamaican and Haitian immigrants in Cuba – who went to work in the sugar industry during the early decades of the twentieth century – was seen by locals as unfair competition since immigrants accepted low salaries and the work regulations imposed by the sugar companies. Some said the presence of the Antilleans represented a disruptive element for the Cuban laboring class, but this is only one version of the story of the relationships between Cubans and other Antillean workers; the tensions between them were exploited by the sugar companies and manipulated by the local elite. Apart from labour competition, the elite defended a national identity to which the arrival of Black foreigners was a threat, as illustrated in the discussions published by conservative media. Evelio Telleria explains that Cubans used "*Antillanos*" (Antilleans) to refer to immigrant workers coming from the islands of Jamaica and Haiti, as well as from other islands. According to him, the sugar industry imported more than 250,000 Black immigrants from the neighboring islands to work for lower wages than the local Afro-Cubans. These immigrant workers were employed cutting sugar cane under miserable conditions that some compared to slavery. (Telleria 1973).

What would be the interest of the sugar companies in destabilizing the Cuban labor movement by hiring Jamaican and Haitian workers? Were those Antilleans not integrated into the labor movement?

The development of the dominant Cuban discourse on immigration is ambivalent and can be explained in ethno-racial terms (Torres 2001; Molina 2001). In 1912, a year before the start of the massive influx of immigrant workers from Haiti and the Lesser Antilles into Cuba, with the approval of President José Miguel Gomes for the Nipe Bay Company to hire foreign workers, there had been major conflict involving the *Partido Independiente de Color*, composed of Afro-Cubans and led by labor leader Evaristo Esteñoz and Pedro Ivonet, a former colonel in the Liberation Army. The party was created to participate in the elections in 1910 (Martínez 1998).

The party's program listed several demands for social benefits, such as compulsory and universal education, abolition of the death penalty, an eight-hour workday, work nationalization, and land distribution, among others (Martínez, 1998). In effect, the benefits demanded by members of the movement were true labor demands and the very same issues that Cuban labor congresses, for example, in 1914, would call for.

The Black Cubans of the eastern region had a political and social awareness that tempered the existing commercial interests of the national bourgeoisie in the first decade of the republic. Faced with the right to organize around the movement and the creation of a party under a racial banner, Martín Morúa Delgado, one of the few Afro-Cuban Senators, put up strong opposition. He proposed a law prohibiting political organizations based on racial distinctions, aiming to avoid racial segregation as it existed in the Jim Crow United States.

The goal of such prohibition was to avoid political disputes based on racial issues, which seems an ironic strategy since the difference between white and Black citizens, and especially the exclusion of Blacks from national policy and social benefits, was so clear that it motivated Afro-Cuban leaders to organize the *Movimiento de los Independientes de Color*. Historian Martinez Ortiz states that white Cubans, with support from the United States, organized to defeat that initiative, arguing that Cuba would not tolerate another Black Republic, a clear reference to the Haitian Revolution. To Ortiz, the Cuban reaction, with the participation of the Americans, to the political organization of Afro-Cubans reveals that the problem extended beyond the limits of internal affairs, becoming part of the political game of the United States in Cuba (Ortiz, 1929).

The discussion among politicians of the prohibition of a party made up only of Blacks generated a wider debate. People like Salvador Cisneros Betancourt and Lino Dou defended the right of Blacks to fight racial discrimination by means of a political party so long as it did not hold a sectarian, racist position.

In early 1912, Esteñoz revived the movement in reaction to the Morua Law, and in March of the same year, its main leaders were arrested and accused of rebellion. The movement escalated its response, especially in the Las Villas and Eastern provinces, with the confirmation of armed groups in four of the six provinces, leading to violent repression by the authorities. President José Miguel Gomes ordered the national army, the Rural Guard and newly recruited men into action in the eastern region. Managers of the central sugar company in the region, such as Mario Garcia Menocal, offered to help the government by sending men to control the rebellion, followed by others who contributed to the Government's fight against the movement, which at this point transformed itself into a political party (not officially sanctioned).

It is estimated that around 3,000 Black men were killed by the government forces in the clashes of 1912, many wounded, and hundreds arrested (Martínez 1998). The confrontation occurred because the Cuban government and the sugar entrepreneurs, the memory of events in Haiti with slaves taking power still present in Cuba, feared a Black uprising throughout the nation.

Eugene Godfred explains that the *Partido Independiente de Color* (PIC) was the product of demands from *Sociedades de Gente de Color*, which argued for the urgency of a political party independent of the existing parties associated with the bourgeoisie. Its aim would be to improve social, cultural and economic standards for Afro-Cubans. Godfred insisted that a transformation of this kind would mark the complete break between the Black masses and the existing institutions dominated by the elite. A rupture was, in his view, at the same time, a response to and a denunciation of the neocolonial tendencies of the Cuban elite (Godfred, 2000).

Black Cuban workers reacted to the social and political disadvantage generated by the government, which ignored the terrible conditions they faced in the country. After virtually decimating the participants of the *Independiente de Color* Movement, the government used decree number 23 of January 10, 1913, to authorize the Nipe Bay Company to hire 1,000 Antillean workers to work in the sugar industry (Pichardo 1980, 78).

A general fear of Black people, shared by the elite and middle class, which adds to the rebellious attitude of Black Cubans, fed a strong opposition to the companies' introduction of more Black people into Cuba, especially after a period of conflict arising from demonstrations against the movement led by Esteñoz. In fact, the companies' intention and plans to hire Antillean manpower were already in motion from the early twentieth century.

Sugar companies subjected this group of immigrants to terrible working and living conditions that some former workers interviewed in the project coordinated by Olga Cabrera compared to slavery (Cabrera 1969). The campaign against Black immigrants was also taken up in the newspapers, which spread rumors of witchcraft, along with news of robbery, mendicancy, and disorderly behavior in which Jamaicans and Haitians were the villains. The rumors and stereotypes ignited animosity against the outsiders. Particularly after 1913, when the flow of these workers into Cuba started to intensify, discrimination increased. The companies wanted not only cheaper manpower but also a workforce that was less likely to rebel and more prone to control. They sent recruiters to Haiti, Jamaica, and the entire Anglophone Caribbean (St. Kitts, Nevis, St Martín, Saba, St Eustatius, Antigua, Dominica, St Lucia, St Vicent and the Grenadines, Barbados, Grenada, Trinidad etc.) or to francophone Guadaloupe and Martinique and the Dutch colonies of Curaçao, Aruba and Bonaire to recruit workers, creating in the factories a cultural mosaic that hampered the integration of the early migratory flows into Cuban society through Spanish as a language barrier. The companies were confident that these workers would pose no danger because of their linguistic background and the consequent impossibility of influencing or being influenced by Cuban workers, who, despite being few in number, were starting to organize as a class.

Another reason for hiring Antillean immigrants was to reinforce a distorted image of Black Cubans as a disruptive element in the nation because of their (un)civilized, antagonistic behavior, which had been gaining strength as Black workers organized around social issues that could not be resolved by white politicians. We will discuss below the process of Cuban labor organization and its influence on political decisions to hire Jamaicans and Haitians.

Cuban labor movement and Antillean migration

According to the chronology drawn up by Tellería (1973), from 1887 to 1934, eight labor congresses took place, with the first held during the republican period from 28 to 30 August, 1914 in Havana. The country was living through its republican experience governed by then General Mario García Menocal, elected on May 20, 1913. His politics, totally geared to North American interests, left Cuban workers in terrible conditions, unsupported, and subjected to rules established by the companies and entrepreneurs that controlled the internal market. (Telleria 1973; Cabrera 1985).

The conservative media supported the government, understanding its actions as protecting the nation's expansionist desires and praising decisions that favored the United States above their own country. Some newspapers in the United States stated that Menocal "era más americano que cubano" (Tellería 1973, 51).

In 1914, the government froze plans to create a Labor Secretariat, put forward in response to the concerns of the Cuban people articulated since the early Republic. Considering the context in which there had been major growth, the proletariat was controlled by this new progressive order of the economy, and many of the workers' claims were suppressed. Contrary to his position before being elected, President Menocal did not promote social action, instead prioritizing only financial activities implemented by North American companies.

Workers were experiencing miserable conditions in the year of the Congress of 1914, with no class organization and subject to up to fourteen-hour workdays and low salaries. Workers often received vouchers and tokens instead of money, forcing them to buy products only at establishments that accepted such methods of payment. There was no legislation to meet the worker's needs in case of accidents, and the government increased the pressure by supporting the prevention of any protest against the lack of better working conditions.

Iglesia Martinez (1998) argues that the economic recovery of that period contributed to a retraction of workers' demands. In addition, the Platt Amendment imposed by the United States carried the risk of American intervention in case of social disturbances, which made the Cuban government more eager to control the labor movement. According to Martinez, the fear of another American intervention led political and labor leaders to compromise with the government against their own interests.

Among the foreign workers, while Jamaicans (and other West Indians) received some support from the representative of the United Kingdom in Cuba, Haitian workers found no such support, leaving them vulnerable to employers who did not honor work contracts or respect their rights. Compensation in case of accidents was not being paid in a context in which accidents were frequent, as demonstrated in the documents on Central Manati.[1]

The length of time for which workers remained unemployed increased social instability. Many searched for work in other areas, but it would not be enough to meet the workers' demands, especially as several of the Antillean immigrants

---

[1] See: Inventario del Fondo Manatí Sugar Co. Archivo Provincial de Santiago de Cuba, años 1902-1960. This inventory introduces a vast documentation on the national association of Cuban farmers, suspension, and separation of workers and work accident; exportation and importations, correspondence related to the shipment and sales of sugar; correspondence between Salvador Rionda and many people or entities.

remained in the country after the end of the cane harvest. Not all foreign workers remained since work contracts were signed for a limited period but there were cases in which employers did not honor the obligation to pay for workers' repatriation. Haitians, with no means of returning home, would be forced to accept any type of job under unfavorable conditions to survive and could often be seen wandering the streets of Santiago de Cuba looking for work.

Another area for research is the labor congress in 1914, which the historian Sergio Aguirre calls "*extraño Congreso.*" According to him, the Cuban Government, presenting itself as progressive, organized that congress, promoting a watered-down version of the workers' demands, selecting speakers from among intellectuals whose commitment to the workers' causes was limited, and who defended superficial social and economic reforms, without challenging the government. (Aguirre 1965).

Historian Rolando Álvarez Estévez explains that powerful sectors of the bourgeoisie in the eastern province – fundamentally the sugar sector – faced a clear contradiction at a crossroads for their own class interests. If, on the one hand, they saw that Antillean immigration considerably increased the Black population in the eastern region, on the other, they were unable to condemn this immigration, thus sacrificing their racist assumptions to prevent damage to their economic interests (Álvarez 1988).

Such overlapping of economic and racial factors is temporary; that is, it serves to create a satisfactory reserve of manpower and thus does not interrupt industrial production but does not mean the end of the race issue. On the contrary, race frequently surfaced even inside factories with segregated spaces for Black workers. The Rural Guard violently repressed workers, especially Black immigrants, even suppressing their religious celebrations through official letter number 35, which prohibited the use of drums by Black workers.

Stratification of the workers was imposed by the companies, based first on racial division and later on other criteria. Francisco García Moreira, a sugar worker, in his book *Tiempo Muerto: memorias de un trabajador azucarero* explained the meaning of the term "*categoria*" to qualify workers, a trick used as a strategy to divide workers. For Moreira, there were three major categories: the elite, composed of skilled workers, administrative officials, and technicians; an intermediate class, also composed of skilled workers, but at a lower level; and the third class applied to everyone else. The criteria for these classifications included loyalty to the company, political affiliation, personal ties, skin color, class and even nationality (Moreira 1969, 24).

Haitian workers were brought to Cuba to work cutting sugarcane, while mainly Cubans and workers from the Canaries would grow it. Antillean immigrants experienced more severe discrimination because of their skin color, but also for being foreign. Among their own workers, the bourgeoisie took care to promote such discrimination in an effort to break the weak base of the embryonic Cuban labor movement.

In the case of Antillean workers, racial discrimination would combine with salary discrimination, harder jobs, and miserable survival in every sense in *bateyes* and shacks (Álvarez, 1988) to turn these workers into a modern version of the slaves from the nineteenth century. The racial issue introduced damaging elements in the workers' fight for better salary, housing conditions and awareness of their growing demands as a class that lived racial conflict more intensely and distracted workers from the true economic conflict and its class implications (Álvarez 1988).

Historian Ariel James (1976) describes the actions of companies such as the United Fruit Company (UFC) to suppress and hold onto the workers controlled by the factory. The tactics used with salaries were only one among the many forms of duress. Similarly, Alberto Arredondo states that in Cuban neocolonial society, racial discrimination had an objective nature.

> "... en la industria azucarera, el negro mayoritariamente podia ser cortador de caña y carretero. Sin embargo, en los cargos de pesadores, puntistas, oficinistas, etcétera, el negro era discriminado. Con grandes obtáculos podia obtener un cargo de maestro en las ciudades, siempre era designado para el campo, para el interior de la Republica". (Arredondo 1939, 149).

In 1933, Rúben Martinez Villena wrote a paper in the magazine *Mundo Obrero*, under a headline that called for unity among workers regardless of their color or origin: "La unión del blanco y el black, del nativo y el extranjero". The article defends the position of Antillean workers and criticizes those who objected to their presence in Cuba. The author affirms that Haitians and Jamaicans had played an important role in unifying the working class by many times joining with their demands, to the point of establishing a "perfect union" between Black and White workers in the provinces of Santa Clara and Oriente.

> En las huelgas de los centrales azucareros, como en las demostraciones de las ciudades y, en general, en la lucha por sus reivindicaciones inmediatas, se ha establecido una unión perfecta entre los obreros blancos y negros. Esto es notable principalmente en las provincias de Santa Clara y Oriente, donde las clases dominantes han llevado la división a un mayor grado. Por otra parte, las teorias comunes entre reformistas y anarquistas referentes a que los jamaiquinos y haitianos son culpables de la situación del obrero azucarero en Cuba, han sido desmentidas una vez más con la participación activa de estos obreros extranjeros en la lucha común. (En 1924 también participaron en muchos

sítios). Un grupo de obreros jamaiquinos llevados al central Habana para iniciar el trabajo en los cortes, con objeto de que rompieran la huelga en preparación, pidió las mochas y, una vez armados, se negaron unánimente a comenzar el trabajo (Villena, 1933).

There were two views on the participation of Antillean workers: one that these workers kept to the sidelines of the Cuban labor movement; another that claimed Antilleans participated in the movement. In fact, what can be clearly shown is the existence of different stages in the process of integrating Antilleans into the movement, which can be looked at in terms of the different stages of their migration into Cuba.

Regarding the first decade of migration of Antillean workers, it is difficult to speak of any integration of these workers as a class with the other workers in the sugar industries since the language barrier hampered communication between Antilleans and Cuban and Spanish workers who spoke no French, Créole or English. The first flow of Antillean immigrants represented a bridge for more effective participation in the Cuban labor movement in the twenties.

Such integration clearly started largely among those who remained in Cuba during the inter-harvest period. Others who returned to their homes introduced labor demands in their home countries based on their experiences. Jacques Roumain provides an example in his book *Masters of the Dawn* (1978), which tells the story of Manuel, who returned to Haiti questioning the conditions in his community and trying to show his parents and neighbors the need to change.

The labor congress conducted in Cuba between February 15 and 19, 1925, discussed the immigration issue in the country. Participants could not bring themselves to oppose the entry of foreign workers but then recommended that Cuban labor organizations communicate with labor organizations in the countries of origin of the immigrants and direct them to discourage workers from looking for work in Cuba, where the situation of workers was deteriorating day by day (Pichardo 1980).

The Cuban economic crisis was hard on the working class. The presence of immigrant workers offering their labor in exchange for miserable wages, with lower demands and expectations, affected salaries in general. The *Segundo Congreso Obrero Nacional* denounced the terrible living and working conditions of Black immigrants. At the end of the congress, it was agreed that a formal protest would be presented to the government for allowing the shameful conditions for Antillean workers (Pichardo 1980).

The Cuban government's solution to unemployment caused by the sugar crisis and to guarantee jobs for Cubans was a decree to approve the repatriation of Antillean workers. Decree number 1404 from July 20, 1921, contained clauses by which the government justified the repatriation decision based on an article of the Law of Immigration from August 3, 1917, which approved the entry of Antillean immigrants in Cuba. That law established that the entry of immigrants would be allowed so long as they did not become a public burden or threat to the national health status. If either should occur, workers would then be shipped back to their country of origin.

With the economic downturn experienced by the sugar industry in 1921 – when the number of field jobs had fallen considerably, leaving hundreds of workers, especially immigrants, in a true state of misery – this provision in the law was used to start repatriation. According to the Decree, these facts contributed to the immediate curtailing of the Immigration Law of 1917 since the sugar industry was unable to employ the manpower available. Weighing a solution to such an issue, the government adopted the following argument:

> Por cuanto: las condiciones de vida de la mayoría de esos inmigrantes, debido a la aglomeración originada por el hecho de haberse reconcentrado en las poblaciones, constituye un serio peligro para la salubridad pública, según reiterados informes y declaraciones de la Secretaría de Sanidad y Beneficencia.
> Por tanto: en uso de las facultades de que me hallo investido por la Constitución y las leyes, a propuesta del Secretario de Agricultura, Comercio y Trabajo y oído el parecer del Consejo de Secretarias,
> RESUELVO:
> Artículo I. Reembarcar por cuenta del Estado a los braceros procedentes de Haiti, Jamaica y demás Antillas menores, contratados para la producción agrícola al amparo de la Ley de Inmigración de 3 de agosto de 1917, por constituir en la hora presente una carga pública para la nación (Pichardo 1980, 22).

The legislation did not aim to solve the problem of over-exploitation of Black immigrants. It considered those immigrants responsible for problems of public health and proposed their deportation to solve the problem. The Secretariats of Agriculture, Commerce and Labor, Health and Benefits, and Finance would oversee the process of repatriating the immigrants.

The *Federación Obrera* of Havana summoned all labor organizations to a national assembly congress on December 14, 1924. One of the resolutions of this congress was to support Antillean immigrants against oppression and over-exploitation. In the item referring to immigration, it stated that the federation could not restrict the entrance of Antilleans into Cuba and that it recognized that those immigrants were misguided, arriving in the country ignorant of working conditions and unwittingly contributing to worsening the situation of Cuban workers (Pichardo 1980).

Using an argument based on the work of Jacques Roumain, who had also been in Cuba as an immigrant, Jorge Ibarra (1983) highlights some sections of the work *Masters of the Dawn* (1978) describing how the immigrants, in this case Haitians, become aware of their role as workers and gradually incorporate into the labor movement. He notes that at first, the Antillean workers in Cuba, like himself, were defenseless and could not resist oppression. They were divided, some seeing themselves as white, others as Black.

> Voy a contarte, en los comienzos de Cuba, estábamos indefensos y sin resistencia, este se creía blanco, aquel era black, y había no poca desintegración entre nosotros: estábamos dispersos como la arena los patrones marchaban sobre ella, hasta que finalmente nos reunimos para organizar las huelgas (Roumain 1978, 168).

Ibarra (1983) points to episodes in which Antillean workers participated, such as in 1919 when Menocal's government decided to expel a leader of the Jamaicans and another of the Haitians. Another event occurred in 1920, in Central Preston, when a group of around 2000 Haitians rebelled following a series of encounters with the army (Primelles 1955).

Another confirmation of Antillean immigrant participation in the Cuban labor movement is the presence of Enrique Shakleton, a Jamaican, at the 2nd National Workers Congress from 15 to 18 February 1925. Regarding his participation in the congress, Ibarra states that Shackleton was a great leader among the foreign workers who denounced the tense situation created by violent repression by government forces. His ideas were accepted by the other leaders and the Congress agreed to a motion of solidarity. Enrique Shakleton – spokesman for the *Unión de Obreros Antillanos de Santiago de Cuba* – along with Manuel Ochoa represented the eastern region during the Congress. Their description of the situation of Antillean immigrants was highlighted by the representatives of the eastern region and gained the support of the other workers. (Ibarra 1983).

Traditionally, Cuban historiography on labor relations has perpetuated the idea that Antillean immigrants were passive workers who avoided involvement in the Cuban labor movement. The historian George Ibarra presents a new perspective in which Haitians and Jamaicans influenced and even participated in the labor movement during that period, a view I can confirm from a review of sources.

Migrant workers from the Lesser Antilles participated actively in the Cuban labor movement, but that is not to say that their political awareness started in Cuba. Haitians participated in political activities in their own country, resisting the intervention of the United States in Haiti in 1915, while Jamaicans were known in the labor movement of immigrant workers in Panama and Costa Rica, in addition to the political influence of Marcus Garvey in the region. Similarly, Afro-Cubans had actively participated in the political struggles of their country since the independence wars of the late eighteenth century. The aim of this article is to present evidence of the relationship between Haitians and Jamaicans in Cuba, the existing racial debate, and their political actions – all factors that provided a racial element in the debate around national development during the early decades of the twentieth century and that influenced labor organization in Cuba.

References

Aguirre, Sérgio. Algunas luchas sociales en Cuba Republicana. *Revista Cubana*, La Habana, nº49, septiembre, 1965.

_____. Nacionalidad, nación y Centenario. *Revista Cuba Socialista*, La Habana, v. 7, nº 66, p. 75-96, 1967.

Álvarez Estevez, R. *Azúcar e inmigración 1900-1940*. La Habana: Editorial de Ciencias Sociales, 1988.

Arredondo, Alberto. *El negro en Cuba*. La Habana: Ed. Alfa, 1939, p.147.

Cabrera, Olga. *El movimiento obrero cubano en 1920*. La Habana: Instituto del Libro, 1969.

_____. *Los que viven por sus manos*. La Habana: Editorial de Ciencias Sociales, 1985.

Godfried, Eugene. "Cuba en una perspectiva caribeña: una reseña histórico-critica de la posición y papel de los cubanos de descendencia africana en el proceso del cambio social". *Afrocuba*. Last modified June 2000. https://www.afrocubaweb.com/eugenegodfried/cubacaribbeanesp.htm

Ibarra, Jorge. Notas sobre nación e ideologia. In: *Ideologia mambisa*. La Habana: Instituto del Libro, 9-76, 1967.

James, Ariel. *Banes, imperialismo y nación en una plantación azucarera*. Habana: Editorial de Ciencias Humanas, 1976.

Martínez, Ortiz, R. *Cuba. Los primeros años de independencia*. Editorial Le Livre Libre: Paris, 200, 1929.

Pichardo, Hortencia. Documentos para la Historia de Cuba, 4 vols. La Habana: Editorial de Ciencias Sociales, 1980.

Roumain, Jacques. *Los gobernadores del rocio*. La Habana, 1978, p.168.

_____. *Nación y cultura nacional*. La Habana: Editorial Letras Cubanas, 1981.

_____. La inmigración antillana: ¿Desproletarización y desnacionalización del proletariado cubano o aceleración de las contradiciones sociales? ¿Disgregacion y marginalización del antillano o progresiva integración de este em las luchas de la clase obrera? IV Encuentro de Historiadores Latinoamericanos y del Caribe, 1983.

_____. *Cuba, 1898-1921: partidos políticos y clases sociales*. La Habana: Editorial de Ciencias Sociales, 1992.

_____. *Una analisis psicosocial del cubano, 1898-1925*. La Habana: Editorial de Ciencias Sociales, 1985.

Sierra, Torres G; Rosario Molina. Juan Carlos. *Los canários en Cuba: juntos pero no revueltos*. Gran Canária: Centro de la Cultura Popular Canária, 2001.

Telleria, Evelio. *Los congresos obreros en Cuba*. La Habana: Instituto Cubano del Libro, 52; 55, 1973.

Villena, Ruben M. La unión del blanco y el negro, del nativo y el extranjero. *Revista Mundo Obrero*, Mayo, 1933, New York.

Yglesias, Martínez T. Organización de la republica neocolonial. *In: La neocolonia: organización y crisis, desde 1899 hasta 1940*. La Habana: Editora Política, 1998.

CHAPTER EIGHT

No Ugly People in The Paradise: Undesirable Immigrants in the Brazilian Racial Democracy

Elaine P. Rocha

The University of the West Indies, Cave Hill Campus, Barbados

Abstract

This article examines the Brazilian historical rejection of black immigrants, starting from the 19th century and continuing through the twentieth century until 2010 when a wave of Haitian immigrants caused great debate among Brazilians, divided into those who rejected what they considered an undesirable immigration and those who argued for a more humanitarian reception of immigrants escaping from hardship exacerbated by the earthquake. The first important wave of black immigrants – post slavery – arrived in Brazil between 1900 and 1915, during the implementation of projects of modernisation in the Rain Forest region. Those Caribbean immigrants entered Brazil despite the prohibition, some illegally, some as immigrant workers under temporary contracts. Their presence, although not significant in numbers, has left its mark on the history of places like Manaus, Belem and Porto Velho.

Keywords: Haitian migrants, Amazon, Modernization, Caribbean, racism

***

Brazil is a country known for its easy-going people and the racial democracy that has created the largest mixed-race population in the world. Brazilian culture also promotes this image, with *samba* as the national rhythm that provided the basis for the *bossa nova*, the samba schools, and the *batuques* that attract hundreds of thousands yearly to carnivals in Rio de Janeiro, Salvador, and other capitals. The country has also invested millions of dollars over the past sixty years to create an image of a harmonious and peaceful society.

Considering the history of Brazil, its public image as a country without racial barriers is a contradiction: slavery was abolished only in 1888, the last country in the continent to do so. Before that, Brazil was the last country to stop the traffic of slaves from the African continent (1857) and to end the internal trade (1880s). These facts have deeply affected the way in which society sees the descendants of Africans and the way social and racial hierarchies were established and maintained throughout the twentieth century.

Brazil was the major destination of enslaved people taken from Africa between the sixteenth and the nineteenth centuries, receiving about 40% of all enslaved who arrived on the continent. Some estimate that the South American country received about 4 million people, others estimate up to 5 million; the difficulty in determining numbers with any precision lies in the fact that many papers were lost, many people were introduced into the territory illegally and after the prohibition of the slave trade, a few groups continued to bring slaves into Brazil until around 1860.

From about the 1870s on, the world changed: neo-colonialism together with philosophical and scientific progress, started to impose new theories and approaches to the question of racial diversity and power. By the end of the nineteenth century and up to approximately 1920, Brazilian society found, in the theories of Positivist philosophy emphasizing social and racial hierarchies and in "scientific racism", the intellectual justifications for the economic, political and social exclusion of Blacks and the need to exercise close control over the former slaves and all people of African descent, reinforcing the stigma of ignorance, lack of skills, low intellectual abilities, and criminality among these groups. It is important to note, however, that the population of African descent in Brazil was at that time much larger than that of European descent.

The situation was aggravated by the maintenance of the "Land Law" of 1850, which acknowledged property rights only to those who could prove its purchase. This would exclude most of the poor people, including those of mixed race and Blacks, who had occupied and used available land for years but were eventually expelled by anyone who would claim its purchase. The former slaves also ran the risk of losing their jobs and their homes every time the land they worked, usually for very low pay, was sold. For those expelled from farms, the main option was to migrate to the cities and try to survive there as part of the lowly paid workforce. In the four decades following abolition, the quality of life of Blacks in Brazil improved little, given the maintenance of the plantation oligarchy, the lack of investment in public education and the absence of a policy that would facilitate access to land ownership.

As slavery came to an end, Brazil started to import European immigrants to fill an imagined gap in workers and farmers since the elite believed that Blacks would never adapt as freed workers and that European workers, with their labor and miscegenation, would bring the society the element of modernization and civilization it needed. During the last decades of the nineteenth century and the first of the twentieth century, Brazil was obsessed with the idea of "whitening" its society and population.

The "ideology of whitening" was not created or practiced exclusively in Brazil and was in fact, very popular in Latin American societies keen to be considered as modern nations through leaving their colonial roots behind. This involved special attention to the racial composition of their societies at a time when racial groups were arranged on a developmental scale with Europeans at the top as the model for modernity, civilization and progress. Several countries in Latin America invested in importing immigrants from Europe to increase their white population. At the same time, Latin American intellectuals elaborated a version of "scientific racism" different from places that condemned miscegenation as a form of degeneration. In the Latin version, miscegenation created a stronger race, adapted to the challenge of the tropics, free of the Old Continent diseases and vices. In Mexico, José Vasconcelos called it "the cosmic race," celebrating *mestizaje* as the creation of an Ibero-American (Vasconcelos 1997).

Brazil embraced the same theory as its neighbors but, given that the Black population in Brazil was much larger than the indigenous, a different version had to be created to accommodate the fact that its mixed population was mostly Black and indigenous. In 1933, Gilberto Freyre's seminal work *Casa Grande e Senzala (The Master and the Slaves)* came to the rescue of the intellectuals by acknowledging the contributions of African cultures in Brazil and the importance of African slaves in society. At the same time, it reinforced white hegemony, creating what is today known as the "Myth of the Three Races," in which Brazil was the product of the mixing of African, Indigenous and Portuguese people, with little conflict and relationships where Europeans overpowered the other groups and were recognized as superior (Freyre 1988).

The nationalist government of Getúlio Vargas (1930-1946) came to power with the promise of breaking up the oligarchy and establishing a government of unity, focusing less on the elites and the needs of the southeast, where economic development was higher. It was during this period that Afro-Brazilian culture became Brazilian culture, with the acceptance of samba as the national rhythm and the promotion of the Samba School parades as part of the carnival supported (and controlled) by the government. Vargas also invested in promoting Brazil externally, creating the image of a congenial society free of racial conflict. In the context of a dictatorship, any mention of racial discrimination or racism in Brazil could be condemned as an act of subversion.

The government of the United States, keen on increasing its commercial and political influence in South America, accepted the image of Brazil and even promoted it through the movie industry, as in Disney's portrayal of the exoticism and originality of Brazilian society and culture in the films "*Saludos Amigos*" (1942) and "*The Three Caballeros*" (1944). A few years later, Bossa Nova, the Brazilian mixture of samba and jazz, consolidated the image of the racial paradise and contributed to concealing the contradictions in society.

The Brazilian policy on immigration

After independence in 1822, Brazil made efforts to control immigration, determining desirable and undesirable immigrants based on their religion, nationality, criminal record and race and successfully imposed a barrier against the immigration of Africans and the descendants of Africans. The first legislative challenge to this policy took place between the 1850s and 60s when representatives of the United States government presented a proposal to move free Black people from the United States to what was then the Brazilian province of Amazonas. The project was proposed as a solution for problems in both countries: it would help to occupy and colonize the Amazon, in need of a labor force, and it would solve the problem of racial conflicts in the United States amid the Civil War. The idea was rejected by Brazilians, who expressed concerns about receiving African Americans in a period when the question of slavery in Brazil was very sensitive. The government also saw in this proposal pressure to support the northern colonies of the United States in their Civil War and declined any involvement, opting for neutrality (Sampaio 2008).

Only two years after abolition, the first republican constitution of 1890 instituted a decree on immigration that specified that Asian and African immigrants should not be freely granted entry into Brazil and could only be admitted by authorization of the National Congress and that diplomatic and consular agents and the police at the ports should prevent the disembarkation of those individuals, as well as beggars and indigents (Skidmore 1974).

In 1921, attracted by the absence of segregation laws in Brazil and by the large "mixed" population, a group of African Americans attempted to emigrate to Brazil, supported by the Brazilian American Colonization Syndicate which planned to buy land in the state of Mato Grosso in central Brazil to accommodate the families. The news of such a project was presented not only to Brazilian authorities but to the general public through the newspapers, causing general commotion and great debate, while diplomatic authorities fought to avoid this type of immigrant into the territory (Gomes 2003).

The racist propaganda claimed that if Brazil wanted to reach the level of developed countries, the country needed to invest in modernizing its labour force by favouring white (European) immigrants in contrast to the national (mixed) workers. In this context, Black immigrants were unacceptable, with the elite and intellectuals arguing that Brazil already had a large population of descendants of Africans and accepting more Blacks would keep the country back in the race for modernity. There was also the availability of European workers, given the harsh economic and political conditions in countries like Italy, Germany, Spain, Portugal, Russia and Poland between 1870 and the 1930s. During that period, thousands of Europeans migrated to the Americas in search of a better life, demanding very little.

> Facing insistent demands from their former slaves for new work regimens – shorter and more flexible hours, no work for women or children, increased autonomy and freedom from direct supervision – employers responded by seeking out alternative sources of workers. These could easily have come from within Latin American societies themselves, but dictates of scientific racism, combined with the availability of millions of European workers ready and willing to leave their native lands, led governments to invest state funds not in locally born non-whites but in European immigrants (Andrews 2004, 136).

At the turn of the century, the republican government invested in creating the modern infrastructure for a transport network that included roads, railroads, river and sea ports, as well as a system of telegraph communications. In the urban areas of the biggest cities, there were projects for public lighting, electricity and telephone, as well as sanitation, wide avenues, and public buildings. The economy was booming with the production of coffee in the southeast, cocoa in the northeast and rubber in the north of the country, all for the external market. Apart from that, the production food for internal consumption created opportunities for raising cattle and growing cassava, corn, rice and other products. However, the working conditions in rural areas were still poor and more and more people would move away from the plantations and farms to try life in the cities.

In the urban areas, once more, Black workers had to compete with European workers who had also decided to leave the farms and go to the city. In Sao Paulo, where industry was in full development most of the employers, some of them Europeans, preferred white workers. Afro-Brazilian workers were under-employed in jobs that no one else wanted: cleaning, washing horses, carrying loads at the train stations and ports, working as domestic workers, shoeshines, and more. Their culture was still marginalized, and they could suffer police violence when enjoying their *batuques* or *sambas*. Marginality, criminality, and violence were part of their daily lives.

Modernizing the Amazon

As the Brazilian government and primarily the state governments of Sao Paulo, Minas Gerais, Rio de Janeiro, Paraná, Santa Catarina and Rio Grande do Sul created funds to finance the importation of European workers, other regions of Brazil complained about the lack of white immigrants in their states and the absence of funds to bring in desirable immigrants. In the northern states and territories where there was not enough money to import workers, except for Japanese immigrants. The Union government, to stimulate internal migration to solve labour force problems, frequently resorted to moving people from drought-stricken north-eastern states to the states of Amazonas and Pará and the territories of Rondonia, Roraima, Acre and Amapa.

The *seringais* of Amazonas were also the destination of unwanted people during the first decades of the republic. In 1906, Black sailors in Rio de Janeiro rebelled against the Brazilian Navy authorities that denied them higher posts and maintained corporal punishments. The sailors received popular support, but the government betrayed the agreement made with them and sent the rebels to prison or into exile as forced labour in the Amazon. About two hundred sailors convicted during the revolt and who made the long trip from Rio de Janeiro to Amazonas under terrible conditions were offered to the railway company constructing the Madeira-Mamoré railroad in Rondônia but were refused given their poor health. Some *seringalistas*, the entrepreneurs who invested in the extraction of rubber, employed those who appeared to be in reasonable physical condition. Along with the rebels were 292 others convicted of idleness and 44 prostitutes (Rodrigues and Oliveira Filho 1999). Before that, in 1904, a people's riot against mandatory vaccinations imposed upon the population of Rio de Janeiro also ended with hundreds of those involved sentenced to exile in the Amazon region. Some went to the *seringais*, and some were employed in the construction of the Madeira-Mamoré railroad, in Rondônia. According to scholars like Francisco Bento da Silva, these were people from the lowest class, not exactly criminals, but also not citizens. Many of them died during the trip, others arrived there without being registered, not even named in official documents (Silva 2006). The conditions of work for those condemned to the Amazon region were close to slavery.

As Barbara Weinstein (1983) and Warren Dean (1987) stated, during the rubber boom, people from several parts of Brazil and other countries went to the Amazon, mostly illegally. Another important characteristic of the Amazon occupation is that, unlike in other regions of Brazil, there were no official colonization or development projects until around the 1940s. Workers extracting latex to produce rubber were expected to produce as much as possible, which implied moving from place to place and enduring very difficult working conditions. The lack of governmental control and the nature of that vast region made it impossible to keep track of all the workers and adventurers who took risks associated with living in such a hostile environment, and immigrants from neighbouring countries were among them.

Despite what is widely believed, the northern region of Brazil known as the Amazon, comprising the states of Pará, Amazonas, Rondônia, Amapa, Roraima and Acre, had also employed slave labour from the seventeenth century and lasted well into the nineteenth century, with a concentration in the more developed provinces of Amazonas and Pará. Ygor Rocha Cavalcante (2013), discusses the strategies used by Blacks to resist and escape from slavery in the Amazon during the nineteenth century, while Marco Antonio Teixeira (2009) examines slavery in the western Amazon, a region known as the Guapore Valley. This meant that the undesirable (Black) people the Republican government started sending to the region were not the first Blacks to arrive there.

Modernization was a great project for the world at the turn of the twentieth century, the apex of the second industrial revolution, when steam-driven machines demanded fuel, iron, rubber, and markets. There was also the need for roads and the means to move products from one point to another. The Panama Canal was built during this period, and construction companies were created in England, Canada and the United States to take over huge construction projects in Latin America, thanks to commercial and diplomatic agreements among governments. At that time, the demand for rubber made the Amazon a target for the investments that would eventually build the basis for progress and economic development. However, there was the challenge of creating a workforce capable of building the necessary structures in the jungle under time constraints. The companies decided to apply in Brazil the same systems that they were using in other parts of the continent, like Panama and Costa Rica and brought in cheaper workers recruited from the Caribbean.

Black immigrants

How did Caribbean immigrants manage to enter Brazil despite the legislation prohibiting Black immigrants? The answer is they were hired under contract, as part of the agreement between foreign companies – who needed skilled workers who could speak, read and write English – and the Brazilian authorities, with the promise that they would return to their countries once the work was done.

Compared to other groups of immigrants who arrived in Brazil during the same period, Caribbean immigrants came in much smaller numbers, spread over a period of 50 to 60 years starting in the 1870s when a few individuals entered Brazilian territory from British Guiana pursuing fortunes in (imaginary) gold mines or in rubber production. Only later did groups of those immigrants start arriving in the port of Belem as part of personnel contracted by big construction companies like Light and Power Ltd., the Port of Pará, and the Madeira-Mamore Railroad Co. They were not sponsored by the local government and were not expected to put down roots in Brazil, since many of them arrived under a contract for a limited time. In Barbados, emigrant records from 1907 revealed at least one contractor, the Hidalgo Co. Ltd., who may have been acting on behalf of American, British or Brazilian companies in contracting workers from Barbados and the neighbouring islands, but there must have been other contractors in the region.

> In fact, there was not a conventional immigration. The migratory movement of Barbadians was directed by British capitalists who were granted successive contracts to carry on urbanization projects in Para and Amazonas. For that they needed skilled laborers, probably some who could speak the language and shared the same culture. The Barbadian Blacks, tamed by the English, were brought by ships from the Booth Steamship Co. Limited, travelling from New York to Manaus, stopping in Barbados and Belem. Many of those workers were also taken to work in the construction of the Madeira-Mamore railroad. (Salles 2005, 84)

Among the reasons for leaving their homes were the lack of available land for small farms, limited job opportunities beyond the sugar cane plantation and low wages, factors that led to a situation of poverty and exclusion, to which natural disasters like hurricanes or droughts would contribute to worsening the living conditions and stimulating the pursuit of better opportunities away from the British colonies. George Andrews (2004) points to an increase in emigration from Jamaica after the earthquake of 1907 and the hurricanes of 1915 and 1917 when small farms and houses were destroyed, and the great plantations dismissed their employees to counter economic losses.

Barbados, for example, with a territory of 430 square kilometers dominated by plantations owned by the white elite until the 1950s and even later, offered limited access to small properties or for Black entrepreneurship. The living standards of the majority of the population were characterized by living in a small, easily movable house (chattel house) located on rocky, rented plantation land and labouring for meager wages for the plantation. Lucky tenants were able to rent an extra piece of land to plant food for the household or for marketing. Additionally, some male tenants had artisanal skills or were fishermen and were able to earn an extra income, while women would seek employment as maids or washerwomen in upper-class houses or try to make some money as hucksters (Beckles 1994). Emigration would, therefore, become the natural outlet for the frustrated Black citizens of Barbados and the West Indies.

In Jamaica, the situation was similar in terms of the white oligarchy. However, the Jamaicans had to compete for work with indentured workers brought in from Ireland and India, and low wages and high rents were behind the tensions between Black workers and the elites. Skilled workers such as masons took the opportunity to leave the plantations for work in the construction of bridges and railroads during the last decade of the twentieth century (Bryan 2000). These workers would be among those hired to build the Panama Canal and, later, for the construction of railroads and other modernization projects in South America.

The Madeira-Mamore railroad project was undertaken by the American investor Percival Farquhar to build a railroad in the heart of the Amazon, connecting the eastern border of Bolivia to the Atlantic port of Belem, the capital of the Brazilian state of Para. While some authors, like Hoyos (1984), argue that during the construction (1907-1912), the project took about 5,000 Black West Indian workers, most of them from Barbados, it is difficult to be precise from the existing sources about the number of immigrant workers from the West Indies who entered Brazil between 1870 and 1930, given the scanty of the official documents registering those migrants either in Brazil or in their countries of origin. Some moved from the Caribbean directly to Brazil, some were imported from among workers on the Panama Canal, while others are believed to have entered Brazil via British Guiana.

Vicente Salles, among others, argues that at the start of the twentieth century, the Black population in the northern regions was in large part mixed with indigenous and white, which for many, made the appearance of those Afro-Brazilian more acceptable, in comparison to the newcomers from the Caribbean (Salles 2005). Citing the writings of Raimundo Morais, a local journalist from the turn of the twentieth century, in Belem, Salles explains: "They were not beautiful, but they were not as ugly as those from the open current of migration from Barbados to Belem." He continues to explain the benefits of miscegenation and the risk that the Afro-Caribbean represented, in the view of Morais: "Those people of scowling faces interfered with the process of miscegenation of our brownish blacks born here, darkening the happy expressions and the agreeable faces [of the Black people of Para]". (Salles 2005, 114).

Brazilian researchers Nilza Menezes (1998) and Roseane Pinto Lima (2006) explain that "*barbadiano*" was a generic name given to all Black immigrants from the West Indies, among whom would be found people from Grenada, St. Vincent, Jamaica, Trinidad, Saint Lucia and, of course, Barbados. The reason for this generalization was probably that immigrants from the Caribbean would board ships in Barbados to go to Brazil. An oral history project centered on the history of the Madeira-Mamore railroad recorded testimonies of some of the *barbadianos*, as follows:

> I tell you more about the island of Grenada where daddy was born... what happens is that here in Porto Velho... they think that all people of color are Barbadians... everybody that speaks English here, they say that he is Barbadian... (Menezes 1998, 32).

The Caribbean immigrants arrived in Brazil as Black workers with superior status. First of all, they were British subjects, and most were workers under contract and somehow under the protection of the foreign company. Data from official documents and newspapers between 1907 and 1911 show that the Barbadian immigrants were hired together with workers from the neighboring islands, that most of them had at least four years of formal education and were between 19 and 32 years old, a fact that caused discontent in some quarters in Barbados who complained in the newspapers that the island was losing its best people. It is important to note that a large number of immigrants from the Caribbean to the Amazon arrived without contracts and struggled to find jobs in the region. Some men opened small businesses like bars, barber shops and small hotels in the railroad construction area. Some ventured into the jungle to seek their fortune in rubber production; some Caribbean women found jobs as laundrywomen, nannies, cooks and maids for the families of the foreign managers, and others found work as seamstresses and teachers among their own community (Menezes 1998; Lima 2006; Fonseca and Teixeira 2009; Sampaio 2010).

Despite their status as British people and their professional skills, they had to face the same obstacles met by all workers in the rainforest region: malaria, yellow fever, attacks by wild animals and snakes, diseases like tuberculosis caused by the humidity and the lack of sanitation and proper shelter. For those lucky enough to stay in the two major cities of Belem or Manaus, employed in urbanizing projects undertaken by the Para Electric Railway and Lighting Co., the Amazon Telegraph Co., and the Para Harbour Co., the conditions were better and the possibility of finding employment outside the foreign companies was greater. In Belem, for example, the community built the Anglican Church of Saint Mary and founded their own school. In both cases, the services were in English.

However, the better conditions of the cities did not protect the Caribbean immigrants against racism, openly expressed by the local population, who were unhappy over receiving these kinds of immigrants, rather than the Europeans who were arriving in the southern states. Proposals against Black immigrants were voted in the Congress. In 1923, one of these proposals against Black immigrants was based on the danger represented by African American immigrants who, in their view, would not only delay the plan for whitening through miscegenation but would also put order at risk because they were not as submissive and docile as the Brazilian Blacks who had accepted and adapted to white superiority. Or, as the popular saying went in Brazil, *O bom preto é aquele que sabe o seu lugar* (A good Black is one who knows his place). During the first years of the 1920s, Brazilian politicians debated on nationalities and ethnicities that should not be allowed to migrate to Brazil. Member of Congress Fidelis Reis, in 1923, emphasized the need to implement means to avoid foreign immigrants who represented risks to Brazilian nationhood. In his view, shared by the majority, Black immigrants would put at risk Brazilian ethnicity and morality; they also represented risks to the "bodies" of Brazilians, implying that such immigrants were carriers of diseases.

Such prejudicial views of Black immigrant workers, found mostly in the newspapers of Rio de Janeiro and Sao Paulo, contradict the opinion expressed by a journalist in *Alto Madeira*, a newspaper published in Rondonia, a northern territory that received immigrant workers from the West Indies during the first decades of the twentieth century. In that newspaper, one can read of the good impression of that society created by those workers employed by the Madeira-Mamore Railroad Co. The newspaper refers on more than one occasion to the "hardworking Barbadians" and as an example of workers who are literate, in contrast with the majority of illiterate Brazilians.[1]

In 1924 and 1925, rural associations directly interested in attracting immigrant workers to Brazil came forward to request a complete prohibition of Black immigrants of any nationality. Among those associations were the Sociedade Rural [Rural Society], the Liga Agrígola Brasileira [Brazilian Agricultural League], and the Sociedade Nacional de Agricultura [National Agricultural Society]. This last launched a national survey of opinions on the importation of Black immigrants with questionnaires distributed in all Brazilian states and involving the Brazilian Geographic Society, the Medical Academy and other institutions. The results, published in 1926, showed massive rejection of Black immigrants and limited acceptance of Japanese, who were considered superior to Blacks. (Ramos 1996).

The inauguration in 1927 of the American project "Fordlandia" - Henry Ford's settlement to grow rubber trees in the Amazon - also fuelled the argument, as the enterprise managed to import Black immigrant workers from the Caribbean and to employ others already in Brazilian territory, former workers of the Madeira-Mamore Railway Co. who stayed behind after the construction of the railroad ended.

> In search for labor, Oxholm also looked to the British Caribbean, which had a long history of supplying workers to large-scale construction projects throughout Latin America, such as the Panama Canal. In the first couple of months he managed to attract a number of West Indians from the upper Amazon who had survived the construction of the 228-mile Madeira-to-Mamore train line...
>
> At the news that Ford was hiring, many headed down the Amazon and then up the Tapajos to the plantation. Added to these stranded West

---

[1] "Grupo Escolar", *Alto Madeira*, (Porto Velho, Rondonia), August 23, 1925, p. 1-2. Biblioteca Nacional, Brazilian Digital Library, Periódicos.

Indians rail workers were migrants who came directly from Jamaica, Barbados and Saint Lucia. (Grandin 2009, 161-162).

In 1929, a fight between a West Indian and a Brazilian worker at Fordlandia resulted in the death of the Brazilian and the retaliation of local workers against the immigrants. The case attracted the attention of the British Consul, who defended the reputation of West Indian workers against accusations by the plantation manager, Einar Oxholm, that the Caribbean workers were known troublemakers. Somehow, the argument found space in newspapers.[2] Maria Helena Capelatto refers to a letter by the editor of the newspaper *O Estado de Sao Paulo*, in which he sided with the Norwegian Oxholm, condemning the idea of Black immigrant workers. His argument contains, in part, what was previously said, "Blacks do not constitute strong elements of civilization, (in the process of miscegenation) they do not contribute to the racial upgrading with physical, mental and moral strength." (Capelatto 1980, 120).

The debate was finally settled in 1934 when the new constitution introduced a law limiting the number of immigrants and defining undesirable types of immigrants. This was the period of the nationalist government of Getulio Vargas and a time when the world was highly influenced by ideas in Nazism, fascism and neo-colonialism on "pure" and "superior" races. Endrica Geraldo remarks that between 1930 and 1945, the Vargas government increased restrictions on immigration and passed nationalist laws that imposed difficulties on those intending to move to Brazil and on foreigners already resident in the country except for those, other than Jews, of European origin (Geraldo 2009).

Article 121 of the 1934 Constitution of Brazil, in paragraph 6, imposed an annual limit on the number of immigrants of each nationality, forbidding the concentration of immigrants from a group in any one place or area of Brazilian territory. The issue of the undesirable immigrant again generated debate; various amendments were presented in which Black immigrants were banned because of hygienic, ethnic or even medical reasons. The idea was to prevent the immigration of individuals who would jeopardize the Brazilian project of constructing a national race and order that would reunite all the elements needed for progress and civilization (Geraldo 2009).

The Sociedade Nacional de Agricultura's report of 1926 already contained some elements found in the constitution above, as in the statement of Antonio Carlos Simões da Silva:

---

[2] "O que vae pelo mundo. Pará", *Jornal do Commercio*, (Manaus, AM), June 9, 1929, p. 7. Biblioteca Naciona, Brazilian Digital Library, Periódicos.

> I don't accept black immigration because Brazil already has in its population a number of people of this race that exceeds the other existing racial groups. It seems just to consider that the entrance of a mass of individuals of the same race (blacks) in large groups would upset the balance of the wonderful harmony existing between these races. (Blacks) would in time reproduce in a manner to take over the entire country, to the prejudice of the other races. Even for the benefit of black Brazilian we should not facilitate this type of immigration, because it would bring immigrants of different religions from the black Brazilian, who are fervently catholic, and would lack the patriotic enthusiasm that our blacks have for Brazil. (*Apud* Ramos 1996, 79).

It is important to note, from the above extract, that at this point the black Brazilian population is seen like any other group of immigrants, the number of newcomers from which should be controlled to defend national sovereignty. In other words, almost 400 years after the first importing of Africans into Brazil, Black Brazilians were considered, under that law, as foreigners. This rule remained valid until 1967, when a new constitution was put in place, with no reference to desirable or undesirable immigrants according to their nationalities (Baraldi 2011).

West Indian immigrants endured difficult conditions, from social isolation – due to cultural issues like the language barrier and religious practices – to racial discrimination. On the railroad construction sites of the railroad, challenging conditions included diseases like malaria, tuberculosis, parasites, yellow fever, cholera, alcoholism, and dysentery (caused by spoiled food), among others. Attacks of jungle animals were also a risk, as were insects like mosquitoes and voracious ants that could devour a person in hours, in addition to accidents in construction or in navigation and fights between workers, all listed in the memoirs of survivors (Kravigni 1911; Craig 1907, Neeleman and Neeleman 2011). The poor conditions continued in the Fordlandia project:

> They arrived at the camp where many of the same conditions that sparked the riot in late 1928 persisted – poor housing and working conditions, particularly for those hired to clear the jungle, confusing pay schedules, and bad food – aggravated by strident attempts to regulate hygiene and enforce Prohibition. (Grandin 2009, 162).

Away from working campsites, living conditions were also precarious. The testimonies of those immigrants refer to police raids in the neighbourhood called *Morro dos Barbadianos* (Barbadian Hill), where most West Indian immigrants lived during and after the construction of the railroad. (Menezes, 1998; Fonseca and Teixeira, 2009; Sampaio, 2010). In Belem, capital of Para state, the second generation of immigrants faced racial discrimination (Lima,

2006). Some of them returned to their islands at the end of their contracts, but most did not, since over time, sometimes as much as ten years later because of contract renewals, they had married women and had children, and the company would pay only for the worker's return ticket (Menezes, 1998). Moreover, the research points to very minimal social advancement among the descendants of immigrants, especially after the second generation. While research on Italian, German, Portuguese and Spanish immigrants and their descendants pointed to social advances reflected in political and economic power, these being, besides the Lebanese, among the richest families and part of the political elite in Brazil, the same did not occur among Barbadians.

A hundred years later: No "ugly people" in the paradise!

In the past fifty years, especially from the 1990s onwards, Brazil has progressively addressed the problem of racial inequality, with overall improvements in policies of social and racial inclusion because of campaigns and demands from Black movements that managed to secure internal and external support. The society is still behind in comparison with the United States and South Africa, where segregation was enforced by laws. There is no significant number of Black Brazilian politicians and Afro-Brazilians are still predominantly at the bottom of the social pyramid, with limited access to employment, education, health, property and sanitation.

Based on the 2000 census, Marcelo Paixão has shown that Blacks in Brazil are a majority among the illiterate and that Afro-Brazilians spend fewer years in school than those classified as whites. This affects their economic inclusion and reinforces poverty and discrimination against Blacks. He suggests that any policy to curb illiteracy must also tackle racism in the educational system and in the job market, considering that even after acquiring an education, many Blacks and mulattoes are discriminated against in the labour market, which also contributes to low self-esteem and discourages them from pursuing higher levels of schooling (Paixão 2004). In the 1990s, Costa Ribeiro (1995) has shown in his statistical analysis of racial discrimination in Brazil that for those Blacks who achieve higher levels of education, the prospect of equal payment and position in the job market is low. Moreover, for the minority who manage to overcome poverty, the possibility of losing their economic status is greater than for whites.

Even though Brazil has publicly faced the contradictions of "racial democracy", the country has still managed to keep the image of racial tolerance, happiness, and economic opportunities for all. It is a fact that Brazilians, in general, avoid discussing their internal contradictions with outsiders, with the racial problem being the number one topic to be avoided in any discussion. The image of a "paradise" is extraordinarily strong in the nationalist/patriotic discourse, from politicians to the common citizen and, to a certain extent, in academia.

In 2004, the Brazilian military arrived in Haiti as part of the United Nations' efforts to control the violence that arose after the fall of President Aristide. Since then, the Brazilian presence in Haiti has been constant and has been remarkably accepted by the Haitians, who see Brazilians as "friendly soldiers." The Brazilian government then decided to extend the military security and control operations to technical support from military engineers in construction and restoration projects, as well as in projects to provide water and electricity, and important support in areas of health. However, the most popular event was the football match of 2004, when Brazilian football stars – supported by the Brazilian government – went to Port-au-Prince in a period of unrest for a friendly game against Haiti, in what was called the "peace game."

Brazilian presence in Haiti has grown from then and was critical during the earthquake of 2010 and the hurricanes of 2006, 2008 and 2012. On one side, the economic conditions in that country push part of the population into pursuing a better life in other countries; from the other side, Brazil is a very attractive destination, not only because of the positive image but because of international reports on economic development in Brazil. Haitian migration to Brazil started to attract the attention of local and federal authorities from 2010, when large groups of immigrants started to cross the Brazilian border at several points. According to a report by the United Nations, in the 12 months following the earthquake, Brazilian authorities received about 2,150 requests for visas from Haitians seeking refugee status, a category that Brazil does not recognize in the case of natural disasters. Between 2010 and 2014, the number of illegal immigrants from Haiti continued to grow. The majority opted to enter the country through the northern frontiers of the Amazon region via Peru or Bolivia. That created a problem of overpopulation in towns around the borders and local authorities started to press the Brazilians for a solution.[3]

In 2012, the Brazilian President, Dilma Rousseff, signed documents regularizing the status of illegal immigrants in the Northwest border, affecting the states of Acre, Amazonas and Rondonia. Political and popular pressure forced the government to limit visas to 100 work permits per month or 1,200 per year. However, months after that decision, another crisis erupted at the border when thousands of Haitians crossed into Brazilian territory. To deal with the problem,

---

[3] ONU/IOM- International Organization for Migration. Brazil – IOM Crisis. Regional Response Plan on Large Movements of Highly Vulnerable Migrants in the Americas from the Caribbean, Latin America and other regions. October 2021. https://brazil.iom.int/sites/g/files/tmzbdl1496/files/documents/oim-global-appeal-2021-10-25-v2_0.pdf

the limit was erased as the migration authorities tried to regularize the situation of Haitians and ease the pressure.[4] Religious institutions supported the immigrants by providing shelter and food and helping to find them jobs, while the population was divided about taking in the immigrants. Local authorities argued that the region could not absorb the workers since the job market was limited and, moreover, there was no infrastructure to accommodate the number of foreigners who kept arriving with little or no money after paying *coyotes* to take them from Haiti to the Brazilian borders.[5]

Newspapers and NGOs started to denounce the practice of racism against the immigrants and the state of neglect that the refugees faced in Brazilian territory, requesting humanitarian measures to deal with the problem. At the same time, blogs and internet pages reflected the ambiguity among opinions, some stating that the "Haitian invasion" created a crisis at the borders, an issue of national defense.[6]

The image of the Haitian immigrant repeats the rejection that Caribbean immigrants suffered a century ago. Even though among the immigrants there are teachers, engineers, medical doctors, lawyers, masons, carpenters, musicians, and students, the society reflects the fear of contamination from cholera and AIDS and sees the immigrants as dangerous people -beggars, criminals, drug addicts, voodoo practitioners. Some of the skilled workers have managed to get jobs in companies in Manaus (the capital of Amazonas) and in the big cities of the south, but not enough to solve the problem.

In 2013, the government of the state of Acre asked the federal authorities for permission to close the border between Brazil and Peru to stop the movement of around 70 Haitians per day. In the same year, responding to requests from the states of Rondonia, Acre and Amazonas, the Senate included the situation of Haitian immigrants in the northern states as one of the issues to be discussed in the Commission for Foreign Relations and National Security. Nonetheless, Brazil remains far from a solution to the problem.

It is important to note that the Haitians were only another nationality among the increasing number of immigrants seeking work permits in Brazil in the past five years, resulting from economic growth. In fact, Brazilian companies are recruiting workers in Europe and the United States, arguing that the national

---

[4] Edson Luiz. "Vistos ilimitados para haitianos". *Correio Braziliense*, (Brasília, DF), April 30, 2013, p.7. Biblioteca Nacional, Brazilian Digital Library, Periódicos.

[5] Juliana Braga. "Fonteira fechada para os haitianos". *Correio Brasiliense*, (Brasília, DF), January 11, 2012, p. 6. Biblioteca Nacional, Brazilian Digital Library, Periódicos.

[6] "O Brasil fecha fronteiras para conter 'invasão de haitianos'", *O Globo*, (Rio de Janeiro), January 11,2012, p. 1, 3 and 4. Biblioteca Nacional, Brazilian Digital Library, Periódicos.

market does not have the level of specialization that the companies demand. The European workers recruited by those companies receive work permits almost immediately, and the "employment package" includes housing, transportation, and, in some cases, paying for a private school for the children of the employee. As was done in the past, Brazilian companies are paying other companies specializing in recruiting those desirable immigrants.

An example of racial discrimination against immigrant workers was in the debate generated by the news article published in May 2014, entitled: "Waiting for a job, Haitians dream of bringing families to Brazil,"; which discussed the increased number of qualified immigrants, working and living in the city of São Paulo. Some defended the rights of Haitians, comparing them to European workers who arrived in the country around the 1900s. The majority, however, expressed opinions against Haitian immigrants. Here is one of the answers:

> There is a lot of difference between Haitians and Italians, this comparison is not valid. There's something called the hidden curriculum, the family unit, and literacy. They [the Haitians] are not coming from a developed country to develop an unexplored part of this immense Brazil, they are arriving in a region that is already economically developed (…) with overpopulation. They come with their indigence, and criminality. (Silva 2014).

It is significant that in a society still struggling against racial exclusion and still dealing with issues related to racism and social and economic inequalities, the recruitment of professionals from Spain, Portugal, Italy, the United States and Canada, among others, has stirred up the debate about "racial democracy." Between 2010 and 2011, the number of work permits for foreigners in Brazil increased by almost 20%.[7] The economic boom of that period attracted workers from developed nations as much as immigrants from Haiti and African countries, but their experiences were very different.

In the case of the Haitian immigrants, the argument is that Brazil cannot afford the "charity" of accepting these miserable immigrants. An article in the *Jornal do Brasil* in January of 2012 called attention to the fact that Brazilians should not be accused of racism when they are trying to control immigration; yes, there was racism in the society, but the government could not neglect security. It explicitly mentioned the fact that among immigrants from Nigeria to the country in the past few years, there were drug dealers and other criminals

---

[7] "Veja como vivem e onde moram os estrangeiros no Brasil". *Ultimo Segundo*. Last modified September 21, 2011. https://dialogospoliticos.wordpress.com/2011/09/21/veja-como-vivem-e-onde-moram-os-estrangeiros-no-brasil/

and that among Asian immigrants, there were "notorious smugglers" challenging the Brazilian authorities.[8]

Among Haitian immigrants in 2011, according to Brazilian government records, there were teachers, engineers, lawyers, musicians, athletes, doctors, nurses, carpenters and other professionals. There were also some less qualified professionals, students and young children. As religious institutions, government offices and NGO entities were making efforts to find accommodations to obtain work permits and jobs for qualified immigrants, the public debate revealed xenophobia and racism against the Haitians. Below, I am sharing some opinions expressed in blogs:

> Reader 1
> I'll speak the truth: When despair hits and these Haitians start robbing and killing, [than] we will have measures. If he kills a middle-class white girl who is struggling to pay for college and help at home with the mortgage payment for her own house: NOTHING will happen. Probably some will say the "Haitian" also has sexual desires and needs to let them out. [But], I he kills some TV celebrity, journalist, or daughter of a judge, then they will react and so everyone is deported.
>
> Reader 2
> Who is feeling sorry take a Haitian home. And what about Brazilians dying in the drought in the northeast, without water, without food, without government help, they don't want a family allowance, they want water, because with water they can manage and still produce for Brazil. Give land and conditions for Haitians to plant, but don't send them to São Paulo. Sampa [Sao Paulo] is already overpopulated, there is even a shortage of water. To pay for their ticket and send them away [from the northern state] is easy, because they are close to the borders. (Ribeiro 2014).

Although the entry of foreign workers of various nationalities in Brazil has increased since 2010, a continuous debate revolves around the growing presence of Haitian immigrants and the risks that those workers represent to the society.[9] While employment agencies continue to look for workers in Europe, Canada, the United States and Australia, Black immigrants from Haiti and African

---

[8] "A chegada dos haitianos e o racismo contra os pobres". *Jornal do Brasil*. Rio de Janeiro, January 10, 2012, p. A6. http://www.jb.com.br/coisas-da-politica/noticias/2012/01/10/a-chegada-dos-haitianos-e-o-racismo-contra-os-pobres/

[9] "Situação de imigrantes haitianos no Acre será debatida pelo Senado". *Agência Senado*. Last modified December 16, 2011. https://www12.senado.leg.br/noticias/materias/2011/12/16/situacao-de-refugiados-haitianos-no-acre-sera-debatida-pela-cre

countries, as well as those from neighboring countries like Venezuela, Bolivia and Peru, are seen as a burden on the Brazilian social system and a security risk. (Lenders 2019).

Already in the fifth generation, the saga of the Caribbean people who emigrated to Brazil has not followed the path of their compatriots who went to places like the United States, Canada, or England. They are -middle-class people, proud of their past but still facing the economic limitations that almost a hundred years ago prevented them from going back to their homelands. One can only hope, given the progress that Afro-Brazilians have managed to achieve in the last decades, that Haitian immigrants will meet a better fate in the "racial paradise".

References

Newspaper articles

"A chegada dos haitianos e o racismo contra os pobres". *Jornal do Brasil* (Rio de Janeiro), January 10, 2012, p. A6. http://www.jb.com.br/coisas-da-politica/noticias/2012/01/10/a-chegada-dos-haitianos-e-o-racismo-contra-os-pobres/

"Grupo Escolar", *Alto Madeira* (Porto Velho, Rondonia), August 23, 1925, p. 1-2. Biblioteca Nacional, Brazilian Digital Library, Periódicos.

"O Brasil fecha fronteiras para conter 'invasão de haitianos'", *O Globo* (Rio de Janeiro), January 11, 2012, p. 1, 3 and 4. Biblioteca Nacional, Brazilian Digital Library, Periódicos.

"Veja como vivem e onde moram os estrangeiros no Brasil". *Ultimo Segundo*. Last modified September 21, 2011. https://dialogospoliticos.wordpress.com/2011/09/21/veja-como-vivem-e-onde-moram-os-estrangeiros-no-brasil/

Edson Luiz. "Vistos ilimitados para haitianos". *Correio Brasiliense* (Brasília, DF), April 30, 2013, p.7. Biblioteca Nacional, Brazilian Digital Library, Periódicos.

Braga, Juliana. "Fronteira fechada para os haitianos". *Correio Brasiliense* (Brasília, DF), January 11, 2012, p. 6. Biblioteca Nacional, Brazilian Digital Library, Periódicos.

"Situação de imigrantes haitianos no Acre será debatida pelo Senado". *Agência Senado*. Last modified December 16, 2011. https://www12.senado.leg.br/noticias/materias/2011/12/16/situacao-de-refugiados-haitianos-no-acre-sera-debatida-pela-cre

Academic articles, chapters, books, and reports

Andrews, George. *Afro-Latin America, 1800-2000*. New York: Oxford, 2004.

Beckles, Hilary. *Natural Rebels*. New Brunswick: Rutgers University Press, 1994.

Baraldi, Camila. "Cidadania, migrações e integração regional – notas sobre o Brasil, o Mercosul e a União Européia". 3º Encontro Nacional da ABRI – Governança Global e Novos Atores n. 1 v. 1 (2011). http://educarparaomundo.files.wordpress.com/2011/07/baraldi-abri-2011.pdf.

Bryan, Patrick. *The Jamaican people 1880-1902. Race, Class and Social Control.* Kingston: University of West Indies Press, 2000.

Capelatto, Maria Helena. *O Bravo Matutino: imprensa e ideologia no jornal "O Estado de Sao Paulo".* Sao Paulo: Alfa-Omega, 1980.

Cavalcante, Ygor Rocha. "Uma Permanente e Viva Ameaça. Resistência, Rebeldia e Fugas de Escravos no Amazonas Provincial, 1850-1882". Master's thesis, Universidade Federal de Manaus, 2013.

Craig, Neville. *Recollections of an Ill-fated Expedition to the Headwaters of the Madeira River in Brazil.* Primary Source Edition. Philadelphia & London: Lippincot Co., 1907.

Dean, Warren. *Brazil and the Struggle for Rubber.* New York: Cambridge University Press, 1987.

Fonseca, Dante; Teixeira, Marco Antonio. "Barbadianos: os trabalhadores negros caribenhos da estrada de ferro Madeira Mamoré". In *Afros e Amazônicos: estudos sobre o negro na Amazônia* edited by Marco Teixeira; Dante Fonseca and Geralda Angenot. Porto Velho: Edufro/Rondoniana, 2009: 137-66.

Freyre, Gilberto. *Casa grande e senzala: formação da família brasileira sob o regime da economia patriarcal.* Rio de Janeiro: Record, 20a. ed., 1988.

Geraldo, Endrica. "A Lei de Cotas de 1934: controle de estrangeiros no Brasil", in *Cadernos Arquivo Edgard Leuenroth*, vol.15(27), 2009, p. 173-209.

Gomes, Thiago de Melo. "Problemas no paraíso: a democracia racial frente à imigração Afro-Americana (1921)" *Estudos Afro-Asiáticos*, Ano 25, n. 2, 2003, p. 307-331.

Grandin, Greg. Fordlandia. *The Rise and Fall of Henry Ford's Forgotten Jungle City.* New York: Picador, 2009.

Hoyos, F. A. *The Quiet Revolutionary.* London: Macmillan Caribbean & Carib Publicity Co Ltd, 1984, 3.

Kravigni, Frank. *The Jungle Route.* New York: Orlin Tremaine Co., 1911.

Lenders, Sebastian. "Bolivianos, haitianos e venezuelanos – três casos de imigração no Brasil". Blog. Fundação Heinrich Böll. Rio de Janeiro. Last modified April 14, 2019.

Lima, Maria Roseane C. Pinto. "Ingleses pretos, barbadianos negros, brasileiros morenos? Identidades e memórias (Belém, séculos XX e XXI)". Master's thesis, Universidade Federal do Pará, 2006.

Menezes, Nilza. *Chá das cinco na floresta.* Campinas: Kimedi, 1998.

Neeleman, Rose and Neeleman, Gary. *Trilhos na selva. O dia a dia dos trabalhadores da Ferrovia Madeira-Mamore.* Sao Paulo: BEI Comunicação, 2011.

ONU/IOM- International Organization for Migration. Brazil – IOM Crisis. Regional Response Plan on Large Movements of Highly Vulnerable Migrants in the Americas from the Caribbean, Latin America and other regions. October 2021. https://brazil.iom.int/sites/g/files/tmzbdl1496/files/documents/oim-global-appeal-2021-10-25-v2_0.pdf

Paixão, Marcelo. "O ABC das desigualdades raciais. Um panorama do analfabetismo da população negra através de uma leitura dos indicadores do censo 2000", in *Teoria e Pesquisa* 42/43 (2004):245-264.

Ramos, Jair de Souza. "Dos males que vêm com o sangue: as representações raciais e a rategoria do imigrante indesejável nas concepções sobre imigração da década de 20". In *Raça, Ciência e Sociedade* edited by Marco Mayo and Ricardo Santos. Rio de Janeiro: Fiocruz, 1996: 59-82.

Ribeiro, Bruno. "Expulsão já para os Haitianos, o Brasil deve cuidar apenas dos brasileiros". *Agência Estado/Jornal Flit Paralisante*. Last modified April 24, 2014. https://flitparalisante.wordpress.com/2014/04/24/expulsao-ja-para-os-haitianos-o-brasil-deve-cuidar-apenas-dos-brasileiros/

Ribeiro, Carlos Antonio Costa. *Cor e criminalidade. Estudo e análise da Justiça no Rio de Janeiro (1900-1930)*. Rio de Janeiro: Editora da UFRJ, 1995.

Rodrigues, Danúbio; Arthur Oliveira Filho. "Em tempos de João Candido". In *João Candido, o almirante negro* edited by Marilia Silva. Rio de Janeiro, Fundação Museu da Imagem e do Som/Griphus, 1999: 5-18.

Sales, Vicente. *O negro no Pará sob o regime da escravidão*. Belém, Instituto de Artes do Pará, 2005.

Sampaio, Maria Clara Sales. "Afro-Americanos na Amazônia brasileira: Brasil e Estados Unidos no Projeto de Colonização da Amazônia por escravos e libertos norte-americanos na década de 1860". Anais do XIX Encontro Regional de História: Poder, Violência e ExcluSao. ANPUH/SP: 2008. Cd-Rom.

Sampaio, Sonia M. Gomes. "Uma escola (in)visível: Memórias de professoras negras em Porto Velho no início do século XX". PhD. Dissertation, Universidade Estadual Paulista, Araraquara, 2010.

Silva, Francisco Bento da. "História: degredados, gente sem memória" in *Usos do Passado*, ANPUH/RJ, 2006.

Silva, Vanessa Correa. "À espera de emprego, haitianos sonham em trazer famílias para o Brasil". *UOL Notícias*. Last modified May 1, 2014. http://noticias.uol.com.br/cotidiano/ultimas-noticias/2014/05/01/a-espera-de-emprego-haitianos-sonham-em-trazer-familias-para-o-brasil.htm#comentarios

Skidmore. *Black into white: Race and Nationality in Brazilian Thought*. Durham, Duke University Press, 1974.

Teixeira, Marco Antonio. "Escravidão negra no Guaporé colonial". In *Afros e Amazonicos: estudos sobre o negro na Amazônia* edited by Marco Teixeira; Dante Fonseca and Geralda Angenot. Porto Velho: EDUFRO/ Rondoniana, 2009:43-76.

Vasconcelos, José. *The cosmic race*. Baltimore: John Hopkins University Press, 1997.

Weistein, Barbara. *The Amazon rubber boom 1850-1920*. Redwood City: Stanford University Press, 1983.

CHAPTER NINE

Diasporic Echoes in the Global South: The Italo-Ethiopian War and Brazil

Petrônio Domingues
Universidade Federal de Sergipe, Brazil

Abstract

The Italian invasion of Abyssinia carried out in October 1935, had drastic consequences for European politics in the 1930s and fostered a broad change in public opinion of the African diaspora at a global level, especially in the Atlantic world. The article will seek to address the repercussions that the Ethiopian War had on black Brazilians, especially among activists who participated in organisations in defense of the rights of Afro-Brazilians. Starting from the DEOPS documentation and, mainly, from the analysis of articles published in the regular press and in the so-called black press, the study will focus on the debates held by Afro-Brazilians around the African war, evaluating the positions and actions taken in the light of the dialogues held in the transnational network of the Black Atlantic.

Keywords: Ethiopia, war, diaspora, network, Brazil

***

> We are related—you and I
> You from the West Indies—
> I from Kentucky
> We are related—you and I
> You from Africa
> I from these States
> We are brothers—you and I
> **Langston Hughes**

In the mid-1930s, far-right regimes such as Mussolini's Fascist Italy, Hitler's Nazi Germany and Hirohito's totalitarian government in Japan embarked on escalating expansionism. Among the Fascists, one of the main foreign policy ideas was Italy's right to its "vital space," which meant that Mussolini and his partisans claimed the right to annex territory to foster Italy's economic growth and strengthen its geopolitical position in the world (Paxton 2007). The Fascists' expansionist aims went beyond the sphere of ideas. Starting out from Somalia and Eritrea (Italian colonies in Africa), Mussolini ordered his troops to be at the ready and, without even issuing a declaration of war, invaded Abyssinia on October 3, 1935, under the pretext that that nation's people were a "herd of slaves" clamoring for freedom; a "horde of barbarians" to whom the Italians would bring the benefits of civilization. The reaction in public opinion was immediate. The League of Nations expressed disapproval of Italy's belligerence and even declared sanctions against the Mediterranean country, though they were never imposed.

In late 1935, Abyssinia was at the forefront of the world scene, becoming the planet's main concern. A powerful fascist army armed with modern weaponry and the most advanced military technology of its time, including chemical weapons, was temporarily "detained in the mountains of Abyssinia by the courage of its defenders, who were relatively poorly armed and in militarily inferior numbers. It was a repeat of the story of David fighting Goliath in the greatest colonial war ever fought on African soil" (Akpan 1991, 747). The Abyssinian army was eventually defeated, but the Italians would still have a bloody fight on their hands before occupying the capital, Addis Ababa, and defeating Emperor Haile Selassie's troops. On May 5, 1936, Mussolini officially informed the Italian people of the victory. Two months later, the League of Nations lifted the sanctions against the aggressor state. The war left more than half a million dead among the Abyssinians and sparked unprecedented upheaval among Africans and their descendants.

The aim of this article is to map and discuss how Black people in Africa, Europe and the Americas reacted to Italy's invasion of Abyssinia. It is well-known that they led a wave of protests in several parts of the Black Atlantic (Scott 1993), but what did those protests mean and signify? This paper will focus particularly on Afro-Brazilians, who were not unaware of the connections in the Black transnational network. They, too, expressed identification, support and active solidarity with the African nation.

Ethiopia: Bastion of Africanity

From at least the 1800s until the mid-twentieth century, Abyssinia (or Ethiopia, as it was also known) was an important and symbolic reference to Africa in the process of constructing Black identity in the Atlantic world. Because it was an ancient civilization with a precious cultural heritage and a "glorious" past—the only African country that was not occupied by a major European power during the so-called Partition of Africa—it inspired pride and admiration among many

Blacks in transnational circuits. Ethiopia and its emperors were remembered when they were not constantly celebrated to keep alive the connection between Blacks in the Atlantic and their ancestral continent.

Menelick II, who governed Ethiopia from 1889 to 1913, was one of that country's most outstanding rulers, along with Haile Selassie I, who became emperor in 1928 and adopted the titles of "Kings of Kings" and the "Lord's Anointed", to mention just two of the twelve by which he was known. The heir to a dynasty whose origins historically went back to King Solomon and the Queen of Sheba, Haile Selassie, was clothed in divine aura. His name, incidentally, meant "Power of the Divine Trinity." Already an iconic figure, from that time on he was adored by Blacks from Africa and around the world. Indeed, an anti-colonial religious movement, Rastafarianism, emerged in Jamaica, its followers believing in the divinity of the Emperor (the Lion of Judah), claiming that he was the earthly incarnation of Jah ("Jehovah"). They believed they would return to Africa and saw Ethiopia as the "promised land" for Black nations (Rabelo 2008). Although Rastafarianism never expanded massively on a transnational scale, it was not born in a historical vacuum devoid of sense and meaning. African communities and their descendants in the diaspora traditionally alluded to Ethiopia in pan-Africanist speeches, in the Bible, in Black Christian churches, in parables, prophecies, literature, travelers' accounts, legends, poems, songs and even revelries like a carnival. Therefore, Blacks in the Atlantic world appropriated Ethiopia as a positive symbol, attributing to it ancestral value, and seeing it as a reference to a distant, legendary and mythical, but vibrant, living past that reconnected them to their glorious roots on their ancestral continent. In terms of their imaginary, Ethiopia signified the portentous Motherland of the Africans; the grammar of Africanity for Blacks in the diaspora (Scott 1993).

Furthermore, the actions of Mussolini's Fascist Italy were seen as a flagrant violation of international law and an act of aggression by a white European state against a Black African state. Based on that premise, the Italian invasion took on a racist connotation, typical of a power that spared no effort to perpetuate white supremacy in the world. What had happened in Ethiopia put other parts of Africa at risk and, at worst, posed a threat to the entire Black world. These, briefly, were the reasons why Africans and their descendants in the diaspora were so strongly opposed to Italy's act of aggression.

The Ethiopia Defense Committee (Comité de Défense d'Ethiope) was organized in France, bringing together several groups that were active in the colonial liberation movements. In July 1935, the International African Friends of Abyssinia was established in London, including C. L. R. James and George Padmore, from Trinidad and Tobago; P. McD. Millard, from British Guiana; Amy Ashwood Garvey, Mohammed Said from Somalia; and J. B. Danquah, from the Gold Coast. The aim of that organization was to use all the means at its disposal to help maintain Abyssinia's territorial integrity and political independence (Makalani 2011). The outbreak of hostilities, which put the Italo-Ethiopian War on the front pages of several newspapers around the world, made a profound impression on future African leaders. Kwame Nkrumah, born in Ghana and at the time a student passing through the UK, recalls that he was stunned by posters announcing "Mussolini invaded Abyssinia." Others expressed similar feelings across Africa. The Nigerian intellectual Nnamdi Azikiwe reserved a copious amount of space for the Ethiopian struggle in his newspapers *West African Pilot* and *Comet*. When writing *Renascent Africa*, a book that had a major influence on several generations and was called the "Africans' Bible," he recalls the strong feelings roused in a typical Gold Coast school when the students learned that "black soldiers, aided by the invisible hand of God, were outwitting and overthrowing their enemies" (Akpan 1991, 747). The West African activist press launched several attacks on the Catholic Church's silence on the Italo-Ethiopian controversy, and in South Africa, Zulu volunteers from Durban declared their willingness to enlist in the Ethiopian armed forces and fight in the trenches (Asante 1977).

The outcry in defense of the African nation took on a transnational, Afro-diasporic character. In Canada, several Black people joined the movement and, in a coalition with the Canadian League for Peace, organized activities against Mussolini's fascism. In October 1935, the League and the Italian-Canadian CCF (Co-operative Commonwealth Federation) denounced Italy's aggression against Ethiopia at a major rally held in Queen's Park, Toronto. After listening to speeches from leaders and calling for peace, the demonstrators marched towards the Italian consulate, but the police stopped them and prevented the protest from reaching its target. In Montreal, the largest city in Quebec, the Black community strongly sympathized with the dramatic situation facing the Africans and launched consecutive attacks on Mussolini's fascism through their newspaper, the *Free Lance*. The Italian consul, Giuseppe Brigidi, reported that the *Free Lance* quickly obtained the support of people of varying racial backgrounds and political views. The pro-Ethiopian coalition grew and its protests became more extreme, to the extent that its activists and supporters clashed with fascists in the streets of Toronto. Fearing the impact of this growing movement, the Royal Canadian Mounted Police began closely monitoring Black groups and their activities (Principe 2000, 33).

In the United States, the International Council of Friends of Ethiopia was one of the first organizations to try to channel humanitarian feelings towards Ethiopia. It was founded in Harlem under the leadership of Dr. Willis N. Huggins, a prominent African American educator and director of the Board for Research on African Civilization. Huggins had been interested in Ethiopia and its problems for years when he was put in charge of accompanying the Ethiopian delegation that visited the United States in 1919. On that occasion, Haile Selassie offered him the post of educational advisor. Furthermore, Huggins had met and befriended Ras Desta Demtu, Haile Selassie's son-in-law, who also visited the United States. In August 1935, Huggins went to Geneva as a representative of the International Council of Friends of Ethiopia to ask the League of Nations to take a stand on the East African crisis and ensure that justice was done. The African American educator was reportedly impressed by his reception in Geneva and announced on August 20 in London that he was convinced that the League of Nations would not tolerate a war that endangered world peace (Harris Jr. 1964).

However, many African Americans did not share Huggins's optimism and, driven by increasing expectations of a declaration of war, created American Aid for Ethiopia, established in October 1935. Chaired by Dr. William Jay Schiefflin, this new organization was intended to provide the American people with a channel to express their sympathy and interest in Ethiopia. Its activities included organizing lectures, fundraising and a campaign in the African American press, all calling for the support of the Black masses. In November 1935, the organization sent donations of nearly a ton of medical supplies and a new Ford ambulance to the Ethiopian Red Cross (Ross 1972).

As the conflict on the other side of the Atlantic worsened, the involvement of the African American community intensified and became more radical. Rallies, public events, marches and demonstrations mobilized thousands of people in the streets of Harlem in New York City. Organizations emerged that pointed to the need for Blacks to take up arms to fight for Ethiopia and even considered the possibility of recruiting volunteers for military training. According to the African American press, Malaku Bayen—a nephew of Haile Selassie with a medical degree from Howard University—welcomed this idea and had no doubt that Ethiopia would accept African-American volunteers. It did not take long for groups organized in several parts of the United States to hold rallies aimed at recruiting volunteers to fight for Ethiopia.

The most active organization in this regard was the Pan-African Reconstruction Association (PARA). Headed by Samuel Daniels and based in Harlem, it started its activities in 1934 and declared that its mission was to promote the social and economic uplift of Black people worldwide. When the war broke out in Ethiopia, Daniels sought to use the Pan-African Reconstruction Association to defend the African country and in July 1935 held a plenary session to discuss the recruitment of soldiers. Daniels said that 850 men from New York had responded to the Pan-African Reconstruction Association's call, and that they were ready to ship out to Ethiopia at any time. He also boasted that his organization had branches in 22 US cities, attracting some 30,000 members.

Another group, the Black Legion, reportedly recruited some 3,000 people. After setting up a military training camp in New York State, the Black Legion reportedly trained 500 airmen and two infantry regiments (Kelley 1994; Corbould 2009).

Notified of this "unrest," the US State Department issued an official statement banning its citizens from enlisting in the Ethiopian Army. Nevertheless, some African American volunteers crossed the Atlantic and reached "Mother Africa." Among them were John Robinson and Hubert Julian. A native of Chicago, Robinson, 31, was the first Black man to graduate from the Curtiss Wright Aeronautical University in his hometown. Upon learning of the incident that triggered the Italo-Ethiopian War, he offered his services as an aviator to the government of that African country. Malaku Bayen, Haile Selassie's nephew, contacted the Emperor, who in turn sent a telegram to Robinson, asking him to present himself in Ethiopia, which the African-American aviator did shortly thereafter. Standing out as one of the Emperor's most trusted lieutenants, Robinson was promoted to the rank of colonel in the Ethiopian armed forces. His fellow countryman Hubert Julian, from Harlem, better known as the "Black Eagle", also received the rank of colonel, but when he returned to the United States, Julian was disillusioned. He told reporters that the Italian invasion of Ethiopia was an act of God in response to the cries of the suffering of humanity (Harris 1994).

Due to the ban on enlisting in the Ethiopian armed forces, many African Americans shifted their focus to raising funds and sending medical supplies to Ethiopia. For example, the Abyssinian Baptist Church, in Harlem, raised $305,000 for that African country. The Medical Committee for the Defense of Ethiopia sent a field hospital unit there. Furthermore, the African American press provided daily coverage of the Italo-Ethiopian War, never failing to extoll the African nation's "heroism" while systematically denouncing Italy, Europe and the League of Nations. In its April 11, 1936 issue, the *Chicago Defender* informed its readers that the Ethiopia Peace Movement, which had its "headquarters" in Chicago, brought together 400,000 members of the "race" with "branches strategically established throughout the country."

There are reports of boycotts and physical attacks on Italians living in the United States. In October 1935, it was reported that 1,000 police officers cracked down on a group of African Americans who insulted and violently attacked Italian merchants in Harlem and Brooklyn. This was repeated on other occasions. In May 1936, Blacks in Harlem started a veritable "riot", and the target was once again the Italians in the neighborhood. Racial tensions and strife grew steadily, with Black activists expanding their activities to Boston, Philadelphia, Detroit, Chicago and the state of New Jersey and multiplying inside and outside the United States (Asante 1973; Bekerie 1997).

Indeed, the movement in defense of Ethiopia helped bolster the Black transnational network. In the Caribbean, the war caught the attention of the people of Barbados, Guyana, Jamaica, and Trinidad and Tobago—among other islands that then formed part of the British West Indies and were part of the British Empire. The Afro-Caribbean people expressed their reactions on a large scale, sometimes passionately. A number of public demonstrations supporting Ethiopia were held in Barbados and an extensive grassroots fundraising campaign collected donations to be sent in aid of the African Red Cross.

In Guyana, several organizations got together in October 1935 and decided to ask George V, King of the United Kingdom and the British Dominions, for authorization to take up arms and go to battlefields in honor of Ethiopia. There was such intense concern in Guyana about the war that the government banned the screening of *The Emperor Jones*, a movie starring the African American actor Paul Robeson, which addressed the racial question. It was feared that the film would serve to incite Black people, who did in fact, attack white residents, believing they were Italian.

In Jamaica, several segments of the population, especially the Ras Tafari, who revered Haile Selassie as a living god, and the followers of Marcus Garvey, took to the streets, evoking their fraternal kinship with Ethiopia and denouncing its usurpation by Mussolini's Fascist Italy. At a rally held in Liberty Hall—the headquarters of the Jamaican branch of the Universal Negro Improvement Association—Amy Jacques Garvey called for a counteroffensive based on the spirit of racial solidarity, arguing that her husband, Marcus Garvey, had been right. Mussolini was an instrument of Divine Providence for encouraging Black people to become aware of their position in the world and the need for unity to achieve liberation. A petition signed by about 1,400 people was sent to the governor of that Caribbean Island, requesting permission for Afro-Jamaicans to join the Ethiopian army to fight for the preservation of the "glories" of the "old and beloved Black Empire." The petitioners called themselves "Africans" in the ancestral sense of their existence because they believed, according to the plans of the Garveyite leaders, that one day they would return to Africa to help build their native land. In Kingston, the Jamaican capital, about 2,000 people heeded the call of the social movements and took part in a rally that denounced not only Italy's aggression but the ineffectiveness of the League of Nations.

In Trinidad and Tobago, the response to the Italian invasion was not overshadowed by those of the other Caribbean islands. Plenaries, colloquia, rallies, demonstrations and speeches were held on behalf of Ethiopia. Dock workers decided to boycott Italian ships and refused to unload them. The boycott by Blacks in Trinidad polarized society to such an extent that a large department store was forced to break its contracts with the Italian Line (a cargo and passenger shipping company) to protect its sales and avoid bankruptcy. In

October 1935, a major demonstration took place in Port of Spain, the Trinidadian capital. After listening to several heated speeches, a crowd marched on the Italian consulate, shouting slogans like "Down with Mussolini" and presented a motion of protest to the consul. In early November, thousands attended an event marking the anniversary of Haile Selassie's coronation. Portraits of the emperor and a colored map of Ethiopia were displayed to the crowd. In December, the newspapers reported that "Yoruba" festive celebrations were being held in a town near Port of Spain. To the rhythm of conga drums, songs in "strange" languages and bloody ritual sacrifices of pigeons, goats, sheep and cows, those celebrations were intended to invoke divine protection for Ethiopia (Yelvington 1999).

Clearly, in several parts of the Atlantic world (such as Europe, Africa and the Americas), Black communities were outraged by Italy's attack on Ethiopia and joined in the chorus of protests in favor of maintaining the African nation's independence. And what about Afro-Brazilians—how did they react to the war?

Ethiopia: The "Lion of Judah"

Brazilians of African descent did not fall outside the Black transnational network. They, too, fervently embraced the Ethiopian cause, not least because Ethiopia was already a role model and inspiration in the Afro-Brazilian imaginary (Germano 2010). When Mussolini's Fascist Italy launched its usurping attacks on the African country, Black leader Orlando Ribeiro turned to the press in Rio Janeiro—then the nation's capital and the center of political power—to send out an appeal "to all blacks in Brazil to raise funds to help Ethiopia purchase arms to repel the twentieth-century invaders" (Marques 2008, 171).

In his memoirs, the former Afro-Brazilian leader José Correia Leite recalled that the fascists' belligerent acts on Ethiopian soil had repercussions in the state of Sao Paulo, causing a certain animosity between Blacks and Italians.

> "At the time, the black milieu in Sao Paulo was angry at the Italian colony that was full of themselves because of Mussolini's action of brutishly invading Abyssinia as a show of strength. They specifically chose a country that was not prepared to confront their troops. The Italians here were all full of themselves. And we were aware of that unequal fight. They said that they had gone there to bring civilization. What sort of civilization could they bring to an ancient country? Abyssinia already had traditions and civilization; it did not need to [be civilized]. It was just an excuse for a show of strength for Italian Fascism" (Leite 1992, 135-136).

For many Afro-Brazilians, coming to the defense of that African nation had special meaning. It was a struggle waged in the workplace, in education, housing, leisure, in short, in all aspects of everyday life (Domingues 2011). In some cases, that defense was ardent and passionate, resulting in exchanges of jibes and street fights. On November 21, 1935, the Sao Paulo newspaper *A Platea* published an article with a revealing title: "An Italian and a black man were at each other's throats yesterday." At around 5:00 pm on November 20, the newsroom received a request for a reporter to go at once to Praça do Correio— in the central part of Sao Paulo City—to cover a "pugilistic demonstration that was taking place there." The contenders were a Black man and an Italian fascist, and their "quarrel" arose from a fierce argument about the "armed robbery that Mussolini has just perpetrated in Abyssinia" (*A Platea*. Sao Paulo, November 21, 1935).

In Sao Paulo, sectors of the Black community would not only take a stand against those events but, according to João Fábio Bertonha, allied themselves with the anti-fascist Italians in that city, taking part in meetings and joint activities. There were even reports that Italians had attempted to enlist Afro-Paulistas to fight the fascists in their war (Bertonha 1999). Indeed, documents reveal that anti-fascist Italians and Blacks took part in public protests shoulder-to-shoulder. "Italians and black Brazilians, men of all races," reported the newspaper *A Platea*, "will attend the monster rally on Sunday in support of the international outcry against the Fascist looting of Abyssinia. The people of Sao Paulo will unleash their vehement and vigorous protest against the most unjust, savage, cowardly and brutish of predatory wars" (*A Platea*. Sao Paulo, October 11, 1935).

The Federação dos Negros do Brasil (Federation of Blacks of Brazil), an organization that fought for Afro-Brazilian rights, was also part of the network of solidarity with the "Lion of Judah." One of its initiatives was to set up the "Black Committee," whose mission was to strive "for unity and for the awakening of the black race" on behalf of Ethiopia. On November 4, 1935, *A Platea* published an invitation from that group: "The 'Black Committee' for the defense of Ethiopia [sic] invites all blacks in Sao Paulo to attend the meeting to be held today, Monday, at 8 pm on Rua Benjamin Constant, no. 5, to discuss the possibility of holding a large public demonstration on the 11th in a place to be announced." The meeting had an anti-fascist tone and, after numerous vehement speeches, slogans and questions about aims, they decided to hold a rally on November 11th. However, the "public demonstration" by Blacks was cancelled at the last minute. Entitled the "Federation of Blacks of Brazil," the announcement was published in *A Platea:* "we hereby communicate:—from the secretary of that entity, that for unforeseen reasons arising at the last minute, the anti-Fascist rally scheduled for today, at 8 pm, in Largo da Pólvora, has been rescheduled for the 15th [of this month] at a place and time to be announced."

In the run-up to the new rally, the Federation of Blacks of Brazil invested in advertising, calling on its members and other civil society organizations to participate in the event, and phampleting on November 12 in downtown Sao Paulo, when a manifesto was distributed. "Blacks of Brazil! Intellectuals, workers, young people and women!" The document began, "The time has come when no longer can blacks fail to participate in the struggle that is taking place all over the world for the liberation of the suffering and oppressed races, and that blacks undoubtedly constitute the majority of these oppressed people, who live as outcasts." After applauding blacks of the most varied backgrounds ("intellectuals, workers, young people and women") using diasporic rhetoric, the manifesto touched on a timely subject: "No one is unaware of the horrors of the war of extermination and plunder that Mussoline [sic] is waging against the last black empire in the world—Abyssinia, for the benefit of a very small group of industrialists which, to fulfill their ambitions, is putting the workers of Italy in the chains of the cruelest of dictatorships." After denouncing the imperialist nature of Italy's attacks on the African country, the document indicated the importance of black people turning to an organization that protected and defended their ideals: "It is high time for blacks to understand the urgent need for a powerful federation of their race to achieve their legitimate aspirations in a more dignified manner, free of the tutelage of those who are directly responsible for the difficult situation in which they now find themselves, they who built the economic foundations of this formidable geographic quadrant of South America, Brazil." In fact, the agency for the protection and defense of the "race" was already being organized and was called the Federation of Blacks of Brazil. With a narrative aimed directly at "people of color," the manifesto declared:

> "(…) the Federation of Blacks in Brazil is the expression of your suffering, it is the interpreter of your pain; it will not agree with the organizations that enlist blacks to sell them in the elections! It will be the outrider who will keep watch on all false leaders who seek to deceive the descendants of this suffering race and will show blacks the path to their true liberation."

The Federation of Blacks of Brazil would not only stop the "descendants of this suffering race" from being manipulated by demagogic leaders and opportunistic organizations but would enlighten them, guide them, lead them on the "path to their true liberation." To this end, Blacks should join, among other things, the anti-fascist campaign in support of Abyssinia:

> "In public rallies that the Federation will sponsor, through the words of their speakers, blacks from Sao Paulo must demonstrate their fervent rejection of Fascism and war, showing their spirit of solidarity with their

brothers of other races, who at this moment are protesting against the criminal assault on defenseless Abyssinia."

Finally, the manifesto called on the "Blacks of Brazil!" and extended this invitation:

"The Federation of Blacks of Brazil (a nationalist movement of the black race) invites you to take to the streets in the next rally once again to affirm your spirit that cannot and should not be subjected to the clutches of the Fascism that massacres women and children in its assault on the black people's homeland."

Aside from Afro-Brazilian activists and groupings, the newspapers of the so-called Black press were also an important tool for mobilizing people to join the Ethiopian cause. We should note that "Black press" *(imprensa negra)* is the expression used in Brazil to designate newspapers produced and maintained by Afro-Brazilians and aimed at addressing their social, economic, political and cultural concerns. According to anthropologist Roger Bastide, *O Menelick* was the first of these publications. Founded in the city of Sao Paulo in 1915, it was named after Menelick II, the legendary king who ruled Ethiopia until 1913 (Bastide 1983). Most of the Black press newspapers were concentrated in Sao Paulo State, but until the 1960s, there were counterparts active in other states, such as Rio de Janeiro, Minas Gerais, Bahia, Paraná, Santa Catarina and Rio Grande do Sul (Ferrara 1986; Domingues 2008). During the Italo-Ethiopian War, four Black press newspapers were circulating in Brazil *(A Voz da Raça, O Clarim* and *A Tribuna Negra,* published in Sao Paulo; *A Alvorada,* in Rio Grande do Sul, and *Raça,* in Minas Gerais), and all of them mentioned the conflict in East Africa in articles and editorials.

In Rio Grande do Sul, the newspaper *A Alvorada,* based in the city of Pelotas, followed the course of the war, encouraging Blacks to fly the Ethiopia flag. The journalists and activists responsible for *A Alvorada* wrote a series of "heated articles"—more than twenty published between June and December 1935—usually on the first page with large-print headlines condemning the imperialist aims of Italian fascism in Abyssinia and intent on keeping the local Black community informed about the situation in East Africa (Marques 2008).

In Sao Paulo State, the newspaper *Tribuna Negra* proclaimed in an editorial that "the great liberating general of the black Haitian people" should be "invoked today when the black masses throughout the world are stirring and extending their eyes avid for freedom and rebellion to ancient Ethiopia *(Tribuna Negra.* Sao Paulo, September 1935, p. 3). In *A Voz da Raça* — the news outlet for the the Frente Negra Brasileira (Black Brazilian Front), considered the most important organization for the defense of Afro-Brazilian rights in the 1930s (Butler 1998; Andrews 2007) — Silvério de Lima wrote an article in which he sounded this warning: "The conquest of Ethiopia by ostentatious and violent means is not only truly iniquitous but directly attacks the pride of a race" *(A Voz da Raça.* Sao Paulo, November 23, 1935, p. 4). In another issue of *A Voz da Raça,* Silvério de Lima pointed out that Ethiopia was the "last bulwark that ensures the independence of the ancient race that in the long curve of its existence tore its own veins to maintain and nourish, with its red-hot liquid, races, civilizations and heritage" that spread over a good part of the planet *(A Voz da Raça.* Sao Paulo, July 1936, p. 4).

The newspaper *O Clarim,* also from Sao Paulo, published an editorial whose suggestive title, "The Case of Abyssinia and the Black World," linked a local issue in Africa to its global, Afro-diasporic implications. According to *O Clarim,* "Abyssinia, the last Black Empire, thanks to Mr. Mussolini, the modern-day Roman Caesar" would feature "on the list of the issues that disturb the world." The call to arms did not just excite the enthusiasm of fascist youth in Italy. According to *O Clarim,* the Black man was also rising up with his "world of thoughts" based on struggles against all sorts of "segregations." And it was this "black world" that, at that very moment, was in the "vanguard" in the defense of the race *(O Clarim,* Sao Paulo, March 1935, p. 1). It seems that *O Clarim* was right: at that moment, the "black world" was rising in a growing racial mobilization.

Regarding the Black press, an article by José Correia Leite published in the newspaper *A Raça* in the state of Minas Gerais perhaps best summarized the Afro-Brazilians' view of the Italo-Ethiopian War. Given the importance of that article, I will quote it almost in full:

> No black man who at this moment has a speck of recognition for his situation, his origins or his self-esteem, can in any way, under any pretext, remain indifferent in the face of this disturbing and decisive hour for his race, from the universal standpoint. The provocation that is being thrown in the face...of the black man...must be taken as an incentive to join the fight. There are, it is true, blacks who have the gall to deny, at this time, their own blood. Blacks who, at times of clear and concrete decisions, embarrass themselves, ashamed of their origins. They will always deserve our pity, because for them, the shadow of the slave quarters is still a dreadful sight. Definitely, black people around the world are challenged to march to win or die. That is quite true. There can be no compromise. If, at this moment, the last Black Empire should fall, exhausted under the weight of this clamorous attack on the freedom of a nation..., with it will inevitably fall the forty-some million blacks spread in the various hemispheres of the Americas. It is a matter of pride and self-esteem, in addition to a duty of honor towards our ancestors *(A Raça.* Uberlandia, December 21, 1935, p. 2).

For José Correia Leite, this was a decisive moment for the future of the Black race from the "universal standpoint." Without hesitation, Afro-Brazilians should take pride in their origins, their "dignity" and their "ancestors" and react vigorously against Fascist Italy's onslaughts on the last Black Empire. It was a question of "blood" and "honor," and there was, therefore, no alternative but to fight—marching "to win or die." In Correia Leite's opinion, Ethiopia was not just the last free and sovereign civilization in Africa, it symbolized the Motherland, the nuclear matrix of an entire race that nourished a redemptive utopia. If Ethiopia should fall due to that "clamorous attack," the aspirations for freedom, the dreams and hopes for freedom of millions of Blacks scattered throughout the "various hemispheres of the Americas" would fall with it.

Conclusion

Despite all the limitations they faced, the political pressure movements, racial mobilizations and rhetorical identities of Blacks in Africa and the African Diaspora played an important role in several respects during the Italo-Ethiopian crisis. Suffice it to say that their legacy was the formation of several Pan-Africanist groups, entities and associations in Europe, the Americas and Africa that helped build up the experience of a transatlantic Black consciousness.

The crisis in Ethiopia encouraged many Black people in several parts of the world to turn their eyes toward Africans, which aroused a feeling of identification with their ancestral "brothers" while bolstering the sense of belonging to a transnational, Afro-diasporic "imagined community". Instead of focusing exclusively on their own problems, people of African descent broadened their world views and fields of action, assimilating into their lives a concern for the fate of Blacks around the world.

Although Black communities' interest in Africa took many forms until the decolonization process began on that continent in the 1960s, the Italo-Ethiopian War was a milestone in the emergence of a Pan-African consciousness. Because many of the cultural ties between Blacks in the diaspora and their continent of origin had been severed or reworked due to transatlantic slavery, and due to the negative stereotypes of Africa perpetuated in the West, some Afro-descendants resisted any kind of identification with the African continent. However, the Italo-Ethiopian War changed the concept of Africa for many Black people. When they learned about the war and Ethiopia and its history and cultural heritage, Blacks in the diaspora realized that the image of Africa propagated in the West was a distortion. The land of half-naked, barbaric people and wild animals they were accustomed to seeing in movies and reading about in literary and mass media publications largely proved to be an invention of Hollywood and the Western ethnocentric imaginary.

Afro-descendant communities were also moved by the resilience of their African "brothers." Although they had occupied Ethiopia, the Italian troops never managed to conquer the people of that African nation. This not only filled the Blacks of the Diaspora with pride but impelled many of them to take up the Ethiopian cause and close ranks in Pan-African movements committed to publicizing the "deeds" and "achievements" of that ancient civilization. By taking that stand, Black people planted the seed of a new consciousness about Africa and, ultimately, themselves. After all, by viewing Ethiopia with enthusiasm and spreading the narrative of revaluing Africa's historical and cultural legacy, they helped forge the image of both the continent and their own positive racial ancestry (Harris 1994; Meriwether 2002).

Finally, it is important to say that Afro-Brazilians sought to combine a number of efforts in the movement for the freedom of Ethiopia. This stance was partly justified by the fact that the "homeland of the Blacks" was portrayed with a mystique of resistance, courage and heroism. From the standpoint of many Afro-Brazilians, it was a matter of honor and dignity to fight for the sovereignty of the last African nation that was free from European colonial rule. In addition to ancestral kinship, Ethiopia was a catalyst for the hopes, dreams and expectations of freedom, emancipation and self-determination of Blacks from all over the Atlantic world. From this perspective, the agency of Afro-Brazilian activists took on a proactive and Afro-diasporic racial sense, intertwining with the network of Black transnationalism.

References

Primary source

"Manifesto da Federação ds Negros do Brasil". (São Paulo, November 12, 1935). Arquivo Público do Estado de São Paulo - Fundo DEOPS.

Articles in newspapers

"Comite Negro". *A Platea* (Sao Paulo), November 04, 1935.
"Federação dos Negros do Brasil". *A Platea* (Sao Paulo), November 11, 1935.
"League of the Nations". *Chicago Defender*, April 11, 1936.
"Um Italiano e um negro iam se engalfinhando ontem". *A Platea* (Sao Paulo), November 21, 1935.

Academic articles, chapters, and books"

Akpan, Monday B. "A Etiópia e a Libéria, 1914-1935: dois Estados africanos independentes na era colonial." In *História Geral da África*. vol. 7, edited by A. Boahen, 717-749. Sao Paulo: Ática: Unesco, 1991.

Andrews, George Reid. *América Afro-Latina (1800-2000)*. Sao Carlos, SP: EdUSCar, 2007.
Asante, S. K. B. "The Afro-American and the Italo-Ethiopian crisis, 1934-1936." *Race & Class* 15, no. 2 (1973): 167-184.
_____. *Pan-African Protest: West Africa and the Italo-Ethiopian Crisis, 1934-1941*. London: Longman, 1977.
Bastide, Roger. "A imprensa negra do estado de Sao Paulo." In *Estudos afro-brasileiros*, edited by Roger Bastide, 129-156. Sao Paulo: Ed. Perspectiva, 1983.
Bekerie, Ayele. "African Americans and the Italo-Ethiopian War." In *Revisioning Italy: National Identity and Global Culture*, edited by Beverly Allen and Mary Russo, 116-133. Minneapolis: University of Minnesota Press, 1997.
Bertonha, João Fábio. *Sob a sombra de Mussolini: os italianos de Sao Paulo e a luta contra o fascismo, 1919-1945*. Sao Paulo: Annablume, 1999.
Butler, Kim D. *Freedoms Given, Freedoms Won: Afro-Brazilians in Post-Abolition Sao Paulo and Salvador.* New Brunswick, NJ: Rutgers University Press, 1998.
Corbould, Clare. "Ethiopia Ahoy!" In *Becoming African Americans: Black Public Life in Harlem, 1919-1939*, edited by Clare Corbould, 196-213. Cambridge, MA: Harvard University Press, 2009.
Domingues, Petrônio. *A nova abolição*. Sao Paulo: Selo Negro, 2008.
_____. "'O caminho da verdadeira emancipação': a Federação dos Negros do Brasil." In *Experiências da emancipação: biografias, instituições e movimentos sociais no pós-abolição (1890-1980)*, edited by Petrônio Domingues and Flávio Gomes, 157-184. Sao Paulo: Selo Negro, 2011.
Ferrara, Miriam Nicolau. *A imprensa negra paulista (1915—1963)*. Sao Paulo: FFLCH/USP, 1986.
Germano, Iris Graciela. "Movimento: Etiópia, resistência cultural e afirmação étnica na pós-emancipação." *Reflexão e Ação* 18, no. 1 (2010): 30-45.
Harris, Joseph E. *African-American Reactions to War in Ethiopia, 1936-1941*. Baton Rouge: Louisiana State University Press, 1994.
Harris, Jr., Brice. *The United States and the Italo-Ethiopian Crisis*. Stanford: Stanford University Press, 1964.
Kelley, Robin D. G. *Race Rebels: Culture, Politics, and the Black Working Class*. New York: Free Press, 1994.
Leite, José Correia. *E disse o velho militante José Correia Leite: depoimentos e artigos. Organizado por Cuti*. Sao Paulo: Secretaria Municipal da Cultura, 1992.
Makalani, Minkah. *In the Cause of Freedom: Radical Black Internationalism from Harlem to London, 1917-1939*. Chapel Hill: University of North Carolina Press, 2011.
Marques, Alexandre Kohlrausch. "'A questão ítalo-abissínia': os significados atribuídos à invaSao italiana à Etiópia, em 1935, pela intelectualidade gaúcha." Porto Alegre, 2008. Thesis (MA). Instituto de Filosofia e Ciências Humanas, Universidade Federal do Rio Grande do Sul.
Meriwether, Jamer Hunter. *Proudly We Can Be Africans: Black Americans and Africa, 1935-1961*. Chapel Hill: University of North Carolina Press, 2002.
Paxton, Robert. *A anatomia do fascismo*. Sao Paulo: Paz e Terra, 2007.

Principe, Angelo. "A Tangled Knot: Prelude to 10 June 1940." In *Enemies Within: Italians and other Internees in Canada and Abroad*, edited by Franca Iacovetta, Roberto Perin, Angelo Principe, 27-51. Toronto: University of Toronto Press, 2000.

Rabelo, Danilo. "Em busca da terra prometida: a Etiópia no imaginário rastafari jamaicano". In *Migrações e fronteiras no Mundo Atlântico*, edited by Olga Cabrera, 217-248. Goiânia: CECAB, 2008.

Ross, Red. "Black Americans and Italo-Ethiopian Relief, 1935-1936." *Ethiopia Observer* 15, no. 2 (1972): 122-131.

Scott, William R. *The Sons of Sheba's Race: African-Americans and the Italo-Ethiopian War, 1935-1941*. Bloomington and Indianapolis: Indiana University Press, 1993.

Yelvington, Kevin A. The War in Ethiopia and Trinidad 1935-1936. In *The Colonial Caribbean in Transition: Essays on Postemancipation Social and Cultural History*, edited by Kevin A. Yelvington and Bridget Brereton, 189-225. Kingston: University of the West Indies Press, 1999.

———. "Dislocando la diáspora: la reacción al conflito Italo-Etíope en el Caribe, 1935-1941." *Estudios Migratorios Latinoamericanos* 52 (2003): 555-570.

Contributors

Elaine Pereira Rocha. Brazilian. Associate Professor (Senior Lecturer) UWI-Cave Hill Campus, since 2007. Historian, with a Master's in history (PUC-SP); PhD in Social History (USP); and a MPhil in Cultural History from the University of Pretoria.

Areas of Interest: Brazilian Black History, Black migrations, Brazil twentieth century, Indigenous History of Brazil, Women's History. Latest books: Rocha, Elaine. (ed.). O Início do Feminismo no Brasil. Subsídios para a História. Leolinda Daltro (2022); Canal de Desvio. Um Estudo da Experiência de agricultores e índios no conflito com a Itaipu Binacional (2021); Ideias fora do lugar. Representações e Experiências de Raça e Gênero (editor, 2021); Mosaico. Construção de Identidades na Diáspora Africana (co-editor 2020); Milton Gonçalves. Memórias Históricas de um ator Afro-Brasileiro (2019). She is also the author of 22 academic articles and more than 20 chapters in books.

Carlos Eduardo Coutinho da Costa is an Adjunct Professor at Universidade Federal Rural do Rio de Janeiro. Has a PhD in History from Universidade Federal do Rio de Janeiro, with thesis about Black migration in Rio de Janeiro state in the post-abolition period. His book on the theme: *"Faltam braços nos campos e sobram pernas na cidade": Famílias, Migrações e Sociabilidades Negras no Pós-Aboliçãodo Rio de Janeiro (1888-1940)*, was published in 2020. He is also the author of academic articles, including: "Raízes Negras Dispersas?: Assenhoreamento no Pós-Abolição do Antigo Município de Iguassú (1888-1940)"(2018); "O registro civil como fonte histórica: contribuições e desafios dos registros civis nos estudos do pós-abolição" (2016); and Migrações Negras no Pós-Abolição do Sudeste Cafeeiro (2015).

João-Manuel Neves is a Research Fellow in the Center for Comparative Studies, University of Lisbon. A Research Associate in the CREPAL, University Sorbonne Nouvelle - Paris 3. Neves holds a Ph.D. in Études du Monde Lusophone, University Sorbonne Paris Cité. Dissertation on colonial literature from the 1920s related to Mozambique (2016); and a M.A. at the University Sorbonne Paris 4. Master's thesis on the literary work of Luís Bernardo Honwana.

Katia Cilene do Couto is a Professor of History at the Universidade Federal do Amazonas, Brazil. She holds a Master's the Federal University of Goias and a PhD in History Graduated in History from the University of Brasília (2006). She has worked mainly on the following topics: migration, memory, identity, work and social movements. Dr. Couto is the author of *Imigração haitiana no Brasil*.

(São Paulo: Paco Editorial, 2016. v. 1. 682p), and of various articles and chapters on the topic of Black migrations.

Karl Monsma is a well known researcher on the field of slavery in Brazil. Professor at the Departament de Sociology, Universidade Federal do Rio Grande do Sul, Brazil. Titular Professor of Sociology at the Federal University of Rio Grande do Sul. Holds a Master's in Sociology - University of Michiga and PhD in Sociology - University of Michigan. He did postdoctoral studies in Sociology at USP (1996) in Social Anthropology at the Museu Nacional/UFRJ (2004) and in Sociology at the Hamburger Institut für Sozialforschung, Germany (2017-2018). He has been Professor of Sociology at Northwestern University, USA (1992-1997), Adjunct Professor of Sociology at the Federal University of São Carlos (1997-2005) and Full Professor of History and Sociology at the University of Vale do Rio dos Sinos (Unisinos) (2005-2010). He was also a visiting professor at USP, UFRGS, UFPel, Universidad Nacional del Centro de la Provincia de Buenos Aires and the Public University of Cape Verde. He has experience in the areas of historical sociology, social theory and research methods, especially quantitative methods and historical methods, addressing mainly the following topics: immigration, racism and ethnic identities. Author of the book: A reprodução do racismo: Fazendeiros, Negros e Imigrantes no Oeste Paulista, 1880-1914, São Paulo, EDUFSCAR, 2021 and of more than 30 academic articles.

Lucia Helena de Oliveira has a Master's in History of Education and a PhD in History, both from the State University of Campinas. She was a fellow researcher at New York University. She is a full professor at the Universidade Estadual Paulista - Assis campus, where she coordinates the Black Research and Extension Center at Unesp. She is a member of the CITCEM Center for Transdisciplinary Research «Culture, Space and Memory» of the University of Porto. She is the author of various books, including *Colonialismo e Cristianidade em espaços missionários em Uganda e Angola séculos XIX e XX."* (São Paulo: FFLCH/USP, 2022); and *Paulistas afrodescendentes no Rio de Janeiro pós-Abolição (1888- 1926);* (São Paulo: Humanitas, 2016). She is also the author of about 50 articles book chapters.

Marco A. Schaumloeffel holds a Master's degree in Linguistics from the Universidade Federal do Paraná, and a PhD in Linguistics from the University of the West Indies, where he studied the creole languages of the Caribbean. He is an Associate Lecturer at the University of British Columbia. Previously, he was lecturer for Portuguese and German at the Barbados Community College (2021-2022), Lecturer of Brazilian Studies at the University of the West Indies in Barbados from 2005 to 2021, and he worked at the University of Ghana, teaching Portuguese and Brazilian Culture (2003-2005). He is the author of the book *Tabom - The Afro-*

Brazilian Community of Ghana (also published in Brazil) about the history of the Afro-Brazilians who returned to Africa after abolition. In addition, he published several articles and chapters of books dealing with Linguistics, Creole languages, especially about Papiamentu and Papiá Kristang, German dialectology in Brazil, Hunsrückisch, teaching foreign languages and Afro-Brazilians returned to West Africa.

Nielson Rosa Bezerra: Holds a PhD in History from the Fluminense Federal University (UFF). He is the first Brazilian to be awarded the prestigious Banting Fellowship Program, obtained from the Canadian Social Sciences and Humanities Research Council (SSCHRC). He is currently an adjunct professor at the State University of Rio de Janeiro (Uerj); director of the São Bento Vivo Museum, in Duque de Caxias – RJ; coordinator of the History course at the Faculty of Belford Roxo (RJ); coordinator of the Research Group A Cor de Baixada. He was a postdoctoral fellow at York University, Canada. Bezerra is the author and organizer of several titles, including: *The keys to freedom: confluences of slavery in the Reconcavo do Rio de Janeiro*, 1833-1888 (EdUFF, 2008); *Another Black Like Me: The Construction of Identities and Solidarity in the African Diaspora* (Cambridge Publish Schollars, 2015), the latter in partnership with Elaine Pereira Rocha.

Patrícia Bosenbecker holds a Masters in History and a PhD in Sociology from the Univesidade Feeral do Rio Grande do Sul. Programa de Pós-Graduação em Sociologia, Universidade Federal de São Carlos, Brazil. Among her publications, the book *Uma colônia cercada de estâncias: a inserção de imigrantes alemães na colônia São Lourenço/RS (1857- 1877)*. Published in 2020 is about German immigrants in Brazil, and more than 25 academic articles and chapters in books, on the topic of migrations in Brazil. In this book, she writes in collaboration with professor Monsma.

Petronio Domingues holds a Master and PhD in History from the University of São Paulo (USP). He is a professor at the Federal University of Sergipe (UFS) and guest researcher at Rutgers State University of New Jersey (USA). He develops research on African Diaspora populations in Brazil and the Americas, post-emancipation, social movements, identities, biographies, multiculturalism and racial diversity. Among his published works, He is the co-editor of *Da escravidão e da liberdade: processos, biografias e experiências da abolição em perspectiva transnacional* (2016); *Políticas da raça: experiências e legados da abolição e da pós-emancipação no Brasil* (2014); *Da nitidez e invisibilidade: legados do pós-emancipação no Brasil* (2013). He is also author of five books, twenty-eight collections chapters and more than eighty articles published in academic journals, not to mention the various reviews and articles published in the daily press. His latest book is *Protagonismo negro em São Paulo: História e historiografia* (Sao Paulo, SESC, 2019).

Index

A

ABC Islands – xxx, 105, 110, 115
Abyssinian Baptist Church – 160
Africa – xix, xx, xxiii, xxiv-xxxv, xxvii, xxviii, xxix, xxxi, xxxii, 3, 4, 5, 7, 9, 11, 12, 13, 16, 18, 29, 30, 31, 38, 39-40, 43, 49, 50, 52, 52, 54-55, 56, 66, 67, 68, 93, 95, 98, 107, 109, 110, 134, 145, 156-158, 161, 162, 165, 166-168; 'Mother Africa' – 160;
African Slaves – xxix, 5, 6, 9, 11, 12, 14, 17, 49, 53, 58, 67, 69, 135
Africanity – 156, 157
Afro-Brazilians – xxviii, xxix, xxxi, 96, 97, 100, 109, 135, 137, 146, 151, 155, 156, 162, 163, 165, 166, 167, 168
Afro-Caribbean migration – xxviii
Alencastro, Luis Felipe – 50, 52, 53, 66
Alto Madeira – 143
Alvarez Estévez, Rolando – 126
Amazonas – 136, 138, 139, 140, 147, 148
Amerindians – 8, 16, 106
Amsterdam – 10, 11, 108, 109
Anderson, Perry – xxv, 13
Andrews, George – 92, 137, 140
Angola – xxix, 18, 43, 49, 50, 51, 52, 54, 55, 57, 66, 68, 69, 107, 110
Antillanos – xxxi, 121
Argentina – xxix, 23, 24, 25-26, 32, 35, 36, 41, 43, 44
Arredondo, Alberto – 127
Aruba – 105, 109-110, 111 -116

asiento rights – 115

B

Baianos – 95-96
Baixada Fluminense – 77, 79, 80, 81-82, 83-84, 85, 86, 87
Barbadian Hill – 145
Barbados – 12, 124, 139, 140-142, 144, 161, 172
Belem – xxxi, 133, 139, 140, 141, 142, 145
Benguela – 13, 43, 49, 50, 53, 54, 55-57, 64, 67, 69
birth registration – 83
Black Atlantic – xxvii, xxxi, 155, 156
Black Committee – 163
Black Migration – xix, xxi, xxiv, xxv, xxvi, xxvii, xxviii, xxx, xxxii, 73, 75, 93, 105, 108
Bonaire – xxx, 105, 109, 112, 113, 114, 115, 124
Booth Steamship Company – 140
Brazilian American Colonization Syndicate – 136
Brotherhood of Our Lady of the Rosary (Confraria de Nossa Senhora do Rosário) – 59, 60

C

cachaça – 45, 50, 51, 54, 56, 58, 59, 62, 67, 68
Caiquetíos – 106
Calabar – 64, 65, 66
Cape Verde – 6, 13, 96, 107, 109
Capoeiras – 99

Caribbean – xix, xxiii, xxiv, xxv, xxvi, xxvii, xxviii, xxx, xxxi, 6, 11, 12, 15, 106-07, 108, 110, 111, 112, 114-115, 124, 134, 139, 141-142, 143-144, 148, 151, 161
Carpata, Bastiaan – 109
Casa de Detenção – xxx, 91, 93
cassava flour – 49, 50-53, 55, 56-57, 58, 59, 60, 61-62, 64, 66-69
Catholic Church – 8, 57, 58, 158
cattle ranches – 42
civil registry – 84
Codigo Penal/Criminal Code – 99, 101
Colombia – xxi, xxii, xxxiii, 11, 113, 114
Congress of 1914 (Cuban) – 125, 126, 129 Congress of labor, 1925 – 128, 130
Congress, National of Brazil – 136
Cosmic Race – 135
cowboys – xxix, 24-25, 27, 29-30, 40, 42-43, 44, 45; black – 23; enslaved – 24, 25, 30, 31, 35, 39, 42, 43, 44, 45, 46
Criminal Code 96
Cuba – xxi, xxviii, xxxi, 74, 111, 121, 122, 123, 124, 126, 128-131
Curaçao – xxx, 11, 105-115

D

Demographics – xxviii, 113; Aruba Demographics –113
diaspora – xx, xxi, xxiii, xxiv, xxv, xxvi, xxvii, xxviii, xxix, xxxi, 49, 54, 67, 155, 157, 167, 168
Disney – 135
domestic workers – 13, 112, 115, 137
Dominican Republic – 111, 114
Dutch Brazil – 11, 108

Dutch conquest – 106
Dutch West India Company, DWIC – 11, 108

E

Eastern Caribbean – 112
economic impact – 111
emancipation – xxii, xxiii, 74, 75, 97, 110, 111, 115, 168
employment – xviii, 26, 27, 29, 39, 44, 78, 112, 113, 140, 141, 146, 149, 150
enslaved Africans – xx, xxx, 6, 7, 23, 49, 56, 61, 105, 107, 108, 109, 110; see also – slaves
entrepôts – xxx, 13, 105, 108
Ethiopia – xxviii, xxx, 156-157, 158-159, 160- 162, 163, 165-166, 167-168; International Council of Friends of Ethiopia – 158, 159; Ethiopia Defense Committee – 157; Medical Committee for the Defense of Ethiopia – 160
Exodus – 111

F

family reunification – 111
Farquhar, Percival – 141
Farroupilha War – 34, 35, 37, 39, 46
favelas – 73, 76, 101
Federacion Obrera – 130
Federation of Blacks in Brazil – 164
forced Black migration – 108
Fordlandia – 143, 144, 145
free migration – 105, 110, 111, 115
free movement of people – 106
Freyre, Gilberto – 135, 136
fugitive slaves – 23, 26, 33, 36, 41, 45, 46

G

Garcia Moreira, Francisco – 126
Garvey, Amy Ashwood – 157
Garvey, Marcus – 131, 161
Ghana – 107, 110, 158
Gilroy, Paul – xxvii
Goebel, Michael – xxiv, xxv
Gorée – 107
Grandin, Greg – 144
Great Migration – xxv, xxx, 73, 74, 75, 80, 92
Guiana, British – xx, xxvi, 139, 141, 158
Guyana – 114, 161

H

Haiti – xxi, xxii, 17, 122, 123, 128, 130, 147, 148, 149, 150, 151; earthquake in – xxxi, 133, 147
Haitian immigrants – xxii, xxxiii, xxxi, 121, 133, 148, 149, 150, 151
Haitian Revolution – xxiii, xxiv, 17, 122
Hidalgo Co. Ltd. – 139
Hispaniola – xxii, 106
Hobsbawn, Eric – xxxi
households – 78, 99, 111,

I

internal migration – 85, 92, 93, 112
interviews – 100, 102, 103, 105, 106, 107, 130
intra-regional migration – 111
Italo-Ethiopian War – xxxi, 155, 158, 167

J

jail house – xxx, 93, 94, 99, 100; see also Casa de Detenção, Rio de Janeiro
Jamaica – 122, 129, 140
jerked beef (*charqueada*): industry – 27, 37; plants – 28, 33, 37, 39, 45; workers – 27, 30, 31, 39
Jews – 10, converted – 9, 108, 109, 144

K

Karasch, Mary – 54

L

Labour – 4, 6, 8, 9, 10, 15, 18, 55, 101, 111, 121, 136, 138, 139, 146
Land Law of 1850 (Brazil) – 24, 134
Law of Immigration (Cuba) – 129
Light and Power Ltd – 139
Lucas, Natasha – xxii

M

Madeira-Mamore railroad –138, 140, 141; Madeira-Mamore Railroad Co – 139
Manning, Patrick – xx, xxv
Manumission – 10, 35, 60, 68, 77
Menelick II – 157, 165; *O Menelick* – 165
Menezes, Nilza – 141, 142, 145, 146
Mexico – xx, xxii, xxiv, 6, 135
migrant women – 81
Migrants – xxii, xxv, xxvi, xxx, xxxii, 73, 74-75, 76, 79-81, 84, 85, 86, 87, 91, 93, 94, 95, 96-97, 98, 100, 111, 114, 133, 141, 144

Movimiento de los Independientes de color – 122
Mussolini, Benito – 156, 158, 161, 163

N

Netherlands (Dutch) Antilles – 112, 113, 114
New Amsterdam – 11, 108,
New York: city – xxv, xxvi, 140, 159, New York state – 160; New Amsterdam – 108
Ngai, Mae – xxv
Nina Rodrigues, Raymundo – 94
Nova Iguaçu – 74, 78, 79, 81, 82, 83, 84, 86, 87

P

Pan-African Reconstruction Association – 159
Pan-Africanism – xxvii, 157, 167, 168
Panama – xxi, xxxiv, 130, 139
Panama Canal – 105, 111, 139, 141, 143
Para – 138, 140, 145; Para Harbour Co. – 142; Para Electric Railway and Lighting Co. – 142
Paraguaná – 106
Paraiba Valley – 73, 76, 77, 78, 79, 80, 81, 82, 83, 84, 87, 100
Partido Independiente de color – 122, 123
Patterson, Tiffany – xxvii
Kelley, Robin – see Patterson, Tiffany
Pernambuco – 11, 50, 61, 66, 95, 97, 108
Pichardo, Hortencia – 123, 128, 129

plantation system – xxiii, xxix, xxx, 3, 4, 8, 9, 11, 12, 14, 15, 17, 18, 74, 75, 96, 105, 106, 108, 110, 137, 140, 144; coffee – 17, 33, 94; eucalyptus – 82; Hato – 109; oligarchy – 134; orange – 85, 87 Pernambuco, in – 11; sugar cane – 4, 5, 75, 140
Platt Amendment – 125
Porto Velho – xxxi, 133, 141
Portuguese – xxix, 5,6, 10, 12, 13, 14, 15, 17, 18, 55, 57, 61, 67, 68, 107, 108, 136; colonies – 10, 15, 28, 32, 49, 51, 53, 54, 55, 57, 58, 61, 67, 106; cultural and political discourse – 3, 18; *fidalgos mercadores* – 5, 10, 14; immigrants – 146; Inquisition – 109; Jews – xxx, 109; literature – 3, 4; military and soldiers – 9, 10; royal family and court – 16, 17, 53, 99; seigniorial society – 7; trade and traders – 7, 9, 10, 11, 15, 16, 55, 107
post-abolition – xxviii, xxix, xxx, 73, 74, 75, 76, 77, 87, 91, 93
post-emancipation – xxx, xxxi, 74, 75, 110

R

racial democracy – xxxi, 133, 146, 149
Reconcavo Baiano – 58, 61, 66, 93
Reconcavo da Guanabara – 51-53, 54, 57, 58, 59, 60, 61, 62, 65, 66, 67-68
Rio de Janeiro – xxiii, xiv, xxvi, xxviii, xxix-xxx, 36, 49-50, 53-55, 56-57, 59, 60, 61-63, 64-65-67, 68, 69, 73, 76-81, 82, 83, 84, 85,

Index

87, 91, 93-96, 99-101, 102, 133, 137-138, 143, 165
Rio Grande do Sul – 24, 25-26, 27, 28, 29, 30, 31, 32, 33, 34, 35, 37, 38, 39, 40, 41, 43, 44, 45, 95, 98, 137, 165
Rondonia – xxvi, 138, 143, 147, 148,
Roumain, Jacques – 128, 130
rubber – 137, 138, 139, 142, 143; rubber boom – 138

S

Salles, Vicente – 140, 141
samba – xxvi, xxx, 95, 96, 133, 135, 136
Segundo Congreso Obrero Nacional – 129
Senegal – 108
Sephardic Jews – xxx, 108, 109
seringais – 138
Shakleton, Enrique – 130
Simoes da Silva, Antonio Carlos – 144
slave ships – 66, 68
slave trade – xx, xxi, xxix, 3, 4-5, 6, 9, 10, 11-12, 15, 17, 25, 26, 27, 51, 52, 53, 54, 55, 57, 58, 59, 66, 67, 95, 105, 106, 107-08, 109, 134
slaves – xx, xxi, xxix, 4-6, 7-9, 10-11, 12-13, 14, 15, 16-17, 23-46, 49-50, 52-53, 54-56, 57, 58, 59, 60-61, 62, 63, 64, 65, 66, 67, 68-69, 73, 74, 75, 76, 77, 79, 80, 81, 82, 87, 91, 92, 93, 94, 96, 99, 101, 107, 108, 109, 110, 115, 123, 127, 134, 135, 137, 156; ex-slaves – 28, 92, 93, 98, 99, 100
Soares, Mariza – 50, 51, 59

South America – xxvi, xxvii, 18, 108, 114, 135, 141, 164
Spaniards – 17, 106
St. Vincent – 112, 141
standards of living – 114
Surinam – 111, 112, 113

T

Thornton, John – 54
Tia Ciata – 96, 97
tourism industry – 113, 114
Transatlantic slave trade – 17, 106
Tula Rigaud – 109

U

Union de Obreros Antillanos de Santiago de Cuba – 131
Universal Negro Improvement Association – 161
Upper Guinea – 13, 107, 109
Uruguay – xx, xxix, 23, 24, 25-27, 28, 30, 32-33, 35, 36-37, 39, 41-42, 43-44, 45-46

V

Venezuela – xxiii, xxiv, 106, 111, 113. 114, 151

W

West Africa – 12, 49, 50, 107, 109, 110
whitening – 94, 135, 142
Willemstad – 108
workforce – 5, 12, 49, 124, 135, 139

www.ingramcontent.com/pod-product-compliance
Lightning Source LLC
Chambersburg PA
CBHW061445300426
44114CB00014B/1847